P9-BYV-949

The

KOWALSKI'S
30th ANNIVERSARY COOKBOOK

Edited by Rachael Perron
Designed by Julie Goetzke with Photography by Phil Aarrestad

Copyright © 2013 Kowalski's Companies

All rights reserved. No part of this publication may be reproduced, stored in a retrieval system or transmitted in any form or by any means – for example, electronic, photocopy and recording – without the prior written permission of the publisher. The only exception is brief quotations in reviews.

First printing September 2013.

Printed in the United States of America.

Library of Congress Control Number: 2013914332

Distributed by Kowalski's Companies
8505 Valley Creek Rd.
Woodbury, MN 55125

www.kowalskis.com

ISBN 978-1-4675-7717-5

Design by Julie Goetzke.
Photography by Phil Aarrestad.
Food styling by Maggie Stoppera.

10 9 8 7 6 5 4 3 2 1

Front cover photos, clockwise from top left: Grilled Corn on the Cob with Fresh Herb Butter, Honeycrisp Apple Spinach Salad, Bison Bistec au Poivre, Porcini & Mascarpone Risotto
Back cover photo: Pears Foster

DEDICATION

To our customers and our partners, who are our neighbors and our friends, and to our employees, thank you for sharing these first 30 years with us. *It's been a joy.*

- Jim and Mary Anne Kowalski and Kris Kowalski Christiansen

FOREWORD

As is the case in every family, food brings the Kowalskis together. There's the Christmas Eve tradition of *Betty's Beef Stroganoff* (first made by Jim Kowalski's mother) and the traditional chocolate fudge recipe that Mary Anne Kowalski attributes to her own mother. Even Jim has a specialty his family raves about. ("His French Toast is the best," Mary Anne boasts. "The secret is Master English Muffin Toasting Bread.") Not just as Kowalski's Chief Operating Officer, but as a shopper and a working mom, Kris Kowalski Christiansen knows the importance of having top-quality ingredients and prepared foods to serve at home. She brings her own family to the table with a modern approach. Her go-to *Family Favorite Pasta Dinner* is one that is likely familiar to many busy households.

Family recipes have been a fundamental element of the Kowalski's customer experience and a key point of difference for the brand since the very beginning. Recipes for some of our all-time best-selling and most beloved foods originated in the kitchens of the Kowalskis or in those of our families and our family of employees. From *Grandma Betty's Famous Chip Dip* to *Mary Anne's Family Favorite Buttercream Icing*, we've been sharing our best with you from day one.

As these "Family Favorite" recipes became popular in every market and every department, customers began to ask for them – stopping in, calling or emailing, oftentimes to get a second or third copy of a favorite Kowalski's recipe card that they'd held on to for years but had misplaced. The recipe card program has been a unique facet of the relationship between Kowalski's and our customers for many years. Card kiosks in each store are often the first place customers stop to find new favorite recipes to add to their collections at home. We've always been happy to share our best recipes – on the cards, in At Home with Kowalski's (our in-store magazine) and in our electronic newsletter ("In Touch with Kowalski's"), as well as on the company website and through various other media.

This book presents a special celebratory collection of some of the best recipes we've shared over the years, including several never-before-published but often-requested recipes. It's our way of saying thank you for bringing us into your homes and your kitchens over the past 30 years. We look forward to sharing more delicious foods and recipe ideas with you in the years to come.

ACKNOWLEDGEMENTS

Thank you to all those who served as diligent taste-testers of these recipes over these 30 years, our families and coworkers chief among them.

FROM THE EDITOR

Every special celebration needs great food, so for me there is no better way to celebrate the Kowalski's anniversary than with recipes that have continually connected Kowalski's and its customers over the past 30 years. As a longtime customer at the White Bear Lake market and now as a member of the Kowalski's team, I am thrilled to recognize not only the contributions the company has made to the communities they serve, but to also honor Jim and Mary Anne – the very special people who brought the company to life – and the passionate people I work with who sustain the Kowalski's vision and purpose to this day.

I would like to offer special thanks to the people who had a hand in creating this book:

- Linda Day Anderson should be especially recognized, as she was the original author of many of the recipes in this book during her tenure as Director of Culinary Promotions before me.

- Julie Goetzke is to be congratulated on designing a beautiful book.

- Phil Aarrestad and Maggie Stoppera are sincerely appreciated for contributing their creative talents in photographing and styling the food in the pictures.

- Deb Kowalski, Laurie Bell, Pam Kasprzyk, Chris Momsen, Mary Carlson, Steve Beaird, Roxanne Kielbasa, Casey Munsen, Kris Kowalski Christiansen, Mary Anne Kowalski, Terri Bennis and Sue Moores contributed valuable time, knowledge and support to this effort.

- Finally, Rachel Carlson served as my proofreader, and I cannot thank her enough. I rely more than I probably should on her gift for incredible attention to detail.

INTRODUCTION

KOWALSKI'S COMPANIES – THE FIRST 30 YEARS

Kowalski's Companies Identity Statement

Kowalski's Companies is a civic business. All stakeholders are obligated to organize, educate and set policy according to democratic principles and standards. We do this in partnership with other demonstrations of the Minnesota Active Citizenship Initiative to renew and sustain democracy and to create a world that is abundant and just.

Learn more at www.activecitizen.org.

Success in business may be a complicated formula, but the practices and values shared by Jim and Mary Anne Kowalski have sustained them from the very beginning, with their focus on common good at the heart of the Kowalski's brand. As the Kowalskis celebrate 30 successful years in the Twin Cities grocery market, we take a look back at six constant themes in the Kowalski's story.

Jim and Mary Anne Kowalski at the opening of the Woodbury Market in 2000.

A COUPLE WITH COURAGE

The Kowalski's story centers around Jim and Mary Anne Kowalski. In 1983, they risked their life savings to buy the then struggling Red Owl grocery store on St. Paul's Grand Avenue. Though Jim had worked for years in the grocery industry and had his share of successes, the challenges facing the market when Jim and Mary bought it were very real. The early days at this first Kowalski's store might have been stressful, but they were confident in the venture. Jim understood that "the most important difference is courage. Having courage in your convictions is the most important asset you can have. There's an awful lot of people who get stopped because of fear." That approach to risk-taking defines much of the company's strategic and operational decision-making to this day, with stakeholders responsible for acting quickly and decisively to create opportunities, manage challenges, and stay ahead of trends.

Jim in front of the Red Owl Country Store in White Bear Lake, which would later become the second Kowalski's Market.

A FOCUS ON THE CUSTOMER

Initially Jim had wanted to call that first store *Mary Anne's*, a tribute to his business partner-wife. He and especially Mary Anne (who had grown up just blocks away from the store) felt an innate sense of connection and responsibility to their local community. From the beginning, the couple focused on building relationships with loyal customers as well as employees. Accordingly, the first thing the Kowalskis did was talk to these stakeholders to discover what they thought would improve the store. Jim and Mary Anne's entire approach to running their new place was, in a single word, neighborly. When the neighborhood's electricity went out for three days, for example, the Kowalskis offered free freezer space to those with foods that would otherwise have spoiled at home. This customer-centric approach continues to this day in all Kowalski's Markets, where employees still not only bag but also carry out groceries and have even been known to walk neighboring customers home. In 2011, Kowalski's was named the Outstanding Community-Based Retailer of the Year by Progressive Grocer Magazine.

COMMUNITY GIVING

Kowalski's has many charitable partners in the communities they serve. Over time, the company has given to causes important to those who shop the markets through their Groceries for Good Causes program, whereby shoppers choose the local non-profit organizations to which each store donates. The company's success has also allowed Jim and Mary Anne to found Kowalski's 4 Kids, which has donated generously over the years to Mary's Place/Sharing and Caring Hands, Hazelden Youth Foundation and many other charities helping at-risk youth. In 2013, Kowalski's was also recognized by Second Harvest Heartland for their contribution of one million meals through their Food Rescue Program.

LOCAL CONNECTIONS

Before it was trendy to offer local, natural, artisan or specialty foods, Kowalski's looked for ways to connect customers to their communities through the products it offered. As a family-owned business with a love and passion for delicious, healthy foods, Kowalski's found it important to partner with honest, hard-working local people who go the extra mile

A few of Kowalski's many Signature products

to produce unique, superior-quality foods – especially those sustainably grown or produced and those made with fresh, natural ingredients. Over the years, Kowalski's even enjoyed the privilege of helping launch and/or foster many area businesses. For some, Kowalski's was their first major customer. For others, a true partnership with Kowalski's helped launch their startup, with Kowalski's advising on everything from product development, packaging, labeling and marketing to finding suppliers, distributers and even other customers.

Since the beginning, sandwiches, salads, hot foods, value-added meats, bakery items and much more have been prepared daily in each market using locally made ingredients and products when available. In 1991, Kowalski's opened a private kitchen and bakery in Mahtomedi, to prepare fresh foods and baked goods. To this day, the facility helps the company maintain its very high standards for the freshest, highest quality products possible. Over time, the company has also grown a Signature Products line, looking specifically for local partners to produce them wherever possible.

The Deli Department at Kowalski's Woodbury Market

THE SHOPPING EXPERIENCE
Since the first market opened, the Kowalskis have been driven to give their customers places where they truly love to shop – markets these shoppers regularly refer to as "my Kowalski's." Today there are nine Kowalski's locations in the Twin Cities, each uniquely designed and operated as a hyper-local retailer. From product selection to décor, each store reflects the personality and needs of the community it serves.

Design is a particular passion for Jim. According to the company's COO, Kris Kowalski Christiansen, the company aims to bring customers "an environment that wraps itself around you from the time you walk in until you leave the parking lot." Over the years, the well-planned physical and aesthetic elements of the Kowalski's stores have been awarded over and over, with their markets called everything from a "gotta-see retail concept" to "The 8th Retail Wonder of the World."

CIVIC BUSINESS

Ensuring that the business will be sustained into the next generation, Mary Anne worked in partnership with the Minnesota Active Citizenship Initiative (which includes demonstrations from the Citizens League and the Islamic Civic Society of America) to develop the civic approach that defines the company above all else. Jim describes the company's civic identity as something much bigger and broader than selling groceries:

Mary Anne Kowalski receives the 2002 Woman of the Year Award from the National Grocers Association

According to Jim, "We realized there was a bigger obligation to the greater world than merely being a good business partner or employer. As an institution, we are obligated to remind people of their role not only as employees, but also as citizens of a democratic society. This puts more of a transcendent purpose to people's daily work, which translates to great service not only to themselves, but to customers and the community as well."

Kowalski's has recieved several Employer of the Year Awards over the years, in large part due to this philosophy. In 2011, Kowalski's was awarded the Family Business of the Year Award from the University of St. Thomas Opus College of Buisiness and has also been recognized by the state of Minnesota with the Governor's Award for Outstanding Community Service & Participation.

Through civics, Jim and Mary Anne have passed on the values and practices that have guided them for 30 years. Today the day-to-day operations of the business lie in the capable hands of the couple's daughter, Kris Kowalski Christiansen. Mary Anne's nephew, Kowalski's VP of Operations, Mike Oase, plays a key role, working closely with Kris to ensure that Kowalski's civic identity carries into the next generation. Top-of-the-line perishables, great facilities, taste and quality you can trust will continue to define the Kowalski's key points of difference. According to Kris, success in the next 30 years means "staying true to our identity and our organizational principles."

MILESTONES

1983   Kowalski's purchased a 22,000 sq. ft. market in a former Red Owl store on Grand Avenue in St. Paul, Minnesota

1986   Kowalski's purchased a 27,000 sq. ft. market in a former Red Owl store in White Bear Lake, Minnesota

1991   Kowalski's opened their Central Bakery and Kitchen in Mahtomedi, Minnesota

1993   Kowalski's built a freestanding Cub Foods franchise in White Bear Township, Minnesota

2000   Kowalski's opened their first freestanding store, built from the ground up: a 48,000 sq. ft. market in Woodbury, Minnesota

2002   Kowalski's acquired GJ's SuperValu markets in Minneapolis, which included the Hennepin (18,000 sq. ft.), Lyndale (18,000 sq. ft.) and Parkview (12,000 sq. ft.) neighborhood markets

2004   Kowalski's opened a 16,000 sq. ft. market in a former Driskill's New Market in Eden Prairie, Minnesota

2005   Kowalski's opened a 40,000 sq. ft. market in Oak Park Heights/Stillwater, Minnesota

2008   Kowalski's opened a 36,000 sq. ft. market in Eagan, Minnesota, including the first Wine Shop and Catering by Kowalski's

2010   The Wine Shop opened at the Woodbury Market

2012   Wine Shops were opened at the Hennepin and Stillwater Markets

Kowalski's has been honored with many industry and community recognitions, including numerous "Best Grocery" awards as well as the prestigious President's Award for Industry Vision and Leadership.

NOTES

ON THE INGREDIENTS, PREPARATIONS, EQUIPMENT, MEASUREMENTS AND DIRECTIONS USED IN THIS BOOK

Important guidance for use of the recipes in this book appears below, related to *Ingredients, Preparation, Equipment, Measurements* and *Directions*. Successful execution of any recipe begins with reading it carefully, then reading it again. And again. Visualize your progress and performance – prepare mentally! Gather and prep all the necessary ingredients and equipment before cooking starts. Assemble the ingredients as indicated. If the recipe calls for "peeled, seeded and diced cucumber," peel, seed and dice before starting in. You may not have time to pause your work later to do this prep without negatively impacting your results.

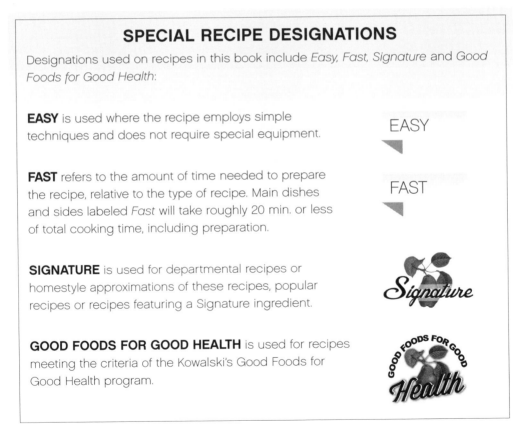

SPECIAL RECIPE DESIGNATIONS

Designations used on recipes in this book include *Easy, Fast, Signature* and *Good Foods for Good Health*:

EASY is used where the recipe employs simple techniques and does not require special equipment.

EASY

FAST refers to the amount of time needed to prepare the recipe, relative to the type of recipe. Main dishes and sides labeled *Fast* will take roughly 20 min. or less of total cooking time, including preparation.

FAST

SIGNATURE is used for departmental recipes or homestyle approximations of these recipes, popular recipes or recipes featuring a Signature ingredient.

Signature

GOOD FOODS FOR GOOD HEALTH is used for recipes meeting the criteria of the Kowalski's Good Foods for Good Health program.

GOOD FOODS FOR GOOD *Health*

INGREDIENTS

FINDING INGREDIENTS IN OUR MARKETS

For assistance in finding specific ingredients in your local Kowalski's Market, staff will be happy to help you. Recipes featuring less-frequently used ingredients will indicate where in the stores those ingredients are generally found. Where it may not be obvious, we have included below the locations of ingredients commonly used in this book:

Produce Department
prepared produce (see "Preparing Produce" below)

Bulk Foods Section
roasted salted, raw, chopped, whole, sliced and halved nuts and seeds (including almonds, cashews, peanuts, walnuts, pecans, filberts [hazelnuts], pine nuts, flax seeds, pepitas [pumpkin seeds], sunflower seeds, etc.)
Kowalski's Cinnamon Spiced Almonds
Kowalski's Honey Toasted Pecans
Kowalski's Praline Pecans
grains, including basmati rice and quinoa
dried fruits (including apricots, cherries, dates [including Medjool dates], figs, cranberries, mango and more)

Meat & Seafood Department
Kowalski's North Woods Grill Seasoning Blend
Kowalski's Kalbi Marinade
Kowalski's Chile Lime Seasoning

Grocery Department
almond flour
Kowalski's Roasted & Salted Jumbo Cashews
Kowalski's Honey Roasted Peanuts
Kowalski's Citrus and Balsamic Vinaigrettes and other dressings
Kowalski's Coleslaw Dressing
pomegranate molasses
balsamic glaze

International Foods Aisle
Sriracha (Asian hot sauce)

Asian peanut sauce
Asian chile-garlic paste (or chile-garlic sauce)
chipotle chiles in adobo sauce

Deli Department
prosciutto (including Prosciutto di Parma) and pancetta
a variety of pita breads and flatbreads
Kowalski's Salsa di Parma

Imported Cheese Department
crème fraîche
mascarpone cheese
Kowalski's Parmesan Cheese
Kowalski's Fresh Mozzarella Cheese

Bakery Department
soft ladyfingers
Kowalski's Mini Croissants
Kowalski's Take & Bake Breads
Kowalski's Artisan Croutons
Kowalski's Mini Morning Buns
Kowalski's Biscotti

Artisan Bread Table
Italian peasant loaf
French baguette
challah bread

Dairy/Frozen Department
Kowalski's Hummus
Kowalski's Crumbled Gorgonzola Cheese
Kowalski's Blue Cheese Crumbles
Kowalski's Fresh Pastas
puff pastry (frozen)

OLIVE OIL
"Good" olive oil is subjective, the same way you might personally like a particular wine that someone else may not. Like so many things, if you like it, it's good. A big-ticket bottle may not always be the best choice. To find your favorite, start by buying several in your price range to try at home. Once you know you like one, it can be your go-to bottle forever. It is important to buy extra virgin oil if you are going to taste the oil uncooked, as in a salad dressing or as a finishing or dipping oil, because it's fruitier and fresher-tasting

than regular "non-virgin" oil. Extra virgin oil results from the first cold pressing of the olives, whereas regular olive oil is later processed using heat to extract the olives' remaining oil. This is why the oil has a less "bright" taste. Because it is usually more expensive, some people reserve their extra virgin oil and use a less pricey bottle of regular olive oil for cooking (especially where more is often needed). It's fine to do so, but if you cook with extra virgin oil, it will taste more like regular oil due to being heated.

BALSAMIC VINEGAR

As with wine and olive oil, your choice for great vinegar might not be the same as everyone else's. You have to trust your palate. You should like the taste of it straight out of the bottle. If you can't stand the taste of it on a spoon, you aren't going to like it any more in your recipes. For this reason, the least expensive ones probably won't cut it. That being said, try several in your price range to find one that's right for you. There is no need to buy the most expensive brand, but if you are using it as a finishing drizzle, you might prefer the thicker, longer-aged balsamic vinegars, and they are usually the more expensive ones.

SALT AND PEPPER

Most of the recipes in this book call for kosher salt. Generally, kosher salt and the salt most of us know as plain old "salt," or table salt, are the same chemical compound, though kosher salt is less uniform in shape and larger-grained than table salt. Some brands of table salt also include ingredients to help prevent the grains from sticking or clumping together. You can fit more table salt than kosher salt in the same dry measure, so a teaspoon of table salt is technically "saltier." If you want to substitute table salt for kosher salt, use approximately half as much. Mainly older recipes simply call for salt (meaning table salt) and have been tested with table salt. Unless the recipe is very dry (kosher salt doesn't dissolve as easily or as quickly as table salt), you can usually substitute kosher salt – just use 50% more.

Kosher salt is preferred by many people because they like the way it handles for sprinkling.

Coarsely ground black pepper is preferred over finely ground black pepper for these same reasons. If you use finely ground pepper, use a little less than the amount of coarse ground pepper called for. If you prefer freshly ground pepper, it should substitute very well in even amounts for coarsely ground pepper.

Most recipes should be checked for proper seasoning with salt (and pepper, if used) before serving and/or where indicated in the directions.

GOOD QUESTION

Q. What does it mean when a recipe calls for salt "to taste"? Why doesn't it just specify an exact amount?

A. In part, this suggestion lets you know that the indicated ingredient isn't required to produce the recipe's intended final texture or flavor profile. It also accounts for different seasoning preferences, but that's not all. A recommendation to add salt "to taste" also accounts for differences that can result from other ingredients in a recipe. Think of ingredients like broth, canned vegetables, dairy products (including cheeses), prepared condiments, pasta, bread, etc., which can vary in their saltiness depending on the brand or type you select. Minor variations in cooking technique, temperature, etc., may also cause different amounts of salt to be required.

HERBS

Fresh herbs are preferred if they are called for, but you can substitute them for half as much dried herbs if you don't have them on hand. If the recipe doesn't indicate fresh herbs, then dried herbs have successfully been tested in the recipe. If an herb is added before cooking, dried will typically substitute well. As is also the case with spices, your dried herbs should be fragrant and are best if used within six months of purchase. You can lengthen the life of your spices and dried herbs by keeping them in the freezer.

Some herbs fare better than others in dried form. In general, deep, woodsy, earthy herbs with durable leaves retain good flavor when dried – thyme, rosemary, oregano, sage and marjoram are good examples. Brighter, fresher herbs with fairly delicate foliage are best used fresh – think parsley, cilantro, chervil, chives and basil. To substitute dried herbs for fresh, use about 1/3-1/2 the amount of fresh herb called for.

SPICES

If a whole spice is needed, the recipe will call for that. If not, assume you need a ground spice. Such is the case with commonly ground spices like cinnamon, ginger, cloves, cardamom, coriander, nutmeg, allspice, etc.

GOOD QUESTION

Q. I have some old spices in my cabinet. How long do spices really last?

A. The unfortunate answer is, "It depends." It depends on how it is stored, used and the particular spice you are concerned about. Generally use your nose as a guide – if you pour a bit in your hand and can smell it from about chest height, it's probably okay. Spices don't really go "bad"; they just lose pungency and flavor as they lose essential oils/moisture. Keeping them in a cool, dark and dry place will ensure freshness as long as possible. Labeling your dried spices with the date of purchase is a good idea, especially for lesser-used spices. A leading national manufacturer claims ground spices should be good at least two years and whole spices at least three. If you've had them much longer than that, it might be a good time to replace them. If you want to maximize the life expectancy of your spices, try freezing them.

BUTTER

Most of the recipes in this book call specifically for unsalted butter, but you can substitute with salted butter if that is what you have on hand. You may need to adjust the seasoning level of other salt called for in the recipe downward to accommodate that.

FLOUR

Recipes in this book that call for *flour* refer to *all-purpose flour*. Bleached or unbleached flour will work interchangeably.

SUGAR

Recipes in this book that call simply for *sugar* refer to *white, granulated sugar.*

The term *superfine sugar* refers to a product sometimes labeled *Baker's Sugar.*

Turbinado sugar is a coarse sugar often used for sprinkling on baked goods.

Brown sugar refers to *light brown sugar*. Where dark brown sugar is preferred, the recipe will so indicate. Brown and dark brown sugar may be used interchangeably.

EGGS

Recipes in this book that call for *eggs* mean *large eggs,* unless specified otherwise.

CREAM

The term *heavy cream* as used in this book is the same as *heavy whipping cream* or *whipping cream.* You cannot effectively substitute light cream, half-and-half or any nonfat product for heavy cream.

USE OF FRESH INGREDIENTS

Where fresh ingredients or freshly prepared ingredients (such as fresh produce, fresh squeezed juice, freshly grated cheese or freshly ground black pepper) are specified, using fresh ingredients is highly recommended, as the recipe was tested with the fresh ingredient.

SUBSTITUTIONS

Some of the recipes in this book refer to specific brands or flavors of products. From time to time those brands or flavors may be unavailable or may become discontinued. Effort has been made to exclude uncommonly available items. For assistance making a brand or ingredient substitution, staff in your local Kowalski's Market will be happy to help.

It is suggested that you do not substitute ingredients the first time you try a recipe so that you can establish a baseline for future improvisation.

PREPARATIONS

TOASTING NUTS AND SEEDS

Toast nuts or seeds in a dry sauté pan over medium heat or in a preheated 350° oven until fragrant and golden, stirring occasionally (3-5 min.). Stovetop toasting is recommended because it's easier to keep your eye on them (and harder to forget about them!). Some nuts burn in a flash, and there is nothing worse than ruining an oftentimes pricey ingredient. Also, nuts are easier to smell on the stovetop, and a nutty aroma is a good indicator that they're ready. If you listen closely, some oilier nuts will even start to sizzle and sing (very, very quietly) when they're nearly done. While a faint golden color is easy to detect on some nuts, it's harder to see on others, so let your nose be your guide. Shake or stir your nuts frequently to ensure they toast evenly.

MEASURING CHOPPED, DICED AND MINCED INGREDIENTS

For a number of foods, some of these terms are practically interchangeable (*finely chopped zucchini* and *diced zucchini* could look pretty darn similar), but there are subtle differences in the terms that are important to good recipe writers and, as a result, are important to you. If a specific size chop, dice or mince is important to a recipe's success, it is usually noted. If the size of a cut isn't going to affect a recipe's result, then that judgment may be left to you (in which case it's okay to *use* said judgment). Here's a look at the terms more closely:

> **Chopped** food is typically bigger than 1/4". While people may disagree as to whether chopped ingredients are required to be uniformly shaped (different from cube shaped), really good recipe writers will let you know that by indicating a *rough chop* when uniformity of shape isn't critical. With some foods it's virtually (if not actually) impossible to get a uniform shape, so there would be no point in specifying roughly chopped (instead of just chopped) for an ingredient like cilantro or walnuts. Where a specific size chop is very important, a good recipe will note that. *Coarsely chopped* is generally understood to be larger than *chopped*. An infrequently used term, *medium chop* is understood to mean the same as *chop*.

> **Diced** food may typically be anywhere from 1/8" to 1/4", with the term *finely diced* referring to the smaller end of this scale. More than anything, diced food is distinguished from chopped food by its uniformity of shape – specifically a cube shape (think about how playing dice are shaped). *Medium dice* is also considered the same as *dice*.

Minced food is usually less than 1/8". While it may have a cube shape, the most important thing here is size. *Finely minced* food is noticeably smaller than 1/8", and the infrequently used term *coarsely minced* is pretty interchangeable with just *minced*.

PREPARING PRODUCE

All produce should be washed and dried thoroughly before use.

For often-used selections, the following preparations are assumed for the recipes in this book, unless otherwise specified:

- Peppers – remove and discard any white/pale-colored membrane, seeds, stem and core
- Potatoes – peel only when noted
- Onions – remove and discard ends and peels
- Carrots – remove and discard ends and peels, unless noted
- Garlic – remove and discard ends and peels from each clove

A wide variety of prepared fresh produce is available in the Produce Department, including:

- Halved and trimmed Brussels sprouts
- Washed, chopped greens such as spinach, kale, mixed greens, romaine lettuce, etc.
- Peeled, pitted, sliced mango
- Pomegranate seeds
- Cored pineapple and pineapple spears
- Peeled, seeded, sliced melons
- Chopped onions
- Soup mix (chopped onions, celery, turnips and carrots)
- Mirepoix (chopped onions, celery and carrots)
- Ready-to-eat mixed fruits and berries
- Carrot sticks, jicama sticks and celery sticks
- Bell pepper strips (including Kowalski's Stoplight Peppers and Kowalski's Fajita Mix, which includes onions)
- Peeled, cubed sweet potato
- Peeled, cubed butternut squash
- Peeled sweet potato fries
- Sliced mushrooms
- Several varieties of fresh salsas and guacamoles

Also look for prepared broccoli and cauliflower florets, beets, garlic, beans and much, much more.

USE OF CANNED FRUITS AND VEGETABLES

When used, canned fruits and vegetables should be drained and/or rinsed only where noted.

USE OF FROZEN FRUITS AND VEGETABLES

When used, frozen fruits and vegetables should be thawed and drained only where noted. If you are substituting frozen fruit in a recipe calling for fresh, don't drain the liquid from the thawed fruit unless the recipe specifically says to do so. Freezing ruptures the cell walls of produce, especially with delicate fruits and veggies; when thawed, the liquid in those cells is released as juice. Since that juice was in the fruit when it was fresh, it shouldn't be drained off a frozen substitute.

SUBSTITUTING DRIED HERBS INSTEAD OF FRESH HERBS

Fresh herbs are recommended in recipes calling for them. If you elect to substitute dried herbs for fresh herbs, use about 1/3-1/2 the amount of fresh herb called for.

CITRUS ZEST

Many recipes call for *citrus zest*, which may mean either strips or grated bits of peel. To decide which is best, consider the recipe. Strips of zest are most often used for garnish. Modern recipes that call simply for *zest* more typically mean grated zest (made on a Microplane™). Older recipes specifying *zest* probably refer to strips of peel and might specify *grated zest* when that is called for.

EQUIPMENT

Recipes are tested on standard home kitchen equipment, and equipment may vary.

OVEN

Testing the temperature of your home oven is recommended.

Temperatures given in degrees indicate Fahrenheit measure.

Recipes have been tested in a standard nonconvection oven.

Unless noted, pans should be placed in the oven on the center rack. It is not necessary to rotate or switch pans (such as for baking) unless noted. Where multiple pans are to be baked one at a time, the recipe has been successfully tested thusly, and it is not recommended to bake more than one pan at a time.

GRILL

It is not necessary, nor is it recommended, to grease grill grates unless noted (not usually the case with burgers, steaks, sausages, chops, ribs, marinated chicken or tenderloins, etc.). When oiling the grill is necessary, several swipes over hot grates with a paper towel dipped in (but NOT dripping with) oil until they are shiny should suffice.

Grill directly over the heat source (the flame in the case of a gas grill, hot coals in the case of a charcoal grill) unless indirect heat is specified.

Always preheat your oven and grill as directed in the recipes, and wait until it has come all the way up to temperature before proceeding. For grilled recipes in particular, a clean grill is essential. Always heat your grill on high, then clean it while it is at its hottest. Then adjust the temperature according to directions.

GOOD QUESTION

Q. How long should I preheat my gas grill?

A. A full 15 minutes at high heat with the lid down, no matter what you're grilling. Once the grill is super hot, clean it with a stiff wire brush, then adjust the heat to that specified in your recipe.

MICROWAVE

Microwave recipes will not indicate a power setting (such as HIGH), unless a setting less than 100% is to be used.

GREASING PANS

If it is necessary to grease a baking pan or dish with butter or cooking spray, that will be indicated in the recipe. If one method is preferred over another, the recipe will specify that. Where nonstick pans are called for, they are important to the recipe's success.

POT AND PAN DESCRIPTIONS AND SIZES

Rimmed baking sheets are necessary where specified; otherwise, non-rimmed sheets will work just fine.

In general, a small saucepan will hold between ½-1 ½ quarts. A medium saucepan will hold 2-3 quarts, and a large saucepan will hold 3-4 quarts. Larger than that and you have a pot; small pots hold in the range of 5-6 quarts, and large pots hold up to 8 quarts.

Small, medium and large skillets or sauté pans will measure, on average, 8", 10" and 12" in diameter, respectively.

Small, medium and large mixing bowls will hold, on average, 2-3, 4-6 and 6-8 cups, respectively.

Where it is recommended, you may substitute another oven-safe, deep pot with a tight-fitting lid for a Dutch oven.

Sauté pans have rounded sides; skillets (also referred to as frying pans) have straight sides.

MEASUREMENTS

MEASURING FLOUR

Flour does not need to be sifted unless noted. Measure flour by dipping your measuring cup into the container of flour, then use a sturdy, flat edge to scrape across the top of the measuring cup. It is generally more accurate to measure a cup of flour using a single 1-cup measure rather than two 1/2 cup measures or four 1/4 cup measures, etc.

MEASURING BROWN SUGAR

Brown sugar should be lightly packed into your measuring cup, unless the recipe specifies that it should be firmly packed.

MEASURING STICKY INGREDIENTS

Measuring sticky ingredients like honey and maple syrup is easy in a measuring glass or cup sprayed lightly with cooking spray.

HOW TO MEASURE LIQUIDS AND DRY INGREDIENTS

Technically, dry and liquid cups measure the same, so in a pinch you can use liquid measuring glasses to measure dry ingredients and vice versa. Measuring glasses help prevent spilling and may have a useful spout to aid in pouring. Dry measures are designed to allow leveling off of ingredients. When measuring liquid in a dry measuring cup, you may notice that liquid poured right to the top of the measure isn't flat. Surface tension causes a slight convex bulge across the top of the measure, but this is usually only significant in very fussy recipes, such as baking recipes. You can use measuring spoons for liquid and dry ingredients.

GOOD QUESTION

Q. When I am measuring yogurt, should I use a measuring cup made for measuring dry or liquid ingredients?

A. It won't make a huge difference, but it may be easier to use dry measuring cups for yogurt, sour cream, cream cheese, mayonnaise, etc.

MEASURING EQUIVALENTS

Key equivalent measures are listed below:

3 tsp. = 1 tbsp.
2 tbsp. = 1 fl. oz.
4 tbsp. = 1/4 cup = 2 fl. oz.
16 oz. = 1 lb.
1 g = 1,000 mg
1 L = 1,000 ml
1 qt. = 2 pts.
8 pts. = 1 gal.

ABBREVIATIONS FOR MEASUREMENTS

Key abbreviations for measures used in this book are listed below:

°	degree(s) (Fahrenheit)
"	inch(es)
g	gram(s)
mg	milligram(s)
L	liter(s)
ml	milliliter(s)
oz.	ounces(s) (may also mean fl. [fluid] oz. in obvious instances)
lb(s).	pound(s)
pt.	pint(s)
qt.	quart(s)
gal.	gallon(s)
tbsp.	tablespoon(s)
tsp.	teaspoon(s)
sec.	second(s)
min.	minute(s)
hr(s).	hour(s)
pkg.	package

DIVIDED MEASURES

Where the term *divided* appears after an ingredient in the ingredient list, this indicates that the total amount of the ingredient is not used all at once, but is added to the recipe in two or more additions, as specified in the body of the recipe.

USE OF DRY/VOLUME MEASURES, PIECE MEASURES AND WEIGHT MEASURES FOR PRODUCE

Recipes specifying a specific dry measure are usually more sensitive to exactitude than recipes specifying produce by unit. While a medium-sized piece should yield reasonably close dry measures, differences in preparation may cause variances. In recipes where the measure isn't vital, a recipe writer may indicate piece measures to assist a reader in shopping appropriately.

To make shopping easier, some recipes call for a specific number of peppers, onions, etc. If not indicated otherwise, a medium-sized piece is fine, or it isn't terribly critical to the recipes' success. Use judgment.

GOOD QUESTION

Q. Some recipes call for minced garlic in terms of cloves instead of as a dry measurement. How do I know if I am using the right amount?

A. With the variation in sizes of today's cloves, this is an increasing "problem." In general, recipes that specify a clove count probably assume a medium-sized clove, which should equate to roughly 1 teaspoon of minced garlic. Bear in mind, though, that it's probably not necessary to read such a recipe too strictly. If the author wrote the recipe measure as a clove, it probably isn't going to make a huge difference in the outcome. As with basics like salt and pepper, the desirable amount of garlic flavor in many recipes is largely a matter of taste.

DIRECTIONS

ORDER OF OPERATIONS

Always prepare ingredients as listed, in the order listed (think order of operations from algebra class). If a recipe calls for a *cup of herbs*, *chopped*, that is different than a *cup of chopped herbs*. (In the first case, you measure then chop; in the second, you measure the chopped ingredient. Most of the time the second method produces a slightly larger quantity of ingredient.)

MIXING TECHNIQUES

MIX

To *mix* something is to combine it. Most recipes that ask you to mix two or more ingredients together mean to combine them so that the ingredients are evenly distributed. Often mixing is achieved by stirring with a spoon or fork, so the terms *mix* and *stir* are often used interchangeably. *Mixing* may also refer to the use of an electric mixer, though recipes that require that will often specify its use.

STIR

To *stir* is to mix with a utensil, often a spoon.

BEAT

The aim of *beating* is to incorporate air into a mixture and is best done with a whisk or electric mixer.

BLEND

Blending is similar to, but perhaps a bit less vigorous than, beating. Blending may also refer also to the use of an electric blender.

WHISK

Whisking could refer to mixing or stirring with a whisk instead of a spoon, fork, spatula or other utensil; it's less vigorous than beating.

FOLD

Folding is a gentle mixing technique usually employed to maintain lightness and volume in mixtures into which air has been incorporated (often by beating). It is commonly done with a spatula dragged slowly across and through a mixture and then up and over (turning the mixture over on itself).

ASSESSING DONENESS

In some cases, recipes include not only time guidelines, but also an indication of what to look for in assessing the doneness of certain recipes (such as opacity, color or tenderness). Cooking times are approximate. How your ingredients are prepared may impact your results, and oven and stove temperatures may vary. At times even weather can impact cooking times. Use judgment above all else. Recipes are tested on home kitchen equipment, and equipment may vary.

COVERING FOODS

Foods are cooked or stored uncovered unless noted.

TABLE OF CONTENTS

BREAKFAST & BRUNCH

KOWALSKI'S COFFEE CAKE A LA MARY ANNE'S

COFFEE CAKE:

3/4 cup brown sugar

1/2 cup sugar

3 tbsp. margarine

4 tbsp. shortening

1/2 tsp. kosher salt

1 tbsp. corn syrup

1 tbsp. honey

3 tbsp. water

2 oz. sliced almonds

36 ½ oz. pkg. unbaked frozen cinnamon rolls (such as Rhodes), icing packets discarded

- *Maple Icing*

MAPLE ICING:

1/2 cup confectioner's sugar

1 ½-2 tsp. milk, approx.

- maple flavor, to taste

COFFEE CAKE: In an electric mixer fitted with the paddle attachment, cream first 7 ingredients (through honey) on medium-high speed. Add water 1 tbsp. at a time, scraping bowl between additions. Mix 2 min. on medium-high. Smear caramel evenly into two deep 9" round pans sprayed with cooking spray; sprinkle caramel evenly with almonds. Divide frozen dough evenly between pans, cutting a roll in half if necessary. Cover loosely with plastic wrap sprayed with cooking spray. Let rise overnight in the refrigerator 10-12 hrs., then at room temperature 1-2 hrs. Remove plastic wrap. Bake on a rimmed baking sheet in a preheated 350° oven until dark golden (25-30 min.); invert cakes onto a baking sheet immediately upon removing them from the oven. Cool; drizzle with *Maple Icing*.

MAPLE ICING: Whisk all ingredients together in a small mixing bowl until smooth. Add more or less milk as needed to reach desired drizzling consistency.

> ## NOTE
> • Mary Anne's recipe was inspired by her favorite Maple Sticks, from the Old Dutch Bakery on St. Paul's Cleveland Avenue.

SERVES 12

Signature

APPLE STREUSEL COFFEE CAKE

1 cup brown sugar

1 cup chopped Kowalski's Honey Toasted Pecans

2 tsp. Kowalski's Ground Cinnamon

3/4 cup softened butter

1 ½ cups sugar

3 eggs

1 ½ tsp. vanilla

3 cups flour

1 ½ tsp. baking powder

1 ½ tsp. baking soda

3/4 tsp. kosher salt

1 ½ cups sour cream

2 cups peeled, cored, chopped baking apples

2 tbsp. cold butter, cut into small pieces

1/2 cup sifted confectioner's sugar

2-3 tbsp. Kowalski's Pure Maple Syrup

In a small mixing bowl, combine brown sugar, pecans and cinnamon; set aside. In a large mixing bowl, beat softened butter, sugar, eggs and vanilla with an electric mixer on medium speed (2 min.). In a separate bowl, combine flour, baking powder, soda and salt. Add flour mixture, alternately with sour cream, to butter mixture on low speed; fold in apples. Spread half of batter in a greased 13x9" baking pan. Sprinkle with 1/2 of the brown sugar mixture; repeat with remaining batter and topping. Sprinkle cold butter pieces over topping. Bake in a preheated 350° oven until a toothpick inserted in the center comes out clean (40-45 min.); cool slightly in pan. In a small mixing bowl, whisk together confectioner's sugar and syrup; drizzle over warm cake. Serve warm.

VARIATION

Berry Streusel Coffee Cake:
Replace apples with 2 cups raspberries, blackberries or blueberries, and replace maple syrup with milk.

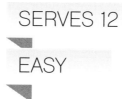

SERVES 12

EASY

BLUEBERRY BANANA-ALMOND PANCAKES

1 cup flour

1/2 cup almond flour

1/4 cup buttermilk powder

1 tbsp. sugar

1 ¼ tsp. baking powder

1/4 tsp. baking soda

- pinch of kosher salt

1 cup sparkling water

1 banana, mashed

1 egg, lightly beaten

1 tbsp. unsalted butter, melted

- canola oil, for greasing the pan

6 oz. blueberries (approx. 1/2 pt.)

In a medium mixing bowl, whisk together flours, buttermilk powder, sugar, baking powder, soda and salt. In a separate bowl, whisk together water, banana, egg and butter. Add wet mixture to dry mixture; whisk until just moistened. Lightly coat a large nonstick skillet or griddle with oil and heat to medium; wipe skillet with a paper towel to coat pan evenly and absorb excess oil. In batches, scoop batter onto skillet, forming 4-5" circles; top pancakes with blueberries. Cook until edges are set and dry and bubbles begin to burst on the surface (2-5 min.). Flip pancakes; cook until golden-brown on the bottom (1-3 min.). Wipe skillet clean; re-oil, wipe and repeat with remaining batter. Serve immediately with desired toppings or keep warm in a 200° oven until all pancakes are done.

GOOD TO KNOW

- If desired, replace almond flour with all-purpose flour. Find almond flour in the Baking Aisle.

- If desired, replace buttermilk powder and water with low-fat buttermilk. Find buttermilk powder in the Baking Aisle.

- Pancakes may be frozen for at least 3 months, tightly wrapped, with freezer or wax paper between pancakes. You can microwave individual pancakes without thawing them (about 1 min. each).

SERVES 4

EASY

FAST

BASIC BUTTERMILK PANCAKES

1 ½ cups flour

1/4 cup buttermilk powder

1 tbsp. sugar

1 ¼ tsp. baking powder

1/4 tsp. baking soda

- pinch of kosher salt

1 cup sparkling water, approx.

1 egg, lightly beaten

1 tbsp. unsalted butter, melted

- canola oil, for greasing the pan

In a medium mixing bowl, whisk together flour, buttermilk powder, sugar, baking powder, soda and salt. In a separate bowl, whisk together water, egg and butter. Add wet mixture to dry mixture, whisking until just moistened and adding more water as needed to reach the consistency of a loose cake batter. Lightly coat a large nonstick skillet or griddle with oil and heat to medium; wipe skillet with a paper towel to coat pan evenly and absorb excess oil. In batches, scoop batter onto skillet, forming 4-5" circles. Cook until edges are set and dry and bubbles begin to burst on the surface (2-5 min.). Flip pancakes; cook until golden-brown on the bottom (1-3 min.). Wipe skillet clean; re-oil, wipe and repeat with remaining batter. Serve immediately with desired toppings or keep warm in a 200° oven until all pancakes are done.

GOOD TO KNOW

- If desired, replace buttermilk powder and water with low-fat buttermilk. Find buttermilk powder in the Baking Aisle.

- Pancakes may be frozen for at least 3 months, tightly wrapped, with freezer or wax paper between pancakes. You can microwave individual pancakes without thawing them (about 1 min. each).

SERVES 4

EASY

FAST

VANILLA-HONEY FRENCH TOAST

6 eggs

1 ½ cups milk

1 tsp. vanilla extract or
vanilla paste

1 tbsp. Kowalski's Pure Honey

1/2 tsp. kosher salt

1 loaf challah bread, sliced
3/4" thick

- unsalted butter

- canola oil

- confectioner's sugar

- warm Kowalski's Pure Maple
Syrup

In a 9x13" glass baking dish, whisk together the eggs, milk, vanilla, honey and salt. Working in batches, soak bread in egg mixture for 1 ½ min., turning once. Melt 1 tbsp. butter in 1 tbsp. oil on a nonstick griddle over medium heat. Use a wadded paper towel to evenly coat griddle with melted butter mixture. Add soaked bread in batches to hot griddle, several slices at a time; cook until dark golden-brown (2-3 min. per side), flipping once. Add more butter and oil between batches, as needed. Serve sprinkled with sugar and drizzled with syrup.

NOTE
• Add up to 1/2 tsp. ground cinnamon to the dipping mixture, if desired.

GOOD TO KNOW
• Find challah bread on the Artisan Bread Table.

SERVES 6

EASY

FAST

JIM'S BEST-EVER FRENCH TOAST

1/2 cup softened butter

1/2 cup light brown sugar

1 cup half-and-half

3 eggs

1 tbsp. vanilla extract

1 ½ tsp. Kowalski's Ground Cinnamon

1/4 tsp. kosher salt

8 slices Master English Muffin Toasting Bread

- confectioner's sugar

- fresh raspberries

- Kowalski's Pure Maple Syrup

In a small mixing bowl, combine butter and brown sugar; set aside. In a shallow dish, whisk together half-and-half, eggs, vanilla, cinnamon and salt. Melt 1/2 cup butter-brown sugar mixture on a large nonstick griddle over medium-high heat. Dip bread slices one at a time in egg mixture, coating both sides. Place bread on griddle; cook until bottoms are deep brown (5-8 min.). Spread remaining butter mixture over tops of bread slices on griddle; turn and continue cooking until bottoms are deep brown (3-4 min.). Serve French toast sprinkled with sugar, topped with raspberries and drizzled with syrup.

SERVES 4

EASY

FAST

Signature

PINEAPPLE RAISIN BRAN MUFFINS

1 ½ cups flour

1 cup bran

2 ¼ tsp. baking powder

1 ½ tsp. ground cinnamon

1/2 tsp. baking soda

1/4 tsp. kosher salt

2 eggs

3/4 cup canola oil

3/4 cup dark brown sugar

2 tbsp. molasses

1 ½ cups grated carrots

1/2 cup chopped pecans (optional)

1/4 cup crushed pineapple

1/4 cup raisins

In a large mixing bowl, whisk together the first 6 ingredients; set aside. In another medium mixing bowl, whisk eggs with oil, sugar and molasses. Gently mix wet ingredients into the dry ingredients using a silicone spatula and a gentle folding technique, just until dry ingredients are moistened (lumps may remain); gently stir in remaining ingredients. Scoop batter into muffin pan lined with 12 paper baking cups. Bake in a preheated 350° oven until a toothpick inserted into the center of a muffin comes out clean with just a few moist crumbs attached (about 25 min.). Cool in pan 5 min. Move muffins to a wire rack; serve warm or at room temperature.

Nutrition Information Per Serving (2 muffins)

Total Calories	264
Total Fat	15 g
Saturated Fat	1 g
Sodium	205 mg
Fiber	3 g

A good source of vitamins A, E and K, selenium and fiber.

GOOD TO KNOW

• Muffins may be frozen for at least 3 months, individually wrapped. Store multiple wrapped muffins in a freezer storage bag or container.

MAKES 12

EASY

CHERRY ALMOND SCONES

2 cups flour

4 tsp. baking powder

1/2 tsp. kosher salt

1/2 tsp. cream of tartar

3 tbsp. sugar

1/2 cup butter, very cold, cut into 1/2" chunks

1/2 cup dried cherries

1 egg, lightly beaten

1/2 tsp. vanilla paste

1 tsp. almond extract, divided

1/2 cup cream, divided, plus more for brushing the scones

1 ½ tbsp. turbinado sugar

1 cup confectioner's sugar

1 ½ tbsp. milk, approx.

- sliced almonds

In a medium mixing bowl, sift together first 5 ingredients. Using a food processor or pastry cutter, cut butter into dry ingredients until butter is in pea-sized pieces; stir in cherries. In a small dish, whisk egg with vanilla paste, 1/2 tsp. almond extract and 2 tbsp. cream. Pour egg mixture into dry ingredients; using a fork, stir remaining cream into dry ingredients a little at a time as needed until a soft but not sticky dough forms, stirring just until dough is uniformly moist (there will be lumps). Move dough to a large sheet of waxed paper; use a second sheet of waxed paper (not your hands) to fold dough in half a few times. Pat into a rough circle about 8" in diameter, taking care not to overwork the dough. Brush scones with a little bit of cream to moisten; sprinkle with turbinado sugar. Using a sharp knife or bench scraper, cut dough into 8 evenly sized, pie-shaped wedges. Place 1 ½" apart on a parchment-lined baking sheet; refrigerate 10 min. Bake in a preheated 450° oven until golden-brown (about 10 min.). Cool on a wire rack. Whisk powdered sugar with milk a few drops at a time until a drizzling consistency is reached; whisk in remaining almond extract. Drizzle icing over scones; sprinkle with almonds while icing is wet.

MAKES 8   EASY   FAST

SIMPLE STRAWBERRY PRESERVES

1 lb. strawberries, rinsed, hulled and halved

3/4 cup sugar

2 tsp. fresh lemon juice

In a large nonstick skillet over medium heat, cook and mash strawberries until softened and fairly chunky. Stir in sugar and lemon juice. Increase heat slightly and bring to a boil; boil and stir occasionally until mixture is thickened and thinly coats the back of a metal spoon without dripping off (5-10 min.). Cool completely in the pan; spoon into a pint-sized container. Cover and refrigerate up to 3 weeks.

NOTE
• The jam will set up slightly as it cools and a tiny bit more so in the refrigerator; be careful not to overcook it or it will be too firm. If the jam seems too loose after cooling, you can cook it a bit longer.

MAKES about 2 cups

EASY

HOMEMADE JAM
CULINARY TIPS & IDEAS

Having won numerous awards for her homemade jam, our Culinary Director is the go-to gal when it comes to prepping preserves. If you've got an abundance of fresh seasonal fruit around and can't eat through it fast enough, consider making some jam of your own; nothing tastes better on your morning toast or PB&J than homemade! Chef Rachael's adapted technique is easy enough for beginners, allowing you to make a small batch of jam without pectin and without a boiling water canner:

1. Wash and rinse ripe fruit thoroughly without soaking.

2. Remove stems, skins and pits from fruit (apricots do NOT have to be peeled); cut into pieces and crush. For berries, you can leave the seeds in or, if you prefer, push them through a sieve or food mill.

3. Add sugar and lemon juice; bring to a boil in a large, deep pan, stirring constantly. Cook at a gentle boil over medium to medium-high heat until mixture thickens to desired consistency. Remember to allow for thickening during cooling.

4. The easiest way to test your jam is to remove it from the heat and spoon a small amount onto a cold plate. Put the plate in the refrigerator for a few minutes. If the mixture gels to your satisfaction, it's ready. If not, cook it a few minutes longer. You may find you prefer your homemade jam a little looser than store-bought jam.

5. While not necessary, you can skim foam from the cooked jam surface for aesthetic reasons.

6. Using a funnel, pour or scoop the hot jam into glass canning jars; cover. Let the jars come to room temperature, then refrigerate up to 3 weeks.

Fruit	Crushed Fruit	Sugar	Lemon Juice	Approx. Yield
Apricots	4 - 4 ½ cups	4 cups	2 tbsp.	3 pints
Berries	4 cups	4 cups	1 tbsp.	2 pints
Peaches	5 ½ - 6 cups	4 ½ cups	2 tbsp.	3 pints

MASCARPONE BERRY BRUSCHETTA

1 loaf Take & Bake French
    Bread, baked according
    to pkg. directions, cut
    into about 30 slices

- melted butter

1/4 cup superfine sugar

2 tsp. ground cinnamon

8 oz. carton mascarpone

- assorted berries, stems
    removed, rinsed
    and drained

- Kowalski's Pure Honey

Lightly brush both sides of each bread slice with melted butter. In a small mixing bowl, completely combine sugar and cinnamon; sprinkle over both sides of each bread slice. Bake in a preheated 375° oven until crisp (10-12 min.), turning halfway through; cool. Spread each bread slice with mascarpone; top with berries. Drizzle lightly with honey.

MAKES 30

EASY

FAST

GOOD TO KNOW
- Mascarpone can be found in the Imported Cheese Department.

HONEY PECAN GRANOLA
WITH DRIED FRUITS

4 cups old-fashioned oats

2 cups sweetened shredded
    coconut

2 cups chopped pecans

1 ¼ tsp. kosher salt

3/4 cup canola oil

1/2 cup Kowalski's Pure Honey

1 cup chopped dried cherries

1 cup chopped dried dates

1 cup chopped dried apricots

1 cup golden raisins

1/2 cup raisins

In a large mixing bowl, toss together first 4 ingredients. In a small bowl, whisk together oil and honey; pour over granola mixture, stirring until well coated. Pour onto a large rimmed baking sheet; bake in a preheated 325° oven until granola is golden-brown (about 35 min.), stirring 1-2 times. Cool on pan 45 min.; stir in fruit. Serve alone or with milk or yogurt; store in airtight container at room temperature up to 3 weeks.

SERVES 16

EASY

BLACKBERRIES & STONE FRUITS **WITH VANILLA-HONEY SYRUP**

1/2 cup water

1/4 cup Kowalski's Pure Honey

1/4 cup sugar

1 tsp. vanilla paste

12 oz. blackberries

2 lbs. stone fruits (such as apricots, nectarines, cherries, plums or combination), pitted, thinly sliced

Place water, honey, sugar and vanilla paste in a small saucepan over medium heat; stir to combine. Bring to a simmer and stir occasionally until sugar is dissolved. Reduce heat to low and continue to simmer until reduced to less than 3/4 cup (about 10 min.). Remove syrup from heat and let cool completely. In a large serving bowl, toss fruit together; drizzle with syrup to taste. Serve immediately.

NUTRITION INFORMATION PER SERVING

Total Calories	125
Total Fat	< 1 g
Sodium	2 mg
Fiber	4 g

An excellent source of vitamins A and C.

GOOD TO KNOW

- Find vanilla paste in the Baking Aisle or substitute an equal amount of vanilla extract.

SERVES 8

EASY

FAST

Blackberries & Stone Fruits with
Vanilla-Honey Syrup (pg 48)

Blueberry Banana-Almond
Pancakes (pg 38)

Honey Pecan Granola with
Dried Fruits (pg 47)

Perfect Scrambled Eggs
(pg 53)

Spinach & Salmon Quiche
(pg 51)

Cherry Almond Scones
(pg 43)

Spinach & Sun-dried Tomato Strata
(pg 52)

Vanilla-Honey French Toast (pg 40)

Gazpacho Bloody Mary (pg 62)

Spinach, Caramelized Onion & Fontina Omelet (pg 56)

Crab, Spinach & Artichoke Dip
(pg 76)

Italian Wonton Bites (pg 80)

Lentil Spread (pg 94) and
Greek Dip (pg 95)

Butternut Squash & Apple
Bisque with Crème Fraîche
(pg 110)

Baked Eggs Florentine (pg 49),
Berry Streusel Coffee Cake (pg 37)
and Brunch Punch (pg 60)

BAKED EGGS FLORENTINE

8 slices Pepperidge Farms
    Very Thin White Bread,
    crust removed

1/4 cup melted butter

2 tbsp. Kowalski's Extra Virgin
    Olive Oil

1 tbsp. finely chopped onion

1 tsp. chopped garlic

1/2 tsp. kosher salt, plus extra

1/4 tsp. Kowalski's Coarse
    Ground Black Pepper,
    plus extra

5 oz. box organic fresh baby
    spinach

1/2 cup julienne-cut sun-dried
    tomatoes in olive oil and
    herbs, drained and
    blotted dry, divided

8 pasteurized eggs

8 tsp. heavy cream, divided

1 tbsp. butter, cut into 8
    small pieces

1/2 cup grated Gruyère
    cheese, divided

Brush both sides of bread with melted butter. Press bread into bottom of each of 8 (6 oz.) ramekins. Bake in a preheated 350° oven (5 min.); remove from oven and set aside. In a large sauté pan, heat olive oil over medium heat; sauté onion and garlic until softened (about 2 min.). Season with 1/2 tsp. salt and 1/4 tsp. pepper. Add spinach; cook until wilted (about 2 min.). Divide spinach mixture evenly among ramekins; top with sun-dried tomatoes. Carefully crack eggs into ramekins; season with salt and pepper. Top each egg with 1 tsp. cream and a piece of butter. Place ramekins in a shallow baking pan; bake until whites are just set but yolks are still runny (15-20 min.), rotating pan halfway through baking time. Sprinkle each ramekin with cheese during last 3 min. of baking. Serve immediately.

SERVES 8

EASY

FAST

FRITTATA BITES

1 tbsp. Kowalski's Extra Virgin
    Olive Oil

1 cup chopped onion

8 eggs

1/4 cup heavy cream

1/2 tsp. kosher salt

1/4 tsp. Kowalski's Coarse
    Ground Black Pepper

1 cup organic fancy shredded
    Italian blend cheese

1 cup fresh baby spinach, torn

7 oz. canned roasted tomatoes,
    drained, chopped

- torn fresh basil

In a small sauté pan, heat olive oil over medium heat; add onions, sautéing until softened (about 5 min.); cool. In a large mixing bowl, whisk eggs, cream, salt and pepper until thoroughly combined; fold in onions, cheese, spinach and tomatoes. Pour mixture into a greased 8x8" glass baking dish; bake in a preheated 325° oven until set in the center (45-55 min.). Cool in pan on cooling rack (20 min.). Place platter over top of baking dish; invert frittata onto platter. Cut into 16 pieces; arrange on a serving tray, top side up. Garnish with basil. Serve warm or at room temperature.

MAKES 16

EASY

SPINACH & SALMON QUICHE

1 refrigerated pie crust

2 tbsp. olive oil, divided

10 oz. salmon fillet(s), about 1" thick

1 small onion, finely chopped

2 oz. fresh baby spinach

4 eggs, beaten

1/2 cup whole milk

1/3 cup grated Parmesan cheese

1 tsp. kosher salt, plus some for seasoning the fish

1/4 tsp. Kowalski's Coarse Ground Black Pepper, plus some for seasoning the fish

Unroll pie crust into 9" pie plate; flute edges. Prick bottom lightly with fork and freeze crust 10 min. In nonstick skillet, heat 1 tbsp. oil over medium-high heat until shimmering but not smoking. Season fish lightly with salt and pepper; sauté fish, skin side up, until it releases easily from pan (about 5 min.). Turn and cook until fish flakes easily with a fork and is opaque throughout (about 5 min.). Cool completely; discard skin and cut salmon into 1" chunks. Put a baking sheet in the oven; preheat to 350°. Meanwhile, in skillet over medium heat, heat remaining oil; sauté onion until softened (about 5 min.). Add spinach, cooking just until wilted (1-2 min.); set aside. In large mixing bowl, whisk eggs with milk and about 3/4 of the cheese; season with 1 tsp. salt and 1/4 tsp. pepper. Spread onion and spinach mixture in the bottom of crust; pour in egg mixture. Top with chunks of fish and sprinkle with remaining cheese. Bake on preheated sheet until filling is just set and pastry is golden (25-27 min.). Let stand 10 min. before cutting.

SERVES 6

EASY

SPINACH & SUN-DRIED TOMATO STRATA

20 oz. refrigerated shredded hash browns

1 cup chopped onion, divided

2 tsp. kosher salt, divided

3/4 tsp. seasoned pepper, divided

2 tbsp. melted butter

1 lb. Kowalski's Bulk Mild or Hot Italian Sausage

3 cups half-and-half

6 eggs, slightly beaten

3/4 tsp. Kowalski's Herbes de Provence

3 cups Kowalski's Shredded Mozzarella Cheese

10 oz. pkg. frozen chopped spinach, thawed and completely drained

6 ½ oz. jar julienne-cut sun-dried tomatoes, drained and blotted dry

In a large mixing bowl, combine hash browns, 1/2 cup onion, 1 tsp. salt and 1/4 tsp. seasoned pepper. Press into the bottom of a 13x9" glass baking dish sprayed lightly with cooking spray; brush with melted butter. Bake in a preheated 425° oven until lightly browned around the edges (20-25 min.). In a large sauté pan, cook and crumble sausage over medium heat until cooked through (10-12 min.); drain fat. Evenly layer browned sausage over potatoes. In a large mixing bowl, whisk together half-and-half, eggs, Herbes de Provence and remaining salt and seasoned pepper. Stir in cheese, spinach, remaining onions and tomatoes. Pour mixture over potato crust. Bake, uncovered, in a preheated 350° oven until center is set (35-45 min.). Let stand, covered, 10 min. before serving.

SERVES 10

EASY

Signature

PERFECT SCRAMBLED EGGS

- unsalted butter, 1 ½ tsp. per egg

- beaten eggs, 2 per person, seasoned with kosher salt and coarse ground black pepper, to taste

In a nonstick skillet over medium heat, melt 1 ½ tsp. butter per egg. Add eggs; using a spatula, stir occasionally and gently while moving the pan on and off the heat. Let the egg mixture heat up, then move it off heat while stirring and distributing that heat throughout. When the eggs appear to stop cooking, move them back to the heat for a few seconds and then off again to stir. Repeat until the eggs are almost done but still quite soft and glossy. Eggs will continue to cook when they are finally removed from the heat; remove them from the hot pan right away so they don't overcook. Serve immediately.

EASY   FAST

DEVILED EGGS

6 eggs

1/4 cup mayonnaise

1 tsp. white vinegar

1 tsp. mustard

1/4 tsp. kosher salt, or more to taste

- Kowalski's Freshly Ground Black Peppercorns, to taste

- paprika

Place eggs in a single layer in a saucepan; cover with water 1 ½" above the eggs; bring to a boil. Remove pan from heat; cover for 14 min. Remove eggs from pan; rinse under cold water continuously for 1 min. Crack egg shells; carefully peel under cool, running water. Gently dry with paper towels. Slice eggs in half lengthwise, removing yolks to a medium mixing bowl. Use a fork to mash yolks; mix in mayonnaise, vinegar, mustard, salt and pepper. Evenly scoop heaping spoonfuls of the yolk mixture into the egg whites; sprinkle with paprika.

SERVES 6   EASY   FAST

CHEESY OVEN SCRAMBLED EGGS

24 eggs

2 cups milk

2 tsp. salt

4 tbsp. butter

4 oz. Kowalski's Fancy Shredded
   Cheddar Cheese

Break eggs into an extra-large mixing bowl; whisk in milk and salt until mixture is completely blended. In a 13x9" glass baking dish, melt butter in a preheated 350° oven. Pour egg mixture into melted butter. Bake approximately 20 min., stirring once after 10 min. to bring the cooked portion around edges of pan into the center (do not overstir). Sprinkle with cheese during the last few minutes of baking.

SERVES 12

EASY

CARAMELIZED BACON

1 lb. smoked pepper-coated
   bacon

1/4 cup brown sugar

Arrange bacon, slightly overlapping, on a large broiler pan. Bake in a preheated 350° oven (10 min.); flip bacon. Sprinkle brown sugar over bacon; continue baking until bacon is crisp and deep golden-brown (15-25 min.). Serve immediately.

SERVES 8

EASY

SOFT SCRAMBLED EGGS
WITH GOAT CHEESE & SMOKED SALMON

2-4 slices Italian peasant loaf, cut 1/2" thick

- Kowalski's Extra Virgin Olive Oil

- freshly ground Kowalski's Sea Salt and Black Peppercorns, to taste

1 clove garlic, peeled

2 ½ tbsp. unsalted butter

4 oz. smoked salmon, flaked

5 eggs, beaten

2 ½ oz. soft fresh goat cheese, diced into 1/2" cubes

- truffle oil

- fresh chopped chives

Arrange bread on a baking tray and brush liberally on both sides with olive oil, seasoning to taste with salt and pepper; bake in preheated 425° oven until crostini are crisp and lightly darkened on the outside but slightly soft on the inside (about 15 min.). Remove from oven and rub crisp edges and surface with garlic clove; allow to cool slightly. In a large skillet, melt butter over medium heat. Add salmon; cook until hot. Add eggs, 1/2 tsp. salt and more pepper to taste; reduce heat to medium-low. Scatter cheese over eggs; stir gently and infrequently as you move the eggs on and off the heat. Allow egg mixture to warm up, then move eggs from heat while gently stirring and distributing the heat evenly. Repeat this several times until the eggs are almost done but still quite glossy and soft. Scoop eggs directly onto prepared crostini; drizzle with truffle oil and garnish with chives. Serve immediately.

SERVES 2

EASY

FAST

55

SPINACH, CARAMELIZED ONION & FONTINA OMELET

1 tsp. Kowalski's Extra Virgin
    Olive Oil

2 tsp. butter, divided

2 thin onion slices, separated
    into rings

2 eggs

1 tbsp. cold water

1/3 cup fresh baby spinach

1/3 cup grated fontina cheese

In a small skillet, heat olive oil and 1 tsp. butter over medium heat; add onions. Sauté, stirring occasionally, until onions are soft and dark brown (about 10 min.); set aside. In a small mixing bowl, whisk together eggs and water. In a small nonstick skillet, melt remaining butter over medium heat; add egg mixture. Shake the skillet with a short forward and backward motion. Using a heat-resistant rubber spatula, pull back a little of the cooked egg around the edge and allow uncooked egg to run over until egg mixture in center is moist (15 sec.). Spread the onions, spinach and cheese down the center of the omelet. Roll 1/3 of the omelet over onto itself, then slide it out of the skillet onto a warm plate, making the second fold as the omelet falls. Serve immediately or keep warm in a 200° oven while making additional omelets.

SERVES 1

EASY

FAST

HASH BROWN POTATO CASSEROLE

40 oz. refrigerated shredded
    hash browns

1/2 cup chopped onion

8 oz. Kowalski's Fancy Shredded
    Cheddar Cheese

8 oz. sour cream

10 ¾ oz. can cream of
    mushroom soup

1 ½ tsp. salt

1/2 cup crumbled corn flakes

2 tbsp. melted butter

In a large mixing bowl, combine first 6 ingredients. Spread evenly in a 13x9" glass baking dish sprayed lightly with cooking spray. In a small mixing bowl, combine corn flake crumbs and butter. Sprinkle evenly over top. Bake in a preheated 350° oven until heated through (40-45 min.).

SERVES 12

EASY

BEVERAGES

SPARKLING LEMONADE

1/2 gal. lemonade

750 ml chilled sparkling wine

SERVES 8

EASY

FAST

Pour lemonade into Champagne flutes about 3/4 full; top off with wine.

NOTES
• Garnish the rim of each Champagne flute with sliced star fruit, strawberries, lemon or orange slices.
• Make mini ice cubes by freezing lemonade in small ice cube trays along with lemon, lime or orange peel, strawberry slices or grape halves. Place one or two ice cubes in each Champagne flute before filling with lemonade and wine.

BRUNCH PUNCH

1/2 gal. Kowalski's Fresh
    Squeezed Orange Juice

1 orange, halved and thinly
    sliced

1 cup halved green grapes

1 cup fresh pineapple cubes

1 cup fresh quartered hulled
    strawberries

Pour orange juice into a 3 qt. glass pitcher; stir in fruit. Serve immediately.

SERVES 8

EASY

FAST

SPARKLING POMEGRANATE COCKTAILS

12 oz. Pom Wonderful
      Pomegranate Juice

1/4 cup fresh squeezed lime juice
      (from about 2 small limes)

750 ml sparkling wine (such as
      Riondo Prosecco), very cold

4 tbsp. fresh pomegranate seeds

10 fresh lime slices, sliced less
      than 1/4" thin, cut into halves

In a 2-cup spouted measuring cup, stir together juices. Divide mixture evenly between 12 sparkling wine flutes; slowly pour wine into each flute, taking care to minimize fizzing. Stir gently. Float a few pomegranate seeds and a lime slice in each glass; serve immediately.

GOOD TO KNOW

- Ready-to-use pomegranate seeds are available in the Produce Department.

SERVES 12

EASY

FAST

GAZPACHO BLOODY MARY

1 medium cucumber, peeled, seeded, cut into 1" pieces

1/3 cup coarsely chopped onion

1/2 red or yellow bell pepper, seeded, cut into 1" pieces

1 clove garlic

1 tsp. prepared horseradish

2 cups tomato juice

1 tsp. kosher salt, divided

1/2 tsp. Kowalski's Coarse Ground Black Pepper, divided

- vodka

In a blender container, purée cucumber, onion, bell pepper, garlic, horseradish, tomato juice, 1/2 tsp. salt and 1/4 tsp. black pepper; refrigerate in a large covered pitcher. On a flat plate, combine remaining salt and pepper. Wet the rim of 6 martini glasses; dip each in the salt mixture. Fill glasses with ice; divide Bloody Mary mixture among glasses. Pour in a shot of vodka in each glass; serve each with cocktail stirrer.

SERVES 6

EASY

FAST

GINGER MARGARITA

GINGER SIMPLE SYRUP:

1 cup sugar

1 cup water

4 oz. fresh ginger, peeled,
    thinly sliced

MARGARITA:

1/2 cup *Ginger Simple Syrup*

1/4 cup tequila

2 tbsp. fresh squeezed
    lime juice

2 tbsp. Cointreau

GINGER SIMPLE SYRUP: Bring the sugar and water to a boil in a medium saucepan over medium-high heat, stirring to dissolve sugar. Add ginger; bring to a simmer. Remove from heat; let steep 30 min. Strain syrup; discard ginger. Store covered in the refrigerator.

MARGARITA: Put all ingredients in a cocktail shaker over ice. Shake; pour into a margarita glass over ice.

VARIATION

Ginger Martini:

1/2 cup vodka

2 tbsp. *Ginger Simple Syrup*

1/2 tsp. fresh squeezed lime juice

Put all ingredients in a cocktail shaker over ice. Shake; pour into a martini glass.

NOTE
• You can also use this simple syrup to sweeten lemonade, iced or hot tea, coffee or hot chocolate.

SERVES 1

EASY

HOT CHOCOLATE
WITH PEPPERMINT WHIPPED CREAM

4 mint-flavored hard candies

1/2 pt. heavy cream

2 tbsp. confectioner's sugar

1/2 tsp. pure peppermint extract

3 ½ cups milk

1 cup half-and-half

8 oz. dark chocolate bar

1 tsp. vanilla

Unwrap mints and place in a small zipper-closure food storage bag; close bag. With a rolling pin, crush mints; set aside. In a medium bowl, beat cream until soft peaks form; add sugar and peppermint extract. Continue beating until stiff peaks form; cover and refrigerate. In a medium saucepan over medium heat, bring milk and half-and-half just to a boil. Add chocolate; continue cooking, stirring with a whisk until chocolate melts and is smooth. Stir in vanilla. Divide hot chocolate among 6 mugs. Top with a dollop of whipped cream; sprinkle with crushed candy.

SERVES 6   EASY   FAST

FROZEN HOT CHOCOLATE

1 cup milk

1/2 cup cream

1/2 cup cocoa powder

3/4 cup confectioner's sugar

3/4 tsp. vanilla extract

1/4 tsp. espresso powder (optional)

- pinch kosher salt

3 cups crushed ice cubes

4 tbsp. shaved chocolate

Blend first 7 ingredients in a blender; add ice and pulse until slushy. Pour into 4 serving glasses or mugs and garnish with chocolate.

SERVES 4   EASY   FAST

HOT CHOCOLATE

CULINARY TIPS & IDEAS

Only one thing beats chocolate: *hot* chocolate. And only one thing beats hot chocolate: hot chocolate with stuff in it. So we're turning hot chocolate into an excuse to party with some ideas for a fun make-your-own hot chocolate bar:

TRY THESE TOPPINGS & MIX-INS:

- Mini marshmallows
- Jumbo marshmallows (try broiling them in the oven for 30 seconds just until golden)
- Peppermint sticks
- Flavored syrups (blueberry, cherry, orange, vanilla, mint, etc.)
- Ground cinnamon or cinnamon sticks
- Orange twists or rinds
- Chopped chocolate or other candy bars
- Crushed chocolate-covered espresso beans
- Chocolate chips
- Caramel squares

- Toasted coconut
- Crushed chocolate sandwich cookies
- Peanut butter
- Chopped almond toffee
- Nutmeg or ginger
- Ground cardamom
- Instant coffee or espresso granules
- Mint chocolate chip or peppermint candy cane ice cream
- Fresh mint
- Sweetened fresh whipped cream
- Crushed malt balls
- Candied ginger

HOLIDAY MARTINIS

2 tbsp. superfine sugar

1/2 tsp. lime zest

1 fresh lime, cut into slices

- ice

1/2 cup vodka

1/2 cup cranberry juice

1/4 cup limeade

1/4 cup triple sec

In a small bowl, combine sugar and lime zest; spread sugar on a flat salad plate. Rub a lime slice around the rim of 2 martini glasses to moisten it. Dip the rim of each glass in sugar to coat; set aside. In a cocktail shaker filled with ice, combine vodka, cranberry juice, limeade and triple sec; shake to thoroughly combine and chill. Carefully pour mixture into sugar-rimmed martini glasses; garnish each glass with a slice of lime.

SERVES 2

EASY

FAST

FRUIT SPRITZERS

2 cups mango peach juice (or similar 100% juice)

1 cup sliced fresh or frozen rhubarb

1/4 - 1/2 cup superfine sugar, to taste

2 tsp. freshly grated ginger

2 cups ginger ale

- ice

In a blender, purée mango peach juice, rhubarb, sugar and ginger; refrigerate in a covered pitcher until ready to serve. Stir in ginger ale. Pour into 4 ice-filled glasses.

NOTE
- 2-3 oz. of Pinot Grigio or Riesling wine can be added to each glass, if desired.

SERVES 4

EASY

FAST

WATERMELON & STRAWBERRY LEMONADE

6 cups cubed seedless
    watermelon (about 1
    personal-sized watermelon)

2 cups hulled strawberry halves

1/4 cup superfine sugar

12 oz. frozen lemonade
    concentrate, thawed

1 ½ cups tonic water or club
    soda

- lemon slices

In a blender, purée watermelon until smooth; pour through a fine-mesh strainer into a large pitcher. In a medium bowl, combine strawberries and sugar; pour into pitcher. Stir in lemonade concentrate; refrigerate, covered, until ready to serve. Stir tonic water into fruit mixture; pour into 8 ice-filled glasses. Garnish each serving with a lemon slice.

SERVES 8

EASY

FAST

NOTE
• 2-3 oz. of Pinot Grigio or Riesling wine can be added to each glass, if desired.

ROSEMARY LEMONADE

5 cups ice-cold water, divided

1 cup sugar

1 cup fresh rosemary leaves,
    plus 4 small stems
    for garnish

1 cup fresh squeezed lemon juice

4 lemon slices

In a small saucepan, mix 2 cups water and sugar; bring to a boil. Reduce heat and simmer until sugar is completely dissolved. Add rosemary leaves; remove the mixture from the heat. Cool completely (about 1 hr.). Strain into a pitcher; add 3 cups water and lemon juice. Stir well; serve over ice with a sprig of fresh rosemary and a lemon slice.

SERVES 4

EASY

ROSEMARY-GIN LEMONADE

1/4 cup gin

1/4 cup *Rosemary Lemonade*

1/2 cup tonic water or club soda

- ice, lime or orange slices
    and maraschino cherries
    for garnish

Stir gin and lemonade together in a glass. Add tonic or club soda. Serve over ice with a lime or orange slice and a maraschino cherry.

SERVES 1

EASY

STRAWBERRY LEMONADE

1 lb. fresh strawberries, hulled
    and halved

4 cups ice-cold water, divided

1 cup sugar

1 tbsp. lemon zest (optional)

1 cup fresh squeezed
    lemon juice

- mint sprigs and whole
    strawberries for garnish

In a blender or food processor, purée strawberries; pour into a pitcher and set aside. In a small saucepan, mix 2 cups water and the sugar; bring to a boil. Reduce heat and simmer until sugar is completely dissolved. Remove the mixture from the heat; chill completely in refrigerator (about 1 hr.). Stir in zest and lemon juice; pour into the pitcher with the strawberry purée. Add 2 cups water; stir well. Serve over ice with a sprig of fresh mint and a strawberry.

SERVES 4

EASY

SUMMER FRUIT SMOOTHIE

1 cup Kowalski's Fresh Squeezed
Orange Juice

1 cup fresh strawberries, hulled

1 kiwifruit, peeled

1 cup nonfat vanilla frozen yogurt

12 ice cubes

Place all ingredients in a blender; process
until smooth.

SERVES 4

EASY

FAST

CITRUS SMOOTHIE

1 banana

1 cup Kowalski's Fresh Squeezed
Orange Juice

1 cup fresh pineapple chunks

6 oz. fat-free vanilla yogurt

1 tbsp. flaxseeds

8 ice cubes

In a blender container, purée all
ingredients until ice is crushed.

Nutrition Information Per Serving	
Total Calories	115
Total Fat	1 g
Sodium	30 mg

Each serving contains 70% of your
daily vitamin C requirement, plus
vitamin B6, potassium and fiber.

SERVES 4    EASY   FAST

ICED TEA
CULINARY TIPS & IDEAS

It's a cooling summer beverage that suits all variety of meals. Make the perfect pitcher of iced tea with these tips and flavor ideas:

- Use filtered water for best results.

- Bring water to a boil, but for white or green tea let it cool slightly before combining with these more delicate teas.

- Steep fresh herbs or whole spices with the tea or tea bags and remove when the bags are removed.

- Be careful not to oversteep; bitter or acidic tastes may result.

- Don't cool your steeped brew too quickly or the tea may become cloudy.

- Sweeten tea with a simple syrup – 1 part sugar dissolved in 1 part hot water.

- Use honey or brown sugar instead of white for a refreshingly different taste, or try replacing a tablespoon of sugar per cup with molasses or maple syrup.

- Add flavored syrups, such as those used for espresso beverages.

- Do not leave citrus fruit rinds in the pitcher if you plan to store it. They will lend a bitter profile to the tea as it holds.

- Iced tea is best stored in glass. Plastic absorbs and releases odors, and metal pitchers can lend a metallic taste.

- Keep pitcher covered in the refrigerator to prevent it from absorbing odors. Drink it within 2 days for freshest flavor.

- Use twice as much tea as you would for the same amount of hot brewed tea.

- Flavor tea with fresh fruit juice or lemonade.

- Use flavored ice cubes – made with juice or lemonade and filled with herbs, edible flowers or fruits.

SUN TEA

6 tea bags or 2 tbsp. loose tea

2 strips lemon zest, each
      1" long

4 ½ cups cold water

2 tbsp. superfine sugar

1 tbsp. fresh squeezed
      lemon juice

Stir first 4 ingredients together in a large jar; cover and place in the sun for at least 4 hrs. Remove tea; add lemon juice. Chill and serve over ice.

SERVES 4

EASY

STARTERS
- HOT -

CRAB, SPINACH & ARTICHOKE DIP

1/2 cup mayonnaise

1/2 cup sour cream

1/4 cup finely chopped onion

1/2 tsp. minced garlic

8 oz. shredded Marble
    Jack cheese

6 oz. julienne-cut sun-dried
    tomatoes in olive oil and
    drained, blotted dry

6 ½ oz. marinated quartered
    artichoke hearts, drained

1 cup roughly chopped
    fully cooked crab meat

1 cup fresh baby spinach

1/4 cup shredded Parmesan
    cheese

1 French baguette, heated,
    sliced

In a 2 qt. casserole dish, combine the first 8 ingredients; bake in a preheated 325° oven until heated through (about 20 min.). Carefully stir in spinach; top with Parmesan cheese. Continue baking 5 min. Serve immediately with warm French bread slices.

SERVES 12

EASY

MAKE-YOUR-OWN BAKED CHEESE DIP

16 oz. cream cheese

1/2 cup mayonnaise

2 cups shredded cheese
(such as Cheddar, Swiss,
Blue, Gorgonzola, Monterey
Jack or combination)

- choice of stir-ins (see list)

1/4 cup shredded cheese, such
as Mozzarella or Parmesan

Beat cream cheese until creamy and smooth; stir in mayonnaise, 2 cups shredded cheese and choice of stir-ins until well blended. Spread in a 9x9" glass baking dish sprayed lightly with cooking spray; sprinkle with 1/4 cup cheese. Bake in a preheated 350° oven until bubbly, golden-brown and thoroughly hot (25-35 min.). Let stand 10 min. before serving with crackers or bread.

STIR-INS:

15 oz. can artichoke hearts, rinsed,
well drained and chopped

10 oz. frozen chopped spinach,
thawed and squeezed dry

1/4 cup shredded rotisserie chicken

1/4 cup chopped cooked shrimp
or crab

1/4 cup crumbled cooked bacon

1/4 cup chopped Genoa salami

1/4 cup chopped sun-dried tomatoes
or roasted red peppers

1/4 cup caramelized onions

1/4 cup chopped, pitted olives

1/4 cup chopped pimentos

1 tbsp. smoked paprika

1 tbsp. taco seasoning

2 tbsp. sliced green onion

2-4 dashes hot sauce or
Worcestershire sauce

2 tbsp. grated onion

1/2-1 tsp. dried herbs

1-2 cloves garlic, finely minced

- kosher salt and/or coarse ground
black pepper, to taste

SERVES 16

EASY

77

ITALIAN GRILLED CROSTINI

1 Kowalski's Take & Bake French Baguette, cut into 24 slices on the diagonal

3 oz. pkg. prosciutto, each slice cut into quarters

7 ⅓ oz. jar Kowalski's Traditional Basil Pesto, divided

7 oz. canned roasted tomatoes, drained

12 oz. fresh mozzarella cheese, thinly sliced

Grill baguette slices over medium-low heat, uncovered, until bottoms are golden-brown and crisp (about 2 min.); remove from grill. With grilled side up, top each baguette slice with a piece of prosciutto, 1 tsp. pesto, a roasted tomato and a slice of mozzarella. Transfer baguette slices back to the grill; continue grilling until bottoms are golden-brown and crisp and fresh mozzarella is slightly melted (about 2 min.). Serve immediately.

MAKES 24

EASY

FAST

GOOD TO KNOW
• Kowalski's Traditional Basil Pesto is available in the Grocery Department.

Signature

78

TWICE-BAKED POTATO MINIS

12 baby red potatoes

2 tbsp. Kowalski's Extra Virgin Olive Oil

1 tsp. kosher salt

3-4 tbsp. milk

1/4 cup plus 1 tbsp. fancy shredded Cheddar cheese, divided

1 bunch green onions, thinly sliced

2 tbsp. cooked crumbled bacon

1 tsp. finely chopped fresh Italian parsley

Cut a slice off both ends of each potato; place in zipper-closure food storage bag with olive oil and salt. Seal bag; toss potatoes in bag to evenly coat with oil and salt. Remove potatoes from bag and arrange in mini muffin pans; bake in a preheated 450° oven (30 min.). Cool potatoes; with small measuring spoon, scoop cooked potato out of each shell. Continue baking shells in mini muffin pans (15 min.). In a medium bowl, mix cooked potato with milk, 1/4 cup cheese, onions and bacon. Spoon filling into another zipper-closure food storage bag. Snip off corner of bag; pipe filling evenly into potato shells. Bake in a preheated 425° oven until tops are browned (15-20 min.); sprinkle remaining cheese and parsley over potatoes. Serve hot.

NOTE
• Mary Anne Kowalski loves this recipe without the cheese.

MAKES 12

ITALIAN WONTON BITES

- Kowalski's Extra Virgin
    Olive Oil

24 wonton wrappers

4 ½ oz. pkg. Boursin Light Garlic
    and Fine Herbs Cheese

1/2 cup pesto

24 pieces julienne-cut sun-dried
    tomatoes in olive oil
    and herbs

1/4 cup shredded Parmesan
    cheese

Lightly grease 24 mini muffin cups with olive oil; press a wonton wrapper into each cup, making a well. Bake in a preheated 350° oven (5 min.); remove from oven. Divide cheese and pesto among wontons; garnish each with 1 tomato and Parmesan cheese. Continue baking until edges of wontons are browned (8-10 min.); serve warm.

MAKES 24

FAST

EASY

PULLED PORK NACHOS

4 oz. (about 32 chips) large
  corn tortilla chips

1/2 lb. Kowalski's Signature BBQ
  Pulled Pork, warmed
  slightly in the microwave

1 ½ cups Kowalski's Shredded
  Mexican Blend Cheese

- thinly sliced green onions,
  to taste

- chopped fresh cilantro,
  if desired

- Ranch salad dressing, to taste

Arrange chips in an even layer on a parchment-lined baking sheet. Top evenly with pork; sprinkle evenly with cheese. Bake in a preheated 400° oven until cheese is melted and bubbly (about 4 min.). If desired, place chips under a preheated broiler just until cheese turns very dark (about 1-2 min.), watching carefully so chips do not burn. Remove from oven; sprinkle with onions and cilantro and drizzle with Ranch dressing. Serve immediately.

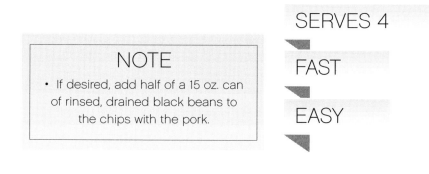

SERVES 4

FAST

EASY

NOTE
• If desired, add half of a 15 oz. can
of rinsed, drained black beans to
the chips with the pork.

BACON-WRAPPED PARMESAN DATES

24 Medjool dates, pitted

24 matchstick-shaped pieces Kowalski's Parmesan cheese, about 1/4" x 1/4" x 1 ½" (cut from a chunk)

12 slices bacon, cut crossways into halves

24 toothpicks

Stuff each date with 1 piece of cheese; set aside. Place bacon on rimmed baking sheet; bake in a preheated 450° oven until starting to crisp but still pliable (about 7 min.); remove from oven, allowing to cool until just warm enough to handle. Wrap partially cooked bacon around each date, securing with a toothpick; place 1" apart on baking sheet. Bake until bacon is fully cooked and lightly crispy (10-12 min.), turning once. Drain on paper towels; serve warm.

GOOD TO KNOW
• Medjool dates are available in the Bulk Foods Section.

SERVES 12

KALBI DRUMMIES

1 tbsp. butter

1 tbsp. olive oil

36 chicken wing drumettes

3/4 tsp. kosher salt

12 oz. Kowalski's Kalbi Marinade

In a large skillet over medium-high heat, melt butter with olive oil. Sprinkle chicken with salt; add to skillet. Cook, turning occasionally until browned on all sides (about 10 min.). Move chicken to a baking sheet sprayed with cooking spray; bake in a preheated 425° oven until chicken reaches an internal temperature of 165°, turning once (20-25 min.). Working in batches, transfer chicken to a large mixing bowl; toss with sauce to coat. Serve immediately.

SERVES 12

EASY

EASY GRILLED PIZZA OR FLATBREAD

- crust, your choice: Golden Home Ultra Crispy & Ultra Thin Pizza Crust, Flat Out Wraps, Toufayan Whole Wheat Flat bread, Stonefire Tandoori Naan or similar

- Kowalski's Extra Virgin Olive Oil

- sauce (such as *Romesco Sauce* or *Pizzaiola Sauce*) and/or toppings and cheese

Brush one side of each crust very lightly with oil. Arrange crust, oiled side down, on the back of a baking sheet or a cutting board; arrange a sparse amount of sauce, toppings and cheese evenly over pizza, taking care not to overload it. Heat grill to high on both sides with lid down. Turn one side off (or move coals to one side). Grill pizzas 1-2 at a time (as space permits), directly over heat, lid down, rotating crust 90° when dark grill marks form (2-3 min. total). Slide pizza to cool side of grill. Let stand, lid down, until cheese is melted and bubbly (about 2 min.). Remove from grill; let stand 1-2 min. before slicing. Serve immediately.

GOOD TO KNOW

- Find flatbreads, wraps and naan in the Deli Department. Also try Toufayan Hearth Baked Multigrain Lavash or Kowalski's 10" Flour Tortillas for the pizza crust.

- Find Golden Home Ultra Crispy & Ultra Thin Pizza Crust in the Grocery Department.

MAKES 1

FAST

EASY

ROMESCO SAUCE:

8 oz. jar roasted red bell
    peppers, drained

1/2 oz. fresh basil

1/4 cup raw skinned almonds

3 tbsp. Kowalski's Extra
    Virgin Olive Oil

3 cloves garlic

1/2 tsp. kosher salt

Pulse all ingredients together in a food processor until well blended but still slightly chunky.

NOTE
• This also makes a delicious alternative to traditional basil pesto on pasta, sandwiches and wraps.

MAKES about 3/4 cup

PIZZAIOLA SAUCE:

2 tbsp. Kowalski's Extra
    Virgin Olive Oil

2 cloves garlic, finely minced

1 tsp. dried oregano

1/4 tsp. fennel seeds

1/4 tsp. crushed red pepper flakes

15 oz. petite diced tomatoes,
    drained

- kosher salt and Kowalski's
    Coarse Ground Black
    Pepper, to taste

Heat oil in a small saucepan over medium heat; add garlic, oregano, fennel and red pepper. Cook 1 min. until fragrant. Add tomatoes; bring to a boil. Reduce heat to low; simmer until thick (8-10 min.). Season to taste with salt and pepper.

MAKES about 1 cup

CLASSIC FONDUE

1 clove garlic, crushed

1 cup dry white wine

1 tbsp. cornstarch

2 tbsp. cold water

1/3 lb. grated Emmental cheese

1/3 lb. grated Gruyère cheese

1/3 lb. soft cheese, such as Brie

1/2 tsp. Kirsch, to taste

- dash freshly grated nutmeg

- coarse ground black pepper, to taste

Rub the inside of a medium saucepan with crushed garlic; discard garlic. Add wine and bring to a simmer. Dissolve cornstarch in water and whisk into wine. Bring to a boil and cook for 2 min. Reduce heat to low and whisk in the cheeses, a little at a time. Stir in Kirsch and season with nutmeg and pepper.

SERVE FONDUE WITH YOUR CHOICE OF DIPPERS:

- Cubes of bread, lightly toasted (such as French or pumpernickel)
- Cornichons (French gherkins)
- Cooked new potatoes
- Cremini mushrooms
- Carrots
- Celery
- Gently blanched asparagus, broccoli or cauliflower

SERVES 6

EASY

FAST

BLUE CHEESE FONDUE

1 tsp. cornstarch

1/2 cup sweet white wine
(Gewürztraminer or
Riesling), divided

1 lb. St. Pete's Select Blue,
Maytag Blue or Point Reyes
Blue Cheese, crumbled

In a small cup, combine cornstarch
and 1 tbsp. wine; set aside. In a medium
saucepan, heat remaining wine to
simmering over medium heat. Stir in
cornstarch mixture and cheese until
smooth.

SERVE FONDUE WITH YOUR CHOICE OF DIPPERS:

- Cooked beef tenderloin
- French baguette cubes
- Bosc pear slices
- Steamed asparagus
- Seared endive

SERVES 6

EASY

FAST

STARTERS
- COLD -

CREAMY YOGURT DIP

1 cup plain yogurt

1 garlic clove, mashed to a
    paste with 1/2 tsp.
    kosher salt

1/2 tsp. dried thyme

1/2 tsp. ground cumin

1/2 tsp. ground coriander

1/4 tsp. ground cinnamon

1/8 tsp. chili powder

- dash cayenne pepper

- coarse ground black pepper,
    to taste

Stir together all of the ingredients in a small bowl. Serve immediately or store, covered, in the refrigerator up to 3 days.

Nutrition Information Per 1/4 Cup Serving

Total Calories	43
Total Fat	1 g
Sodium	45 mg

NOTE

• Serve with grilled spiced meats (such as poultry or flank steak), with pita chips or whole grain crackers or with fresh veggies (such as carrots, celery, peppers, radishes, cauliflower, tomatoes, spring onions or string beans).

MAKES 1 cup

EASY

FAST

FRESH GUACAMOLE

2 ripe avocados

1/4 cup seeded, chopped tomatoes

2 tbsp. minced red onion

1 tsp. chopped garlic

2 tsp. minced jalapeño pepper

2 tbsp. finely chopped fresh cilantro

1 tbsp. fresh lime juice

- kosher salt, to taste

Cut avocados in half; remove pits. Scoop flesh from one avocado into a medium glass bowl. Mash with a fork; stir in tomato, onion, garlic, jalapeño and cilantro. Cut flesh of remaining avocado into 1/2" cubes. Scoop out of skin into the bowl with the mashed avocado mixture. Sprinkle with lime juice, mixing lightly with a fork until combined but still chunky. Season with salt. Serve with tortilla chips.

Nutrition Information Per 1/4 Cup Serving

Total Calories	80
Total Fat	7 g
Saturated Fat	1 g
Sodium	4 mg
Fiber	3 g

GOOD TO KNOW

• To ripen avocados, place in a paper bag; leave on the counter at room temperature, checking each day until they reach the desired softness.

• For variety, stir in cooked shrimp, lump crabmeat, chipotle peppers, tomatillos, sliced red radishes or jicama to the finished guacamole.

MAKES 1 ½ cups

EASY

FAST

GRANDMA BETTY'S FAMOUS CHIP DIP

16 oz. softened cream cheese

1/2 cup Miracle Whip
    Salad Dressing

2 tbsp. grated onion, or more
    to taste

4 dashes Worcestershire
    sauce

1/4 cup half-and-half, approx.

2 dashes Tabasco sauce

Beat cream cheese until creamy and smooth; stir in remaining ingredients until well blended, adding additional half-and-half to reach desired consistency.

NOTE

- Betty Kowalski's original hand-written recipe suggested tasting with a rippled potato chip for best results, and to "taste again and have someone else taste. Now, stop tasting! You'll spoil your dinner!"

MAKES 2 cups

EASY

FAST

92

MAKE-YOUR-OWN CREAMY CHIP DIP

16 oz. softened cream cheese

1/2 cup salad dressing (such as Miracle Whip) or mayonnaise

1/4 cup half-and-half (approx.)

- choice of stir-ins (see list)

Beat cream cheese until creamy and smooth; stir in remaining ingredients until well blended, adding additional half-and-half to reach desired consistency.

MAKES 2 cups

EASY

FAST

STIR-INS:

10 oz. frozen spinach, thawed and squeezed dry

1/4 cup shredded cheese (such as Cheddar, Blue or Parmesan)

1/4 cup finely chopped cooked shrimp, crab or bacon

1/4 cup chopped sun-dried tomatoes or roasted red peppers

1/4 cup caramelized onions

1/4 cup chopped, pitted olives or pimentos

1 tbsp. smoked paprika or taco seasoning

2 tbsp. sliced green onion

2-4 dashes Worcestershire or hot sauce

1/2-1 tsp. dried herbs

1-2 cloves garlic, finely minced

- kosher salt and/or coarse ground black pepper, to taste

LENTIL SPREAD

1 tbsp. plus 1/2 cup Kowalski's Extra Virgin Olive Oil, divided

1 cup Kowalski's Mirepoix

1/2 oz. Kowalski's Fresh Thyme, stemmed and roughly chopped

1/2 oz. Kowalski's Fresh Rosemary, stemmed and roughly chopped

1 bay leaf

1 cup green or brown lentils

1/2 cup dry white wine

4 cups low-sodium chicken broth, divided, approx.

1/4 cup roasted garlic cloves

2 tbsp. fresh squeezed lemon juice

- kosher salt and Kowalski's Coarse Ground Black Pepper, to taste

Heat 1 tbsp. oil in a large saucepan over medium heat; add mirepoix and herbs. Cook until vegetables are soft (about 5 min.). Add lentils; cook and stir for 2 min. Add wine; cook until almost evaporated (4-5 min.). Pour in enough broth to cover lentils by 1"; bring to a boil. Reduce heat to medium-low; simmer until lentils are tender (about 60 min.), adding more broth or water a bit at a time as needed to keep lentils barely submerged. Cool slightly; discard bay leaf. Purée lentil mixture with garlic cloves in a food processor; with processor running, drizzle in remaining oil through pour spout. Stir in juice; season with salt and pepper.

Nutrition Information Per 1/4 Cup Serving

Total Calories	162
Total Fat	11 g
Saturated Fat	2 g
Sodium	19 mg
Fiber	3 g

A good source of vitamins A and K, folate and iron.

NOTE

• Red or yellow lentils will work, too, but will require less cooking liquid and less cooking time.

MAKES 3 cups

EASY

94

GREEK DIP

1 tbsp. Kowalski's Extra
    Virgin Olive Oil

1/2 cup chopped yellow onion

2 cloves minced garlic

1 cup canned Northern beans,
    rinsed and drained

1/2 cup plain Greek yogurt
    (not nonfat)

2 tbsp. olive oil mayonnaise

- zest of 1 lemon

3 tbsp. finely chopped mild
    pickled banana peppers

1 tbsp. chopped capers

- dash cayenne pepper

- kosher salt and Kowalski's
    Coarse Ground Black
    Pepper, to taste

Heat oil in a medium skillet over medium heat. Sauté onion and garlic, stirring constantly until onion is very soft (5-7 min.); cool to room temperature. In a food processor, process onion mixture with beans, yogurt and mayonnaise until smooth. Add remaining ingredients and process until desired consistency is reached (or, for a slightly more textured dip, transfer to a medium bowl and stir in the remaining ingredients by hand).

Nutrition Information Per 1/4 Cup Serving

Total Calories	145
Total Fat	6 g
Saturated Fat	1 g
Sodium	275 mg
Fiber	3 g

A good source of vitamins C and K, folate, potassium and iron.

MAKES 1 cup

EASY

FAST

GOOD FOODS FOR GOOD
Health

SWEET RED PEPPER DIP

3/4 cup chopped walnuts,
   toasted

12 oz. jar roasted red peppers,
   well drained

1 tbsp. molasses, plus extra
   for garnish, if desired

1 tbsp. sugar

1 tsp. lemon zest

- juice of 1/2 lemon

1/2 tsp. whole cumin seeds

1/4 tsp. ground cumin, or more
   to taste

- pinch cayenne pepper

- kosher salt and Kowalski's
   Coarse Ground Black
   Pepper, to taste

1 ½-3 tbsp. Kowalski's Extra
   Virgin Olive Oil, as desired

Combine all ingredients except oil in food processor and process until smooth. Slowly drizzle in oil through oil spout until mixture is glossy, smooth and reaches desired consistency. Adjust seasoning to taste; drizzle with molasses, if desired.

Nutrition Information Per 1/4 Cup Serving

Total Calories	118
Total Fat	10 g
Saturated Fat	1 g
Sodium	91 mg

Provides nearly a day's worth of vitamin C (94%).

NOTE
• Substitute 4 freshly roasted red peppers (stemmed, peeled and seeded) for the jarred peppers, if desired.

MAKES 2 cups

EASY

FAST

GLAMMED-UP HUMMUS PLATTER

12-16 oz. Kowalski's Original
Hummus

1 tbsp. Kowalski's Extra
Virgin Olive Oil

1/2 tsp. crushed red pepper
flakes

1/2 tsp. kosher salt

1/2 tsp. dried oregano or 1 tsp.
chopped fresh oregano

1/4 tsp. coarse ground black
pepper

- zest of 1/2 lemon

2 small stems fresh oregano

- pita chips or fresh vegetables
(radishes, carrots, celery,
peppers, etc.)

Scoop hummus directly onto an 8" serving platter; spread to thickly cover the plate. Drizzle hummus with oil and sprinkle with red pepper flakes, salt, oregano, pepper and lemon zest. Garnish with fresh oregano. Serve alongside a basket or platter of chips or vegetables for dipping.

Nutrition Information Per 1/4 Cup Serving
(Excluding chips or veggies)

Total Calories	62
Total Fat	5 g
Saturated Fat	1 g
Sodium	137 mg
Fiber	2 g

SERVES 12

EASY

FAST

CARAMELIZED ONION & BLUE CHEESE DIP

1 tbsp. Kowalski's Extra
        Virgin Olive Oil

1 tbsp. butter

2 cups chopped yellow onions

1 tbsp. sugar

8 oz. crème fraîche

1 cup mayonnaise

1/2 cup crumbled blue cheese

In a medium skillet, heat olive oil and butter over medium heat until butter melts; stir in onions and sugar. Sauté onions until translucent (about 10 min.); cool. In a medium bowl, combine crème fraîche, mayonnaise and cheese; stir in onions.

SERVES 12

EASY   FAST

BLUE CHEESE SPREAD

8 oz. softened cream cheese

6 oz. crumbled blue cheese

3 tbsp. finely minced shallots

- dash Tabasco sauce

1/4 cup walnuts, toasted,
        coarsely chopped

- rye, flax or multigrain bread,
        your choice

In a large bowl, beat cheeses, shallots and Tabasco on medium speed until well blended. Spoon into serving bowl; garnish with walnuts. Serve with bread.

SERVES 4

EASY

FAST

DATE & BLUE CHEESE SPREAD

8 oz. cream cheese, at room temperature

4 oz. crumbled blue cheese, at room temperature

1 tbsp. milk

8 Medjool dates, pitted and minced

2 tsp. honey

3/4 oz. finely chopped toasted walnuts

1 tsp. grated lemon zest

1/4 tsp. fresh ground black pepper

1 tbsp. minced fresh Italian parsley

Beat together first 4 ingredients using an electric mixer until completely smooth. Scoop directly onto an 8" serving platter; spread to thickly cover the plate. Drizzle with honey and sprinkle with walnuts, lemon zest and pepper. Garnish with parsley. Serve alongside a basket or platter of whole grain crackers for dipping.

NOTE
- This is also delicious on a thin wafer-style lemon, ginger or almond-flavored cookie.

SERVES 12

EASY

FAST

BRUSCHETTA

1 Kowalski's French Baguette

- Kowalski's Extra Virgin
    Olive Oil

1 clove garlic, cut in half

3 medium tomatoes, cored,
    seeded, diced

1/2 cup chopped yellow onion

1/4 cup chopped fresh basil

2 tsp. balsamic vinegar

1 tsp. minced garlic

1 tsp. kosher salt

Slice baguette into 1/2" thick slices on
the diagonal; brush each side with olive
oil. Arrange on a baking sheet; bake in
a preheated 375° oven until crisp and
golden-brown, turning once (8-10 min.).
Rub garlic clove on one side of each
bread slice. In a medium bowl, thoroughly
combine remaining ingredients. Spoon
tomato mixture on bread slices; serve
immediately.

Nutrition Information
Per 2-Piece Serving

Total Calories	132
Total Fat	5 g
Saturated Fat	< 1 g
Sodium	296 mg
Fiber	1 g

SERVES 24

EASY

FAST

SPICY MARINATED PROVOLONE

10 oz. chunk provolone cheese, cut into 3/4" cubes

1/2 cup Kowalski's Extra Virgin Olive Oil

1/4 cup fresh squeezed lemon juice

3 cloves garlic, thinly sliced

1 ½ tsp. fresh lemon zest

1 tsp. Kowalski's Whole Fennel Seeds

1/2 tsp. Kowalski's Whole Mixed Peppercorns

1/4 tsp. Kowalski's Crushed Red Pepper Flakes

Place cheese in a zipper-closure food storage bag. Combine remaining ingredients in a 1 pt. glass jar with a tight-fitting lid; cover and shake well. Pour over cheese in storage bag; seal bag. Refrigerate 8 hrs. or up to 3 days, turning occasionally. Let cheese stand at room temperature at least 1 hr.; stir and pour onto serving platter, serve immediately.

SERVES 12

EASY

MASCARPONE-STUFFED DRIED APRICOTS

8 oz. mascarpone cheese, at room temperature

2 tbsp. yuzu marmalade (or orange marmalade)

16 dried apricots, slit with a paring knife

1/4 cup candied pecans, crushed with the flat end of a chef's knife

In a small bowl, stir together mascarpone and marmalade. With a spoon or pastry bag, fill each apricot with approx. 2 tsp. of the cheese mixture. Refrigerate, covered, 8-24 hrs. One hr. before serving, press the crushed pecans onto one end of each stuffed apricot.

GOOD TO KNOW
- Find yuzu marmalade with the accompaniments in the Imported Cheese Department.

MAKES 16   EASY

GORGONZOLA-STUFFED FIGS **WITH RED WINE SYRUP**

2 cups red wine

24 dried figs

1/4 cup sugar

24 slices Prosciutto di Parma, thinly sliced

3 oz. Gorgonzola cheese, in 24 chunks

- chopped fresh chives

- red grapes, sliced in half lengthwise

In a small saucepan, bring wine to a boil. Lower heat and add figs; simmer until figs are tender (about 5 min.). Remove figs and set aside. Add sugar to the wine in the saucepan; simmer until reduced to 1/2 cup; remove from heat and set aside. Fold each prosciutto slice in half to make 4 ½ x 4" rectangles. Remove stem and cut an "x" in the top of each fig; stuff opening with cheese. Place a stuffed fig in the center of each prosciutto rectangle. Wrap a piece of prosciutto around each fig. Drizzle a serving plate with wine reduction and set wrapped stuffed figs on top. Drizzle with additional syrup; garnish plate with chives and red grapes.

SERVES 8

TENDERLOIN CROSTINI

WITH CAPER AIOLI

1 Kowalski's French baguette, sliced 3/4" thick on the diagonal (24 slices)

- Kowalski's Extra Virgin Olive Oil

1 lb. center-cut beef tenderloin

2 tsp. Kowalski's North Woods Grill Seasoning Blend

1 cup mayonnaise

1 tbsp. capers, drained and rinsed

2 tsp. minced garlic

Brush one side of each baguette slice with oil. Arrange in a single layer on a baking sheet. Bake in a preheated 350° oven 5 min. Turn and continue baking for an additional 2 min.; remove from oven and set aside. Rub tenderloin with seasoning; arrange on a broiler pan. Broil, uncovered, until rare in the center (8-12 min.), turning once. Let stand, covered, 10 min. before slicing 1/4" thick. In a small bowl, combine mayonnaise, capers and garlic. Arrange a slice of beef on each crostini; top with aioli.

MAKES 24

EASY

Signature

TUSCAN-STYLE MELON & PROSCIUTTO

1/2 cantaloupe

6 oz. prosciutto

1 tbsp. honey

1 ½ tsp. finely minced fresh rosemary

2 fresh rosemary stems

Remove cantaloupe rind, scoop out seeds and slice melon into crescent-shaped pieces about 1/4" thick; fan out onto half of a serving platter. Separate slices of prosciutto and loosely arrange in a fluffy pile on the other half of the platter. Drizzle honey over both sides of the platter; sprinkle minced rosemary over honey. Garnish with fresh rosemary stems placed between the melon and prosciutto; serve immediately.

SERVES 12

EASY

FAST

BRIE WITH CARAMELIZED PEARS

6 tbsp. butter

1 cup sugar

2 ripe pears, thinly sliced

1 wheel Brie cheese, top
    rind removed

In a large skillet, melt butter; stir in sugar, cooking until sugar melts and turns brown. Gently stir in pear slices; cook until slightly soft. Spoon over Brie; serve immediately.

SERVES 16

EASY

FAST

106

KOWALSKI'S MEXICAN SHRIMP COCKTAIL

12 oz. container Kowalski's
    Cocktail Sauce

1 lb. fresh cooked, peeled,
    tail-off shrimp, cut into
    bite-sized pieces

1 tomato, cored and seeded,
    diced

1/2 cup chopped fresh cilantro

1/2 cup diced red onion

2 tbsp. ketchup

1 tbsp. chopped garlic

1 tbsp. horseradish

1/2 tsp. Kowalski's Chili Powder

1/2 tsp. Kowalski's Cumin

2 avocados, diced

In a large bowl, combine the first 10 ingredients. Just before serving, stir in the avocados. Serve alone or with tortilla chips.

SERVES 6

EASY

FAST

GOOD TO KNOW

• Kowalski's Cocktail Sauce is available in the Seafood Department.

SOUPS

BUTTERNUT SQUASH & APPLE BISQUE **WITH CRÈME FRAÎCHE**

2 tbsp. butter

1/2 cup finely minced onion

1 ½ lbs. butternut squash, peeled, cut into 1" cubes (about 4 cups)

2 cups apple juice

3/4 tsp. ground cinnamon

1 cup half-and-half

1/2 apple, cored, peeled and very thinly sliced

2 tsp. salt

1/4 tsp. white pepper

7 oz. carton crème fraîche

In a large saucepan over medium heat, melt butter. Stir in onion; sauté until slightly softened (about 2 min.). Add squash, apple juice and cinnamon. Bring to a boil over medium-high heat, covered; reduce heat and simmer until squash is fork-tender (20-25 min.). Cool in pan 15 min. Place squash mixture in a food processor or blender and process until smooth. Return puréed squash to saucepan; stir in half-and-half, apple slices, salt and pepper. Warm over medium heat, stirring occasionally, until heated through (about 10 min.). Ladle soup into cups; top with a small dollop of crème fraîche.

SERVES 4

LENTIL STEW

WITH SMOKED TURKEY SAUSAGE

3 tbsp. olive oil

16 oz. pkg. Kowalski's Soup Mix

3 tbsp. flour

8 cups chicken broth

1 bay leaf

1/2 tsp. dried thyme

1 ½ cups dried lentils

1 tsp. kosher salt

1/2 tsp. Kowalski's Coarse
        Ground Black Pepper

12 oz. smoked turkey sausage,
        sliced

In a large saucepan over medium heat, heat oil; cook soup mix until softened (about 10 min.). Whisk in flour; cook 2 min. Pour in broth; add bay leaf, thyme, lentils, salt and pepper. Bring to a boil; reduce to simmer. Cook until lentils are tender (65-75 min.); stir in sausage; heat through.

GOOD TO KNOW

• Kowalski's Soup Mix is available in the Produce Department. Or you can use approximately 3 cups of finely chopped mixed vegetables, such as carrots, celery, onions, leeks and parsnips.

SERVES 8

EASY

111

ROTISSERIE CHICKEN NOODLE SOUP

1 Kowalski's Signature
Rotisserie Chicken

12 cups chicken broth

1 ½ cups matchstick-cut carrots

1 ½ cups diced celery

1/2 cup minced onion

5 sprigs fresh thyme

2 tbsp. chopped fresh
Italian parsley

1/2 of a 9 oz. pkg. of Kowalski's
Fresh Linguine Noodles,
noodles cut into thirds

Pick chicken meat from bones, removing skin; discard bones and skin and shred meat. In a large stockpot, combine chicken, broth, carrots, celery, onion, thyme and parsley. Bring to a boil over high heat; reduce heat to low and simmer until vegetables are tender (about 15 min.). Return to a boil over high heat; add linguine, cooking until noodles are tender (2-3 min.).

SERVES 8

EASY

FAST

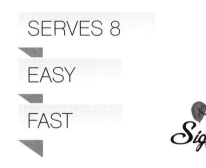

Signature

112

CHICKEN WILD RICE SOUP

1/2 cup butter

1/4 cup finely chopped onion

1/4 cup chopped celery

1/2 cup flour

4 cups chicken broth

2 cups cooked wild rice

1/2 cup grated carrots

1 cup chopped, cooked
Kowalski's Signature
Rotisserie Chicken

1/2 tsp. salt

2 cups half-and-half

1/4 cup dry sherry

In a large saucepan over medium heat, melt butter; sauté onion and celery until tender (about 5 min.). Whisk in flour; cook 1 min. Gradually add broth and bring to a boil, stirring until slightly thickened. Stir in wild rice, carrots, chicken, salt and half-and-half; simmer about 15 min., stirring occasionally. Remove from heat and stir in sherry before serving.

SERVES 8

EASY

FAST

TURKEY WHITE BEAN SOUP

1 tbsp. olive oil

1 cup diced carrot

1/2 cup chopped yellow onion

1/3 cup diced celery

1 tbsp. minced garlic

5 cups low-sodium chicken broth

28 oz. can fire-roasted
   diced tomatoes

2 cups chopped, cooked
   turkey breast

1 ¾ cups dried cannellini
   beans, picked over, rinsed

1 tbsp. finely chopped
   fresh rosemary

1 tbsp. finely chopped fresh thyme

1 tbsp. finely chopped fresh basil

1/2 tsp. Kowalski's Coarse
   Ground Black Pepper

2 tbsp. balsamic vinegar

- shredded Parmesan cheese

In a large stockpot, heat oil over medium-high heat; sauté carrot, onion, celery and garlic until vegetables soften (about 5 min.), stirring frequently. Add broth, tomatoes, turkey, beans, rosemary, thyme, basil and pepper. Liquid should cover the beans by about 1"; add more broth or water if necessary. Bring stock to a boil; reduce heat to low. Simmer, covered, stirring occasionally until beans are tender (2-3 hrs.). If necessary, add additional water so the beans remain covered with liquid the entire cooking time. Stir in vinegar; serve topped with shredded Parmesan.

Nutrition Information Per Serving

Total Calories	205
Total Fat	3 g
Saturated Fat	1 g
Sodium	227 mg

A good source of these heart nutrients: vitamins A and C, fiber, niacin, potassium, calcium, folate, magnesium, zinc and copper.

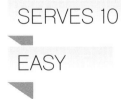

SERVES 10

EASY

THREE BEAN CHILI CON CARNE

2 lb. extra-lean ground beef

1 ½ cups chopped onion

1 ½ cups chopped celery

1 tsp. chopped garlic

46 oz. can tomato juice

29 oz. canned diced tomatoes with chiles

29 oz. canned diced tomatoes

1 tbsp. chili powder

2 tsp. salt

2 tsp. cumin

1 tsp. dried basil

1/2 tsp. cracked black pepper

15 ½ oz. can kidney beans, rinsed and drained

15 oz. can black beans, rinsed and drained

19 oz. can cannellini beans, rinsed and drained

In a large skillet, brown ground beef with onions, celery and garlic; drain. In a Dutch oven, combine ground beef mixture with remaining ingredients except beans. Simmer over low heat for 1 ½ hrs. Stir in beans just before serving; heat through. Serve with toppings, if desired.

SERVE WITH YOUR CHOICE OF TOPPINGS:

- Sour cream
- Diced jalapeño peppers
- Sliced black olives
- Finely shredded Cheddar cheese
- Tortilla chips

SERVES 12

EASY

ITALIAN VEGETABLE SOUP

1 tsp. Kowalski's Extra Virgin Olive Oil

2 cloves garlic, finely minced

1/4 cups diced white onion

1/3 cup thinly sliced carrot

1/3 cup diced celery

15 oz. canned diced tomatoes with their juice

2/3 cups canned light red kidney beans, rinsed and drained

2/3 cups canned small white beans (such as Northern beans), rinsed and drained

4 cups low-sodium vegetable stock

2 cups low-sodium tomato sauce

2 tsp. dried oregano

1 tsp. dried basil

1 tsp. kosher salt

1 tsp. Kowalski's Coarse Ground Black Pepper

1/2 tsp. crushed red pepper flakes

2 tsp. brown sugar

1/2 cup dried small shell pasta

1 ½ tbsp. chopped Kowalski's Fresh Italian Parsley

Heat oil in a deep pot over medium-high heat. Sauté garlic and onion 2 min. Reduce heat to low; add carrot, celery and tomatoes with their juice. Simmer 10 min. Add beans, stock, tomato sauce and next 6 ingredients through sugar; simmer just until carrots are tender (about 40 min.), adding pasta in the last 5 min. Adjust salt and pepper if necessary; stir in parsley and serve immediately.

Nutrition Information Per Serving

Total Calories	130
Total Fat	1 g
Saturated Fat	0 g
Sodium	390 mg
Fiber	5 g

An excellent source of vitamins A, C, K and folate. A good source of iron, potassium and vitamin B6.

SERVES 8

EASY

WHITE CHICKEN CHILI

1 tbsp. vegetable oil

1 cup chopped onions

2 tsp. minced garlic

1 lb. boneless skinless chicken
breasts, cut into 1" pieces

5 ½ cups chicken broth

30 oz. canned cannellini beans,
rinsed and drained

9 oz. canned diced green
chiles, drained

1 tsp. dried oregano leaves

1/2 tsp. cumin

1 1/2 cups shredded Monterey
Jack cheese

- chopped fresh cilantro

In a large Dutch oven or stockpot, heat oil over medium-high heat until hot. Add onions, garlic and chicken, cooking until chicken is no longer pink. Stir in remaining ingredients except cheese and cilantro. Bring to a boil; reduce heat to low and simmer 15 min., stirring occasionally. Serve garnished with cheese and cilantro.

SERVES 8

EASY

FAST

TORTILLA SOUP

6 (6" diameter) yellow corn tortillas

1 tbsp. vegetable oil

- kosher salt

5 cups chicken stock

29 oz. canned roasted, diced tomatoes with chiles

1 lb. boneless skinless chicken breasts, cut into 1/2" cubes

1/2 cup chopped onion

2 cloves garlic, minced

1 tbsp. chili powder

2 tsp. ground cumin

8 oz. Kowalski's Shredded Mexican Blend Cheese

1 avocado, peeled, pitted, cubed

- chopped fresh cilantro

1 lime, cut into small wedges

Brush both sides of tortillas with vegetable oil; cut into strips 1/2" wide. Arrange in single layer on a rimmed baking sheet; sprinkle with salt. Bake in a preheated 425° oven until crisp and golden-brown (5-6 min.); set aside. In a large stockpot, combine stock, tomatoes, chicken, onion, garlic, chili powder and cumin. Bring to a boil over medium heat; reduce heat and simmer until chicken is cooked through (15-20 min.). Break several tortilla strips into bottom of each serving bowl; cover with soup. Sprinkle with cheese, avocado and cilantro. Top with remaining tortilla strips and garnish with lime wedges.

SERVES 6

EASY

FAST

ROASTED CARROT & GINGER SOUP

2 lbs. baby-cut carrots

2 pears, peeled, cored, cut into eighths

2 shallots, peeled, each clove cut in half

1 tbsp. canola oil

1/2 tsp. kosher salt

1/4 tsp. Kowalski's Coarse Ground Black Pepper

14 ½ oz. low-sodium chicken broth

1 tbsp. peeled, shredded fresh gingerroot

2 cups skim milk

- crème fraîche

- chopped Italian parsley

In a large bowl, combine carrots, pears, shallots, oil, salt and pepper, tossing to coat. Arrange on parchment-lined rimmed baking sheet; roast in a preheated 450° oven until tender and beginning to brown (40 min.), stirring twice. In a blender or food processor, purée half of the carrot mixture with chicken broth until smooth. Move to a large saucepan; purée remaining half of carrot mixture and ginger with milk. Add to the saucepan; reheat mixture over medium heat (5-8 min.). Ladle into bowls; top with dollop of crème fraîche and garnish with parsley. Serve immediately.

Nutrition Information Per Serving

Total Calories	158
Total Fat	3 g
Saturated Fat	0 g
Sodium	429 mg
Fiber	6 g

Each serving is an excellent source of the antioxidants beta-carotene and vitamin C and gets bonus points for potassium.

GOOD TO KNOW

• A serrated-tip grapefruit spoon or regular teaspoon is useful for peeling fresh gingerroot.

SERVES 6

GOOD FOODS FOR GOOD
Health

BEEFY MUSHROOM & BARLEY SOUP

1 tbsp. butter

1 lb. beef stew meat

1/2 tsp. Kowalski's North Woods
Grill Seasoning

1 cup minced yellow onion

1/2 lb. sliced mushrooms

2 qts. low-sodium beef stock

1/4 cup dry red wine

1/2 cup pearled barley

In a large stockpot, melt butter over medium heat; add stew meat and seasoning. Cook meat until browned (about 5 min.). Add onions; cook until golden-brown, stirring often (about 10 min.). Add mushrooms; cook until they have released their liquid. Stir in stock and wine; cover and simmer 1 hr. Add barley; simmer, covered, 30 min.

SERVES 8

EASY

Ingredients for Italian Cannellini Bean & Spinach Soup

Italian Cannellini Bean & Spinach Soup (pg 122)

Gazpacho (pg 125)

Tortilla Soup (pg 118)

Turkey White Bean Soup
(pg 114)

Corn & Edamame Lime Vinaigrette Salad (pg 149), Garden Fresh
Veggie Salad (pg 148) and Ginger Mint Melon Salad (pg 150)

Herbed Coleslaw (pg 155)

Citrus Crab Salad (pg 142)

Grape Waldorf Salad (pg 151)

Mexican Picnic Salad with Lime Vinaigrette (pg 146)

Ginger Mint Melon Salad (pg 150)

Southwest BBQ Chicken Salad
(pg 140)

Buttermilk Blue Cheese
Dressing (pg 162)

BLT Pasta Salad (pg 136)

Tossed Caprese Salad in Parm
Bowls (pg 145)

Steak House Tenderloins (pg 170) and
Creamed Spinach Gratins (pg 270)

Gorgonzola & Herb Topped Beef Tenderloin
(pg 171) and Shredded Sweet Potato &
Parsnip Pancakes (pg 292)

BEEF STEW

1 tbsp. vegetable oil

2 lbs. boneless beef chuck, cut into 1" pieces

1 medium onion, chopped

1 tsp. chopped garlic

1/3 cup flour

2 tbsp. chopped fresh Italian parsley

2 tsp. chopped fresh thyme

1 tsp. salt

1/4 tsp. coarse ground black pepper

2 cups chicken stock

1 cup dry red wine

8 carrots, peeled, cut on the diagonal into pieces about 1/2" long

4 baby red potatoes, quartered

2 stalks celery, cut on the diagonal into pieces about 1/2" long

Heat oil in a Dutch oven over medium heat; stir in beef, onion and garlic. Cook until beef is browned and onions and garlic are softened. Stir in flour, parsley, thyme, salt and pepper. Gradually stir in stock and wine; bring to a boil. Reduce heat to low; cover and simmer 1 ½ hrs., stirring occasionally. Stir in carrots, potatoes and celery. Simmer, covered, until beef and vegetables are fork-tender (30-45 min. more).

SERVES 4

EASY

ITALIAN CANNELLINI BEAN & SPINACH SOUP

2 cups

boiling water

1 oz. dried shiitake mushrooms

1 tbsp. extra virgin olive oil

1 large yellow onion, finely chopped

2 cloves garlic, minced

4 cups (about 4 oz.) fresh
    spinach, roughly chopped

1 tsp. finely chopped fresh
    rosemary

1 tsp. finely chopped fresh thyme

1/4 tsp. coarse ground black
    pepper

1/4 tsp. crushed red pepper
    flakes

14 oz. canned cannellini beans,
    rinsed and drained

4 cups low-sodium vegetable
    broth

- kosher salt and coarse
    ground black pepper,
    to taste

In a medium bowl, pour boiling water over mushrooms; allow to stand 10 min. Drain mushrooms, reserving liquid; coarsely chop. In a deep pot over medium heat, heat oil. Cook mushrooms, onion and garlic until softened (about 10 min.). Strain reserved mushroom liquid; add to the pot with spinach, rosemary, thyme, peppers, beans and broth. Bring to a boil; reduce to simmer. Cook until spinach and beans are tender (about 10 min.); season to taste and serve immediately.

Nutrition Information Per Serving

Total Calories	120
Total Fat	3 g
Saturated Fat	0 g
Cholesterol	0 mg
Sodium	480 mg

A good source of fiber, vitamin C, iron, potassium, magnesium and folic acid. One serving offers more than 100% of the daily requirement for bone-building vitamin K.

SERVES 6

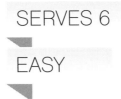

EASY

SALMON CORN CHOWDER

1/2 lb. apple wood smoked bacon

1 cup chopped onion

2 tbsp. flour

3 cups chicken stock

1 lb. Yukon Gold potatoes,
        peeled, cut in small cubes

1 tsp. kosher salt

1/4 tsp. coarse ground black
        pepper

1 lb. salmon, skin removed, cut
        into 1" cubes

16 oz. pkg. frozen organic corn,
        thawed

1 cup half-and-half

1 tbsp. chopped fresh thyme

1 tbsp. chopped fresh Italian
        parsley

In a large skillet over medium-low heat, fry bacon until crisp, reserving 2 tbsp. drippings. Drain cooked bacon on paper towels; crumble. Add reserved bacon drippings to a Dutch oven. Cook onion in drippings over medium heat until tender (about 5 min.). Sprinkle flour over onions; stir to coat. Gradually whisk in stock. Add potatoes, salt and pepper. Bring to a boil, covered; boil 5 min. Add salmon; cook, covered, 5 min. more. Reduce heat to a simmer; stir in corn, half-and-half, thyme and parsley. Cook until heated through (about 10 min.). Serve immediately, topped with crumbled bacon pieces.

SERVES 4

EASY

APPLE BRIE SOUP

1/4 cup butter

1/2 cup chopped onion

1/2 cup sliced celery

1/2 cup flour

1 pt. half-and-half

3 ½ cups chicken broth

15 oz. Brie cheese, rind removed, cubed

1 Gala or Honeycrisp apple, peeled, cored, finely chopped

In a large saucepan over medium heat, melt butter. Stir in onion and celery; sauté until tender (about 10 min.). Whisk in flour; stir in half-and-half and chicken broth. Cook over medium heat (10 min.). Stir in cheese until melted. Pour into a blender or food processor and pulse until smooth. Return to saucepan; stir in apple. Cook over low heat until apples are slightly softened (about 15 min.). Serve immediately.

NOTE

• Soup can be refrigerated several hrs. to overnight before adding apples. Pour refrigerated soup into a large saucepan with apples; reheat about 25 min. over low heat.

SERVES 6

EASY

GAZPACHO

1 ½ lbs. tomatoes, cored, seeded, cut into 1/4" dice

1/2 lb. orange bell pepper, cored, seeded, cut into 1/4" dice

1/2 lb. yellow bell pepper, cored, seeded, cut into 1/4" dice

1 English cucumber, cut in half lengthwise, seeded, cut into 1/4" thick slices

1/2 cup diced sweet onion

2 cloves garlic, minced

1/4 cup Champagne vinegar

2 tsp. kosher salt

46 oz. bottle V8 Vegetable Juice

In a large glass bowl, combine first 8 ingredients; let stand about 5 min. Stir in vegetable juice; refrigerate, covered, to blend flavors (at least 4 hrs.). Serve with with desired toppings.

SERVE WITH YOUR CHOICE OF TOPPINGS:

- Kowalski's Extra Virgin Olive Oil
  - Diced avocado
  - Chopped cilantro
  - Cooked shrimp
- Chopped jalapeño peppers
- Kowalski's Artisan Croutons

SERVES 10

EASY

SALADS

THAI PEANUT CHICKEN PASTA SALAD

1 cup mayonnaise

1 cup prepared Asian peanut sauce

1 tbsp. prepared Asian chile-garlic paste

12 oz. dried penne pasta

2 cups shredded roasted chicken

2 stalks celery, thinly sliced, including leaves

1/2 large red bell pepper, julienned

1/4 cup chopped roasted peanuts

1/4 cup chopped fresh cilantro

1 bunch green onion, chopped

In a small mixing bowl, whisk together first 3 ingredients until well blended; set aside. Cook pasta according to pkg. directions; drain. Cool to room temperature. Combine drained pasta in a large mixing bowl with the next 5 ingredients through cilantro. Mix dressing with salad. For best flavor, cover and refrigerate several hrs. up to 2 days before serving. Garnish with green onion.

SERVES 8

EASY

CASHEW CHICKEN SALAD

1 lb. diced cooked chicken breast

2/3 cup halved grapes

1 cup diced celery

3/4 cup plus 1 tbsp. mayonnaise

- seasoned salt, to taste (about 1/4 - 1/2 tsp.)

- chopped roasted cashews, to taste

In a large mixing bowl, mix all ingredients together until thoroughly combined. Serve immediately or refrigerate, covered, up to 2 days.

SERVES 4

EASY

FAST

KRISPY KALE & CRAISIN SALAD

1/4 cup canola oil

1 tbsp. lemon juice

1 ½ tsp. freshly grated lemon zest

3/4 tsp. kosher salt

6 ½ oz. chopped kale (about 4 cups)

1/2 cup dried cranberries

1/2 cup golden raisins

3 tbsp. toasted pine nuts

In a small mixing bowl, whisk together oil, juice, zest and salt until well blended; set aside. In a large mixing bowl or salad bowl, combine remaining ingredients; toss with dressing.

SERVES 4

EASY

FAST

KOWALSKI'S ANTIPASTO SALAD

16 oz. penne pasta

1 pt. Kowalski's Sweet
    Grape Tomatoes

1 lb. Kowalski's Provolone
    Cheese, cubed

1 lb. Boar's Head Salami, cubed

16 oz. jar pepperoncini
    peppers, drained

12 oz. jar quartered and marinated
    artichoke hearts, drained

6 ½ oz. Boar's Head Pepperoni,
    sliced

1 cup garlic-stuffed green olives

1 cup pitted Kalamata olives

1 cup julienne-cut red
    bell pepper

1 cup julienne-cut green
    bell pepper

1/2 cup coarsely chopped
    red onion

1/2 cup shaved Kowalski's
    Parmesan Cheese

- Kowalski's Italian Vinaigrette,
    to taste

Cook pasta according to pkg. directions; drain. Cool to room temperature. In a large mixing bowl, combine pasta with next 12 ingredients; toss with vinaigrette.

NOTE

• If the salad is made ahead and refrigerated, the pasta will absorb the dressing. Keep additional dressing on hand to moisten the salad before serving.

SERVES 12

EASY

FAST

THAI GRILLED CHICKEN
WITH KALE SALAD

1 tsp. black sesame seeds

2 tsp. Asian hot sauce, such
    as Sriracha

1 tbsp. sesame oil

4 ½ tsp. olive oil

2 tbsp. rice vinegar

2 ½ oz. chopped kale (about
    1 ¾ cups)

1/2 lb. grilled chicken breast,
    sliced (about 2 breasts)

1 cup pea pods, trimmed
    and halved lengthwise
    (about 3 oz.)

2 oz. matchstick-cut carrots
    (about 1/2 cup)

1 tsp. finely chopped fresh
    cilantro

1/2 cup diced celery

1/3 cup dried cranberries

1/4 cup fennel bulb, finely
    chopped

In a small mixing bowl, whisk together first 5 ingredients until well blended; set aside. In a large mixing bowl or salad bowl, combine remaining ingredients; toss with dressing.

SERVES 4

EASY

FAST

Signature

131

BUFFALO CHICKEN PASTA SALAD

1/2 cup plus 3 tbsp. mayonnaise

5 tbsp. buffalo sauce

1 ½ tsp. lemon juice

- hot sauce, to taste

3/4 cup dry penne pasta,
    cooked and cooled

1/2 lb. diced cooked chicken
    (about 2 breasts)

1/2 cup diced celery

2 tbsp. crumbled blue cheese

2 tbsp. sliced green onion

In a small mixing bowl, whisk together first 4 ingredients until well blended; set aside. In a large mixing bowl or salad bowl, combine remaining ingredients; toss with dressing.

SERVES 4

EASY

FAST

SOUTHWEST PASTA SALAD

16 oz. dried fusilli pasta

2 tsp. kosher salt

2 cups Ranch dressing

3 tbsp. taco seasoning

2 tbsp. finely chopped jalapeño
    peppers, seeds removed

2 tsp. minced garlic

30 oz. canned black beans,
    rinsed and drained

22 oz. frozen corn kernels,
    thawed and drained

2 cups cubed Kowalski's Sharp
    Cheddar Cheese

1 bunch fresh cilantro,
    coarsely chopped

1/2 cup chopped red onion

1/2 cup chopped red bell pepper

3 ½ oz. lightly salted tortilla strips

Cook pasta according to pkg. directions using 2 tsp. salt; drain. Cool to room temperature. In medium mixing bowl, combine Ranch dressing, taco seasoning, jalapeño pepper and garlic; refrigerate, covered. In a large mixing bowl, combine pasta with remaining ingredients, except tortilla strips; fold in dressing. Sprinkle with tortilla strips just before serving.

SERVES 12

EASY

FAST

CHERRY CHICKEN SALAD

16 oz. penne rigate pasta

1 lb. grilled chicken breast, diced

8 oz. dried cherries

3/4 cup chopped sweet
    yellow onion

3/4 cup chopped celery

2 cups mayonnaise

2 tbsp. honey Dijon mustard

1/4 cup superfine sugar

2 tsp. salt

1/2 tsp. cracked black pepper

1/2 tsp. poppy seeds

1 cup toasted whole
    almonds, divided

Cook pasta according to pkg. directions; drain. Cool to room temperature. In a large mixing bowl, combine pasta, chicken, cherries, onion and celery. In a small mixing bowl, combine mayonnaise, mustard, sugar, salt, pepper and poppy seeds until thoroughly combined. Stir dressing into salad ingredients along with 3/4 cup almonds; top with remaining almonds.

SERVES 6

EASY

FAST

CHICKEN PASTA SALAD

16 oz. whole grain rotini pasta

2 cups mayonnaise

1 tbsp. heavy cream

1 tbsp. sugar

1/2 tbsp. mustard

1 Kowalski's Signature Rotisserie
   Chicken, bones and skin
   removed, meat chopped
   or pulled by hand into
   large chunks

1/2 stalk celery, diced

1 medium sweet onion, chopped

1 lb. seedless red grapes

1 lb. mild Cheddar cheese,
   cut into chunks

Cook pasta according to pkg. directions; drain. Cool to room temperature. In a medium bowl, combine next 4 ingredients; refrigerate, covered. In a large mixing bowl, combine pasta with remaining ingredients; toss with dressing to coat.

SERVES 6

EASY

FAST

BLT PASTA SALAD

16 oz. applewood smoked bacon

16 oz. penne pasta

3 tsp. kosher salt, divided

10 oz. grape tomatoes

1/2 cup diced red onion

1/2 cup shredded Parmesan cheese

1 ½ cups Ranch dressing

10 oz. hearts of romaine (about 5 cups)

5 oz. Kowalski's Artisan Croutons

In a large skillet over low heat, cook bacon until crisp; drain. Break each slice of bacon into 4 pieces. Cook pasta according to pkg. directions using 2 tsp. salt; drain. Cool to room temperature. In a large mixing bowl, combine pasta, tomatoes, onion, cheese, 1 tsp. salt and dressing; refrigerate to blend flavors. Just before serving, carefully fold in bacon, romaine and croutons.

NOTE

- If the salad is made ahead and refrigerated, the pasta will absorb the dressing. Keep additional dressing on hand to moisten the salad before serving.

SERVES 10

EASY

APPLE MAPLE CHICKEN SALAD

10 oz. chopped hearts of romaine (about 5 cups)

2 ½ cups cubed Kowalski's Signature Rotisserie Chicken, skin discarded, white meat only

1 green apple, cored, thinly sliced

1 red apple, cored, thinly sliced

1/2 cup Kowalski's Honey Roasted Pecans

1/2 cup Kowalski's Dried Cherries

1/2 cup Kowalski's Blue Cheese Crumbles

- *Maple Dressing*

In a salad bowl or on a rimmed serving platter, layer all the ingredients, except dressing, in the order listed; drizzle with dressing. Serve immediately.

> **MAPLE DRESSING:**
> In a small mixing bowl, whisk together 1/2 cup Kowalski's 100% Pure Maple Syrup, 1/4 cup apple juice, 1/4 cup white wine vinegar, 1 tbsp. walnut oil, 1 tbsp. Dijon mustard and 1/4 tsp. kosher salt.
> **Makes about 1 cup**

SERVES 4

EASY

FAST

CITRUS-DRESSED GRILLED CHICKEN & GREENS SALAD

1/2 cup fresh squeezed orange juice

1 tbsp. superfine sugar

1 tbsp. Champagne vinegar

1 tsp. Dijon mustard

1/2 tsp. kosher salt

5 oz. organic baby romaine salad

2 boneless skinless chicken breasts, grilled, cut into strips on the diagonal

6 oz. pkg. gourmet snow peas, ends trimmed

1 cup Kowalski's Roasted and Salted Cashews

1/2 cup julienne-cut Kowalski's Dried Mango Slices

1 cup hulled sliced strawberries

3 red onion slices, quartered, separated into strips

In a small mixing bowl, whisk together first 5 ingredients; refrigerate, covered. In a large salad bowl, combine remaining ingredients. Drizzle dressing over salad; serve immediately.

SERVES 4

EASY

FAST

CHICKEN, CORN & TOMATO SALAD

3 tbsp. tarragon wine vinegar

3 tbsp. chopped shallots

2 tsp. chopped fresh tarragon

1 tsp. Dijon mustard

1/4 tsp. salt

1/8 tsp. freshly ground pepper

1/2 cup canola oil

1/2 lb. small red potatoes

8 cups mixed greens

2 cups diced cooked chicken

1 cup cooked corn kernels

2 large tomatoes, each cut
    into 8 wedges

In a small mixing bowl, whisk together first 6 ingredients; slowly whisk in the canola oil. Refrigerate dressing, covered. In a saucepan over medium-high heat, cook potatoes in salted water to cover until tender (25-30 min.). Drain; cool to lukewarm. Cut potatoes into 1/4" thick slices. In a small mixing bowl, toss potatoes with 1/4 cup dressing; let stand 30 min. or until ready to serve. Divide greens among serving dishes. Layer chicken, potatoes, corn and tomatoes on top of greens; drizzle with dressing. Serve immediately.

SERVES 4

EASY

SOUTHWEST BBQ CHICKEN SALAD

2 ½ cups cubed Kowalski's Signature Rotisserie Chicken, skin discarded, white meat only

1/2 cup Kowalski's Original BBQ Sauce

20 oz. organic hearts of romaine, chopped

15 oz. can black beans, rinsed and drained

2 ears corn on the cob, grilled, removed from cob

18 grape tomatoes, halved

1 ½ cups peeled matchstick-cut jicama

1 avocado, peeled, seeded, diced

8 oz. pkg. Kowalski's Shredded Colby Jack Cheese

1 oz. pkg. fresh cilantro, chopped

1/3 cup toasted pumpkin seeds

- Kowalski's Peppercorn Ranch Dressing, to taste

- tortilla strips

In a large bowl, combine chicken and BBQ sauce; set aside. Divide romaine and chicken among serving dish(es); layer next 8 ingredients in the order listed. Drizzle with dressing; serve immediately, garnished with tortilla strips.

GOOD TO KNOW
- Lightly salted tortilla strips can be purchased in a 3 ½ oz. package in the salad dressing and crouton section of the Grocery Department.

SERVES 6

EASY

FAST

140

CHICKEN SALAD FOR SANDWICHES

1 ¼ cups shredded white meat, Kowalski's Signature Rotisserie Chicken, skin discarded

1/2 cup diced celery

1/4 cup finely diced onion

1/2 cup mayonnaise

1 tbsp. fresh squeezed lemon juice

1/2 tsp. salt

4 mini croissants

- red tipped leaf lettuce

Mix first 6 ingredients in a medium mixing bowl. Slice croissants in half horizontally; line with lettuce. Divide chicken salad among croissants. Serve immediately.

VARIATIONS

Cashew Chicken Salad:
Add 1/2 cup coarsely chopped cashews.

Apricot & Cashew Chicken Salad:
Add 1/3 cup coarsely chopped dried apricots, 1/4 cup coarsely chopped cashews and 1 tbsp. apricot preserves.

SERVES 4

EASY

FAST

CITRUS CRAB SALAD

7 oz. Kowalski's 50/50 Blend
    Organic Salad Mix

1 ½ lbs. fully cooked King Crab
    legs, split, crab meat
    removed, cut into chunks

8 oz. Kowalski's Sliced
    Mango, diced

2 oz. Kowalski's Jicama Sticks

4 oz. Kowalski's Stoplight
    Pepper Slices

1 bunch green onions, sliced

1/4 cup sliced almonds, toasted

- Kowalski's Citrus Vinaigrette

In a large salad or mixing bowl, toss all ingredients, except dressing. Drizzle with dressing; toss lightly and serve immediately.

VARIATION
Citrus Salmon Salad:
Replace crab with grilled salmon.

GOOD TO KNOW
• Find prepared mango, jicama and peppers in the Produce Department.

SERVES 4

EASY

FAST

GRILLED SALMON SALAD

7 oz. Kowalski's 50/50 Blend
  Organic Salad Mix

1 lb. salmon, grilled, skin discarded

1/2 cup shredded carrots

4 radishes, trimmed and sliced

4 roasted baby beets, sliced

4 mini sweet yellow peppers,
  stemmed, seeded and
  julienned

1/2 English cucumber, cut
  in half lengthwise, seeded
  and sliced

1/4 small red onion, very thinly
  sliced, separated

- honey mustard salad dressing,
  to taste

Divide greens among serving dish(es);
place salmon in the center of the greens.
Pile remaining ingredients, except dressing,
in piles around the salmon. Drizzle with
dressing; serve immediately.

GOOD TO KNOW
• Roasted baby beets are available
already prepared in the Produce
Department.

SERVES 4

EASY

FAST

143

GRILLED SUMMER SALAD

1/3 cup kosher salt

1/3 cup sugar

3 cups cold water

1 lb. boneless skinless
    chicken breasts

2/3 cup vegetable or canola oil

1/3 cup fresh squeezed
    lemon juice

1/2 cup superfine sugar

1 tbsp. finely minced onion

1 tbsp. poppy seeds

1 tsp. Dijon mustard

1/2 tsp. kosher salt

1 tbsp. olive oil

20 oz. hearts of romaine,
    chopped

1 cup hulled, sliced strawberries

1 cup slivered almonds, toasted

4 oz. blue cheese, crumbled

1 shallot, peeled, cut into rings

Dissolve 1/3 cup salt and sugar in water in a large zipper-closure food storage bag; add chicken breasts. Refrigerate 30 min. In a jar with tight-fitting lid, add next 7 ingredients (through 1/2 tsp. kosher salt); shake to combine and set aside. Remove chicken from water mixture. Drain and blot dry with paper towels. In a large mixing bowl, toss chicken with olive oil to coat. Grill chicken over medium heat, covered, until no longer pink in thickest part of breast (about 5 min. per side), turning several times. Cut chicken into thin strips; divide chicken and remaining ingredients among serving dish(es). Drizzle dressing over salad; serve immediately.

SERVES 4

EASY

144

TOSSED CAPRESE SALAD
IN PARM BOWLS

1 ⅓ cups shredded Parmesan cheese

2 tsp. chopped fresh chives

2 cups organic mixed baby greens

24 grape tomatoes

4 oz. Kowalski's Fresh Mozzarella Cheese, cubed

2 tsp. thinly sliced fresh basil

1/4 cup Kowalski's Balsamic Vinaigrette

In a small mixing bowl, combine Parmesan cheese and chives. Heat a 10" nonstick skillet over medium-high heat. Sprinkle 1/3 cup Parmesan cheese mixture in a circle into skillet, keeping edges lacey. When cheese is golden-brown around the edges, remove the skillet from the heat; with a narrow metal spatula, loosen cheese around edge, working into center. Place a 3" diameter glass in the center of the cheese circle; invert pan and glass onto the counter, removing skillet. Quickly drape cheese circle over the glass, pressing to form a bowl; cool completely. Repeat with remaining Parmesan to make three more bowls. In a large bowl, combine remaining ingredients; toss with dressing. Divide salad among each of 4 Parmesan bowls. Serve immediately.

SERVES 4

FAST

MEXICAN PICNIC SALAD
WITH LIME VINAIGRETTE

5 pint-sized wide-mouth glass canning jars, with lids

3 tbsp. fresh squeezed lime juice

6 tbsp. Kowalski's Extra Virgin Olive Oil, plus some for grilling

1 tsp. sugar

1/2 tsp. kosher salt

1/4 tsp. Kowalski's Coarse Ground Black Pepper

1 jalapeño pepper, seeded and finely chopped

2 tbsp. finely chopped red pepper

2 tbsp. finely chopped fresh cilantro

1/2 pineapple, peeled, cored and cut crosswise into 4 (1/2") slices

2 cups finely shredded romaine lettuce

1 cup frozen corn kernels, thawed and drained

1 cup canned black beans, rinsed and drained

1/4 cup chopped jicama, in matchstick-shaped pieces

1/4 cup thinly sliced red onion

1/2 pt. grape tomatoes, halved

1/2 cup crumbled Cotija cheese (optional)

MEXICAN PICNIC SALAD WITH LIME VINAIGRETTE (CONTINUED)

In one jar, combine lime juice, oil, sugar, salt and pepper; screw lid on tightly and shake vigorously to blend. Set aside. In a small bowl, mix jalapeño, red pepper and cilantro; set aside. Brush pineapple with oil; grill pineapple over direct heat on grill preheated to medium until pineapple is soft but not falling apart (about 10 min. total), turning once. Chop pineapple; set aside. In each of the remaining 4 glass canning jars, layer an equal amount of lettuce, corn, beans, jicama, grilled pineapple, red onion, tomatoes, cheese and pepper mixture. Shake dressing thoroughly to combine. Drizzle about 2 tbsp. dressing on top of each salad; screw lids on tightly and shake to toss. Pour onto a plate or eat from the jar.

Nutrition Information Per Serving
(without the optional cheese)

Total Calories	332
Total Fat	22 g
Saturated Fat	3 g
Sodium	385 mg
Fiber	8 g

Contains nearly a full day's requirement of vitamin C, plus vitamin B12, vitamin K, folate, magnesium and potassium.

NOTE
• Salad jars are easy to tote to a picnic. Screw the tops on the jars and take them in a cooler with the jar of dressing. When you're ready to eat, dress salad. No trash to throw away!

SERVES 4

EASY

GOOD FOODS FOR GOOD
Health

GARDEN FRESH VEGGIE SALAD

1 pt. Kowalski's Grape
        Tomatoes, halved

2 cups broccoli florets

1 cup diced yellow bell pepper

1 cup diced green bell pepper

1/2 English cucumber, sliced

1/4 cup chopped red onion

1/3 cup feta cheese crumbles

1/3 cup prepared Greek
        vinaigrette

1 tbsp. thinly sliced fresh basil

In a large mixing bowl, combine all ingredients. Refrigerate, covered, or serve immediately.

Nutrition Information Per Serving

Total Calories	180
Total Fat	12 g
Saturated Fat	4 g
Sodium	427 mg

Each serving is also a good source of these brain nutrients: beta-carotene, vitamins B6 and C, folate, selenium and potassium.

SERVES 4

EASY

FAST

CORN & EDAMAME LIME VINAIGRETTE SALAD

1/2 cup Newman's Own Light
    Lime Vinaigrette

1/4 tsp. cayenne pepper,
    or to taste

4 cups frozen sweet corn,
    thawed

12 oz frozen shelled edamame,
    thawed

1 cup matchstick-cut jicama
    strips

1 cup matchstick-cut red bell
    pepper strips

1/2 cup chopped sweet onion

1/3 cup finely chopped
    fresh cilantro

In a small mixing bowl, combine vinaigrette and cayenne; set aside. Combine remaining ingredients in a large salad or mixing bowl; drizzle with dressing, tossing to coat. Refrigerate, covered, or serve immediately.

Nutrition Information Per Serving

Total Calories	230
Total Fat	8 g
Saturated Fat	1 g
Sodium	200 mg

Each serving is an excellent source of these brain nutrients: fiber, vitamin C and folic acid. It is also a good source of iron, thiamin, vitamin B6, magnesium, zinc and potassium.

SERVES 6

EASY

FAST

149

GINGER MINT MELON SALAD

1/4 cup Kowalski's 100% Pure
Fresh Squeezed
Orange Juice

2 tsp. lime zest

3 tbsp. lime juice

2 tbsp. superfine sugar

1 ½ tbsp. finely chopped fresh
mint

2 tsp. minced crystallized ginger

16 oz. container Kowalski's
Honeydew Chunks
(about 3 cups)

16 oz. container Kowalski's
Watermelon Spears,
cubed (about 3 cups)

4 ½ oz. container blueberries
(about 1 cup)

In a small mixing bowl, whisk together first 6 ingredients; set aside. Combine remaining ingredients in a large salad or mixing bowl; gently stir in dressing, tossing to coat. Serve immediately.

NOTE
• One fresh lime will give you enough zest and juice for this recipe. Zest the lime first, then roll the fruit on the counter before cutting and juicing it.

SERVES 6

EASY

FAST

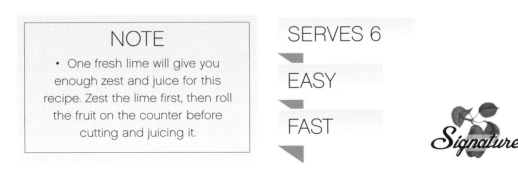

Signature

GRAPE WALDORF SALAD

1/2 cup organic low-fat plain
    yogurt

1 tbsp. sugar or 1 tbsp. Kowalski's
    Pure Honey

2 cups red seedless grapes,
    halved

2 cups green seedless grapes,
    halved

1 cup chopped celery (about
    2 ribs)

1/2 cup golden raisins

1/2 cup pecan halves, toasted

5 oz. organic baby spinach

In a small mixing bowl, whisk together
first 2 ingredients; refrigerate, covered.
Combine remaining ingredients in a
large salad or mixing bowl; gently stir
in dressing, tossing to coat. Serve
immediately.

Nutrition Information Per Serving

Total Calories	142
Total Fat	5 g
Sodium	36 mg

Each serving is also a good
source of vitamins C and K,
manganese and boron – all known
to help support bone strength.

SERVES 8

EASY

FAST

PEAR & BLUE SALAD

1/2 cup almond oil, or another salad or nut oil

1/4 cup Champagne vinegar

1 tbsp. finely minced shallot

- dash salt

5 oz. organic baby lettuces

1 pear, cored, thinly sliced

4 oz. blue cheese, crumbled

1/4 cup Kowalski's Honey Roasted Almonds

In a small mixing bowl, whisk together first 4 ingredients. Divide greens among serving dish(es); layer remaining ingredients, except dressing, on top of the greens. Drizzle with dressing; serve immediately.

SERVES 4

EASY

FAST

HONEYCRISP APPLE SPINACH SALAD

2 tbsp. white wine vinegar

2 tbsp. orange juice

1/4 cup Kowalski's 100% Pure
    Maple Syrup

1 tbsp. walnut oil

1 tbsp. Dijon mustard

1/4 tsp. kosher salt

1 Honeycrisp apple, cored,
    thinly sliced

5 oz. organic baby spinach salad

1 cup red grape halves

1 shallot, thinly sliced

1/2 cup coarsely chopped
    Kowalski's Cinnamon
    Spiced Almonds

In a large salad bowl, whisk together first 6 ingredients; toss with apple slices. Lightly toss remaining ingredients with apples and dressing. Serve immediately.

SERVES 6

EASY

FAST

153

ROASTED SQUASH & ARUGULA SALAD

2 lbs. butternut squash, peeled, seeded and cut into 1/2" cubes

2 tbsp. Kowalski's Extra Virgin Olive Oil

1 tsp. kosher salt, divided

1/2 tsp. Kowalski's Coarse Ground Black Pepper, divided

1/4 tsp. Kowalski's Crushed Red Pepper Flakes

2 tbsp. orange juice

1 ½ tbsp. walnut oil

1 ½ tsp. fresh squeezed lemon juice

8 cups (about 8 oz.) arugula, washed in very cold water and thoroughly spun dry

1/2 cup shelled walnuts, toasted, coarsely chopped

1/2 cup fresh pomegranate seeds

2 tsp. pomegranate molasses

On a rimmed nonstick 15x12" baking sheet, toss squash with oil; season with half the salt and black pepper and the red pepper flakes. Roast in a preheated 450° oven until edges are browned and squash is tender (about 25 min.), turning once. In large salad bowl, whisk together orange juice, oil and lemon juice; season with remaining salt and black pepper. Add arugula, walnuts and pomegranate seeds to bowl; toss. Adjust seasoning if necessary. Mound dressed salad on 6 serving plates, topping with squash; drizzle with molasses.

SERVES 6

EASY

154

HERBED COLESLAW

14 oz. bag Dole Classic Coleslaw

10 oz. bag Dole Shredded
    Red Cabbage

10 oz. bag Dole Shredded Carrots

1 cup mayonnaise

1 cup Kowalski's Coleslaw
    Dressing

1/4 cup Dijon mustard

3 tbsp. sugar

2 tbsp. apple cider vinegar

1 tsp. celery seeds

1/2 tsp. kosher salt

1/2 tsp. coarse ground black
    pepper

1 oz. fresh Italian parsley, chopped

1 bunch green onions, chopped

2 tbsp. finely chopped fresh dill

In a large mixing bowl, toss together cabbages and carrots; set aside. In a food processor, process remaining ingredients. Pour dressing over salad; toss to coat. Cover bowl; refrigerate 1-4 hrs. before serving to allow the flavors to develop.

SERVES 12

EASY

Signature

POTATO SALAD
CULINARY TIPS & IDEAS

It's a picnic standard for a reason – everyone loves potatoes! But this summertime favorite still has a little room for improvement. Perfect your technique and punch up your most-loved basic recipe in a few steps:

1. First, make a basic dressing: for every cup of mayonnaise use 3-5 tbsp. of vinegar (try flavored vinegars, too), 1 ½ tsp. kosher salt and 3/4 tsp. coarse ground black pepper; set aside.

2. Start 3-3 ½ lbs. new, baby or fingerling potatoes (or combination) in enough cold, salted water to cover. They don't need to be peeled. (You can also try sweet potatoes or other large potatoes, but peel them first and cut them into large chunks.)

3. Bring to a boil and cook until barely tender.

4. Drain; cool until cool enough to handle.

5. Cut into evenly sized pieces of approximately the same shape (slices, cubes, etc.).

6. Toss warm potatoes with 1/4 cup rice vinegar to give them flavor.

7. Toss with dressing and any other ingredients. Try these add-ins in a combination that suits your fancy:

- 1-2 cups chopped red bell pepper
- 1-2 cups thinly sliced celery, including leaves
- 2 cloves garlic, finely minced
- 1 chipotle pepper in adobo sauce, finely minced
- 2 tbsp. prepared horseradish
- 1/2 cup diced red onion
- 1-2 cups fresh corn, blanched
- 1/4 cup finely diced dried fruit (such as tart cherries, apricots or raisins)
- 1 cup thinly sliced green onion
- 1 cup chopped sun-dried tomatoes
- 1/2 tsp. crushed red pepper flakes

- 1-2 cups fresh or frozen sweet peas, blanched or thawed
- 1/2 cup toasted nuts
- 1/2 cup hot smoked salmon
- 1/2 lb. cooked pancetta, diced
- 3/4 lb. bacon, cooked and crumbled
- 3-4 hard-boiled eggs, diced
- 3/4 cup blue or Parmesan cheese
- 3/4 cup finely chopped fresh herbs
- 1 cup chopped, pitted olives
- 3/4 cup finely diced pickles
- 3 tbsp. capers
- 2 tbsp. chopped sweet pickled peppers

CLASSIC SWEET POTATO SALAD

1 cup mayonnaise

1/2 cup sour cream

3 tbsp. Dijon mustard

1 ½ tsp. kosher salt

1/2 tsp. Kowalski's Coarse Ground Black Pepper

2 lbs. sweet potatoes

1 ½ lbs. Yukon Gold potatoes

2 tsp. kosher salt

4 hard-cooked eggs, peeled, sliced

1 cup diced celery

1 cup diced sweet red pepper

1/2 cup diced onion

In a small mixing bowl, whisk together first 5 ingredients; refrigerate. Peel potatoes; cut each into quarters, lengthwise. Cut each quarter crosswise into 1/4" thick slices. In a large saucepan, add salt and potatoes to 2 qts. water; bring to a boil over high heat. Boil potato slices until crisp-tender (3-4 min.); drain. Plunge immediately into ice water until cool; drain. In a large mixing bowl, combine potatoes, eggs, celery, peppers and onion; gently fold in dressing. Refrigerate several hrs. before serving.

SERVES 10

EASY

QUINOA SALAD

4 cups cooked and cooled quinoa, cooked in chicken or vegetable stock

1 cup thinly sliced celery, including leaves

1 cup finely chopped red, yellow and/or orange bell peppers

1/2 cup finely chopped green onion

- zest of 1 lemon

2 tbsp. finely chopped fresh Italian parsley

- *Roasted Red Pepper Vinaigrette*

In a large bowl, toss together all ingredients except dressing. Pour dressing over the salad, using just enough to coat thoroughly (save any extra dressing in the refrigerator for up to 2 days). Serve immediately or store for up to 2 days in the refrigerator.

ROASTED RED PEPPER VINAIGRETTE:

Blend 1/3 cup Kowalski's Extra Virgin Olive Oil, 1/4 cup fresh squeezed lemon juice, 1/4 cup Dijon mustard and half of a drained 8 oz. jar roasted red peppers in a blender or food processor until smooth; season with kosher salt and Kowalski's Coarse Ground Black Pepper to taste.

Makes 1 cup

Nutrition Information Per Serving

Total Calories	260
Total Fat	13 g
Sodium	165 mg
Fiber	3 g

A good source of bone-building vitamins A, C and K and magnesium.

SERVES 6

EASY

FAST

158

TRADITIONAL MACARONI SALAD

1 cup macaroni noodles

1/3 cup thinly sliced celery
    with leaves

1 oz. bunch fresh dill, fronds only,
    coarsely chopped

1/2 cup mayonnaise

2 tbsp. fresh squeezed lemon
    juice

- kosher salt and coarsely
    ground black pepper,
    to taste

Prepare pasta in salted boiling water according to pkg. directions. Put drained pasta in a medium mixing bowl with celery; set aside. In another small mixing bowl, whisk dill and mayonnaise with lemon juice; season dressing to taste. Mix thoroughly with pasta and celery. Refrigerate, covered, several hrs. before serving.

NOTE
• Pasta will absorb dressing the longer it is refrigerated. Additional dressing can be added just before serving to moisten the pasta.

SERVES 4

EASY

HERB VINAIGRETTE

3 tbsp. white balsamic vinegar

1 tbsp. Dijon mustard

1 tbsp. minced shallots

3/4 tsp. kosher salt

1/4 tsp. Kowalski's Coarse
        Ground Black Pepper

1/2 cup Kowalski's Extra
        Virgin Olive Oil

2 tsp. finely chopped fresh
        Italian parsley

2 tsp. finely chopped fresh
        chives

2 tsp. finely chopped fresh dill

In a medium mixing bowl, whisk together vinegar, mustard, shallots, salt and pepper. Drizzle in oil very slowly, whisking constantly to form an emulsion. Whisk in remaining ingredients; adjust seasoning to taste.

MAKES 1 cup

EASY

FAST

BASIC CAESAR DRESSING

1/2 cup mayonnaise

1/2 cup freshly grated Parmesan
cheese

2 cloves garlic, finely minced

2 tbsp. buttermilk powder

1 ½ tsp. fresh lemon juice

1 tsp. anchovy paste

1-2 tbsp. water, as needed for
desired consistency

- kosher salt and coarsely
ground black pepper,
to taste

In a small mixing bowl, whisk together
first 6 ingredients until well blended;
whisk in enough water to reach desired
consistency. Season to taste. Serve
immediately or store, covered, in the
refrigerator up to 3 days.

NOTE
• 1-2 tbsp. fresh buttermilk can be
substituted for the buttermilk
powder and water.

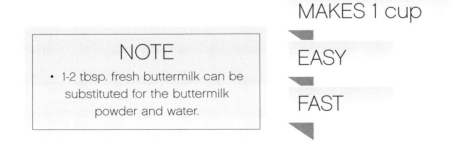

MAKES 1 cup

EASY

FAST

161

BUTTERMILK BLUE CHEESE DRESSING

1/2 cup mayonnaise

2 cloves garlic, finely minced

2 tbsp. buttermilk powder

1 ½ tsp. fresh lemon juice

1/2 tsp. Worcestershire sauce

- kosher salt and coarsely ground black pepper, to taste

1-2 tbsp. water, as needed for desired consistency

1/2 cup Kowalski's Blue Cheese Crumbles

In a small mixing bowl, whisk together all ingredients, except water and cheese, until well blended; whisk in enough water to reach desired consistency. Fold in cheese and additional water, if needed. Serve immediately or store, covered, in the refrigerator up to 3 days.

NOTE
• 1-2 tbsp. fresh buttermilk can be substituted for the buttermilk powder and water.

MAKES 1 cup

EASY

FAST

Signature

SALAD DRESSING
CULINARY TIPS & IDEAS

Nothing beats fresh, homemade salad dressing, and it couldn't be easier to make. You can create a custom vinaigrette with just about any flavor of oil and vinegar, in a ratio anywhere between 4:1 (classic) to 2:1. Just be sure to use top-quality oils and vinegars that taste great on their own. There's no masking off flavors in a salad dressing. From there, just season with salt and pepper, a pinch of sugar and any herbs or spices that compliment the flavors in your salad (finely minced garlic or garlic paste, prepared mustard and shallots are popular whisk-ins). You can also experiment with nut oils such as walnut and flavored vinegars such as fig, apple and ginger when those flavors flatter the ingredients in your salads.

All vinaigrettes will separate over time, but a bit of mustard, a pasteurized egg yolk or a little mayonnaise will stabilize them a little longer. Traditionally, vinaigrettes are made by very slowly streaming in and briskly whisking oil into the other ingredients, but you can achieve the same results by vigorously shaking ingredients together in a screw-top glass jar. When they separate, just shake 'em up again!

Make simple, creamy dressings by whisking together a base of mayonnaise, sour cream or yogurt (or a combination) and the flavorings of your choice. You can thin the mixture to drizzling consistency with a little bit of low-fat buttermilk, citrus juice, vinegar, water or a combination. Mix in ingredients such as cheese (like blue or Parmesan), herbs, salt, pepper, garlic, honey (or other sweetener) and mustard in combinations that suit your fancy. You can make mayo-based creamy dressing healthier by swapping in Dijon mustard, low-fat sour cream, low-fat yogurt (including Greek) or a combination in place of part of the mayonnaise.

RACHAEL'S LIGHT RANCH DRESSING

1/4 cup mayonnaise

1/4 cup nonfat Greek yogurt

2 tbsp. buttermilk powder

1 ½ tsp. dried parsley

1/4 tsp. kosher salt

1/4 tsp. onion powder

1/4 tsp. dried marjoram

1/4 tsp. dried thyme

1/4 coarse ground black
    pepper, to taste

1/4 tsp. apple cider vinegar

1/8 tsp. garlic powder

1/2 cup water, more or less as
    needed for desired
    consistency

In a small mixing bowl, whisk together all ingredients, except water, until well blended; whisk in enough water to reach desired consistency. Serve immediately or store, covered, in the refrigerator up to 3 days.

MAKES about 1 cup

EASY

FAST

ORANGE YOGURT DRESSING

1/2 cup organic fat-free French vanilla yogurt

1 tbsp. fresh squeezed orange juice

1/2 tsp. orange zest

In a small mixing bowl, whisk together all ingredients until well blended. Serve immediately or store, covered, in the refrigerator up to 3 days.

Nutrition Information Per Serving

Total Calories	49
Total Fat	0 g
Sodium	38 mg

Each serving is also a good source of calcium, a mineral known to help support bone strength.

MAKES 1/2 cup

EASY

FAST

MEAT

ARUGULA AIOLI TOPPED SIRLOIN STEAKS

2 cups arugula

1 cup Hellmann's Light
    Mayonnaise

2 tbsp. fresh squeezed
    lemon juice

1 tbsp. prepared horseradish

2 cloves garlic

1/2 tsp. kosher salt

1/4 tsp. coarse ground black
    pepper

1/2 cup julienne-cut sun-dried
    tomatoes in olive oil,
    drained, blotted dry

1 lb. Kowalski's USDA Prime All
    Natural Sirloin Steak

In a food processor bowl or blender, purée first 7 ingredients. Transfer to a small bowl; stir in sun-dried tomatoes. Refrigerate until ready to use. Grill steak over medium heat, covered, to desired doneness (14-16 min.), turning once. Let steak rest 5 min.; slice steak and slightly overlap slices on serving plates. Top with aioli.

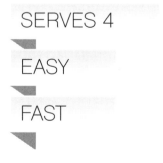

SERVES 4

EASY

FAST

BEEF WELLINGTONS
WITH RED WINE SAUCE

2 cups hot water

1 ½ oz. pkg. More Than Gourmet Gold Classic French Demi-Glace

6 tbsp. unsalted butter, divided

1/2 cup minced shallots

8 oz. pkg. baby bella sliced mushrooms, chopped

1/3 cup chopped Italian parsley

1 tbsp. Dijon mustard

1 ½ tsp. snipped fresh thyme

- salt and pepper, to taste

1 lb. beef tenderloin, cut into 4 pieces

- Kowalski's North Woods Grill Seasoning Blend

3 tbsp. flour

2 tbsp. double-concentrated tomato paste

1 ½ cups red wine

17 ¼ oz. pkg. puff pastry, thawed

1 egg, beaten with 1 tsp. water

In a small saucepan, simmer water and demi-glace until dissolved; set aside. In a large skillet, melt 2 tbsp. butter; sauté shallots until tender (about 5 min.). Stir in mushrooms and parsley, sautéing until mushrooms are tender (8-10 min.). Stir in mustard, thyme, salt and pepper; set aside. In another large skillet, melt remaining butter over medium heat; sauté steaks until browned (3-4 min. per side). Season with North Woods Grill Seasoning Blend; remove from pan. Stir flour and tomato paste into pan drippings; cook 3 min., stirring constantly. Slowly stir demi-glace and wine into pan drippings. Boil and stir until thickened (about 1 min.). Stir 1 tbsp. sauce into mushroom mixture; refrigerate remaining sauce, covered. On a lightly floured surface, cut each sheet of puff pastry in half. Place 1/4 of mushroom mixture onto center of each piece of pastry; top with steak. Wrap pastry around steak, wetting edges with water and pinching to seal. Place, seam side down, on a parchment-lined baking sheet. Refrigerate, covered, several hrs. Brush egg mixture over each pastry; pierce tops several times with a fork. Bake in a preheated 400° oven until golden-brown (about 25 min.). Reheat red wine sauce; spoon over each Wellington. Serve immediately.

SERVES 4

STEAK HOUSE TENDERLOINS

1 tbsp. Kowalski's Extra Virgin Olive Oil

4 (6 oz. each) beef tenderloin steaks

- Kowalski's North Woods Grill Seasoning Blend

Heat an ovenproof skillet over medium-high heat for 5 min.; add olive oil. Sear steaks in oil on one side until a deep brown crust forms (4-5 min.). Flip steaks; season cooked side with seasoning. Move pan to a preheated 425° oven; roast to desired doneness (5-9 min.). Remove pan from oven; rest steaks 5 min. Season second side; serve immediately.

NOTE

• Roast steaks in oven 5 min. for rare, 7 min. for medium-rare and 9 min. for medium.

• If your sauté pan has a plastic handle, cover it with several layers of aluminum foil before placing the pan in the oven.

• It may get smoky when searing the first side of each steak. This is normal, so have the exhaust fan over the stove on.

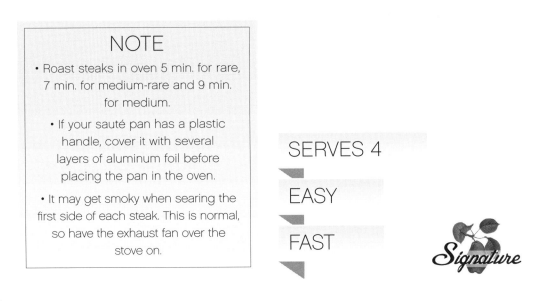

SERVES 4

EASY

FAST

Signature

GORGONZOLA & HERB TOPPED BEEF TENDERLOIN

3 tbsp. Kowalski's Extra Virgin Olive Oil, divided

1/4 cup minced shallots

1/4 cup panko breadcrumbs

1/2 cup Gorgonzola cheese, crumbled

2 tbsp. chopped fresh Italian parsley

1 tsp. Kowalski's Four Pepper Blend Peppercorns, coarsely chopped

1 tsp. kosher salt

2 lbs. beef tenderloin, cut into 8 equal pieces

In a medium skillet, heat 1 tbsp. olive oil over medium heat; sauté shallots until softened (about 2 min.). Place the cooked shallots in a medium bowl; set aside. In the same skillet, heat 1 tbsp. olive oil over medium heat; brown breadcrumbs, stirring often (2-3 min.). Add to bowl with shallots, along with cheese, parsley, peppercorns and salt. In a large skillet, heat remaining olive oil over high heat; brown steaks (2-3 min. per side), turning once. Place on a parchment-lined jelly-roll pan; divide cheese mixture among steaks, pressing to adhere. Roast in a preheated 350° oven to desired doneness (6-8 min. for medium-rare). Serve immediately.

SERVES 8

EASY

THE HEAT IS ON:
TEMPING FOR SUCCESS

No matter what kind of rub, recipe or sauce you're considering, the most important thing to bear in mind when it comes to properly preparing just about any cut or type of meat is temperature. (There's a reason chef jackets come with a thermometer pocket; it isn't a fashion statement.) Cooking may be an art, but there's a fair amount of science happening in your kitchen, too.

The best advice we can give when a customer asks how to ensure the success of their pork roast, veal chops, rack of lamb, Wagyu steaks or just about anything we sell in the Meat Department is to use a thermometer to assess the doneness of their purchase. As unappetizing as undercooked poultry can be, dry, tough or overcooked meats and poultry can be just as bad. Nothing ensures hitting that temperature sweet spot like an accurate instant-read thermometer.

For some customers safety concerns are paralyzing, and that's understandable. No one wants to become or cause another to become ill from improperly cooking a meal. This is why understanding both the safety guidelines for cooking meat as well as the science behind them is so important. While it's true that meat inherently harbors bacteria that can only be destroyed at 160° or higher, even the USDA recommends an internal temperature of 145° for intact cuts of healthy meat tissue. Why is this? *Because bacteria are on meat surfaces, not inside.* Whether you're grilling, roasting or sautéing your meats, surface temperatures rise far above 160° (meat begins to brown at 230°). You are more likely to get sick from the way you handle your meat at home; cross-contamination and holding meat at dangerous temperatures are real issues. Eating a rare steak is a much lesser concern. The fact that bacteria are on meat surfaces also explains why it is recommended to cook ground meat to 160° – with ground meat, the contaminated meat surface has been broken and spread throughout the ground product.

While temperature is a matter of food safety, it's also a matter of taste. As proteins cook they naturally lose moisture, and the longer they cook, the more moisture they lose. Also, as proteins cook, the natural sugars in them add depth of flavor, and the longer they cook, the more flavor is built. Somewhere in the middle is a safe-to-consume and optimally delicious middle ground. This is particularly interesting when considering pork and poultry. USDA guidance has changed in the last two years when it comes to both; safe cooking temperatures have both been revised down from earlier recommendations. This is good news for those wanting to cook pork and poultry safely while maintaining vital, flavorful natural moisture.

The following table shows recommended final internal temperatures* for poultry and meat:

Poultry
      Whole or Parts   165^
      Ground   160^

Meat (Beef, Lamb and Pork)
      Ground   160^

      Steaks, Chops, Roasts
            Rare   125-130 (not recommended for pork)
            Medium-Rare   135-140
            Medium   145^
            Medium-Well   145-150
            Well Done   155-160

* Insert thermometer in the center of the thickest part, away from bone, fat and gristle (sideways in the case of thin cuts or pieces). Test whole poultry in the inner thigh, near the breast.

^ Recommended as safe by the USDA. Of course, extra caution must be exercised when cooking for at-risk groups, particularly the elderly, young children, pregnant women and those with otherwise compromised immune systems. In such cases, we suggest that USDA guidelines be strictly followed.

CONSIDER CARRYOVER COOKING!

Remove intact cuts of protein (not ground meat or poultry) from the heat source before the desired final temperature is reached. During this "rest period," proteins may increase 5-20° or more. Keep them loosely covered with foil to ensure they don't cool too quickly. Larger, denser pieces will increase in temperature more than smaller ones (a 12 lb. turkey, for example, can easily handle an hour of rest and will increase an average of 20° after it's removed from the oven).

GRILLED RIB-EYE STEAKS
WITH GORGONZOLA BUTTER

GORGONZOLA BUTTER:

4 oz. Gorgonzola cheese,
    room temperature

4 tbsp. unsalted butter,
    softened

RIB EYE STEAK:

4 (1" thick) rib-eye steaks

- Kowalski's North Woods Grill
    Seasoning Blend

In a food processor bowl, process cheese and butter until smooth. Use a piece of plastic wrap or waxed paper to roll and form butter into a log shape; seal tightly and refrigerate until firm. Grill or broil steaks over medium-high heat, covered, to desired doneness, turning once just past the halfway point in the cooking time (6-8 min. total for rare; 8-10 min. for medium-rare; 10-12 min. for medium). Season to taste with North Woods Grill Seasoning Blend. Let steaks rest a few minutes, covered.
Top with a slice of *Gorgonzola Butter*; serve immediately.

NOTE
- You can also use a spatula to mash the butter and cheese together in a small bowl if you don't have a food processor.

SERVES 4

EASY

174

NEW YORK STRIP STEAKS
WITH BALSAMIC ONION CONFIT

3 tbsp. Kowalski's Extra Virgin Olive Oil

2 tbsp. butter

3 sweet onions, thinly sliced

1/2 tsp. kosher salt

1/4 tsp. coarse ground black pepper

1 tbsp. balsamic vinegar

4 New York strip steaks

- Kowalski's North Woods Grill Seasoning Blend

In a large skillet over low heat, heat olive oil and butter. Stir in onions, salt and pepper; cook until onions are completely softened, stirring occasionally (35-40 min.). Stir in balsamic vinegar and continue cooking to blend flavors (about 15 min.); cool. Refrigerate, covered, up to 3 days or freeze for later use. Grill steaks over high heat, covered, to desired doneness (8-12 min.), turning 2-3 times. Sprinkle both sides of steak with seasoning blend. Serve topped with onion confit.

SERVES 4

EASY

HORSERADISH STEAK SANDWICHES

1/3 cup plain Greek yogurt
(not nonfat)

1/4 cup mayonnaise

1 tbsp. buttermilk powder

1 tbsp. fresh squeezed
lemon juice

1 tbsp. prepared horseradish

1 ½ tsp. Worcestershire sauce

1 tsp. coarse ground black
pepper, divided

2 tbsp. unsalted butter

2 tbsp. olive oil

2 cloves garlic, finely chopped

1 ½ lbs. sirloin steak, shaved
or very thinly sliced on
the diagonal

1 tsp. kosher salt

1 yellow onion, very thinly sliced

1 lb. mushrooms, cleaned and
sliced (cremini, shiitake,
baby portabella or
combination)

1/4 cup finely chopped fresh
Italian parsley

4 split French demi baguettes,
split horizontally

2 cups mixed baby greens

In a small bowl, whisk together first 6 ingredients and 1/2 tsp. pepper; set aside. In a large nonstick skillet over medium-high heat, melt butter into olive oil. Add garlic and beef; stir-fry until medium-rare (3-4 min.). Season beef with salt and remaining pepper. Remove beef and garlic from pan with a slotted spoon; set aside. Add onion and mushrooms to the pan. Cook until onion is translucent and mushrooms are golden (3-5 min.). Stir in beef and parsley. Load buns with greens; top with warm steak mixture. Drizzle with dressing; serve immediately.

GOOD TO KNOW
• Find buttermilk powder in
the Baking Aisle.

SERVES 4

FAST

EASY

BISON BISTEC AU POIVRE

2 tbsp. Kowalski's Coarse
    Ground Black Pepper

4 (8 oz. each) bison rib-eye
    steaks

2 tbsp. unsalted butter

2 tbsp. dry sherry

2/3 cup heavy cream

2/3 cup beef broth

1 tbsp. Dijon mustard

Rub pepper into both sides of meat. In a large oven-proof sauté pan, heat butter over medium-high heat; sear meat on both sides (3-4 min. total). Transfer to a preheated 400° oven; roast to medium-rare (9-14 min.). Remove pan from oven. Transfer steaks to a plate and cover with foil; let rest 10 min. Put pan on stovetop over medium heat; stir sherry into drippings, scraping up browned bits at bottom of pan. Whisk in remaining ingredients; cook, stirring until sauce is thickened and reduced by half (about 5 min.). Return steak to pan and turn to coat. Slice steak on the diagonal, arranging on a serving platter; pour hot sauce on top.

GOOD TO KNOW
• Bison producers often recommend cooking bison steaks to 115°. As with grass-fed meat, bison texture is best when it is not cooked past medium. USDA guidelines recommend cooking to 145°.

SERVES 6

EASY

TUSCAN MEATLOAF

1 ½ lbs. 93% lean ground beef

1 cup Italian dry breadcrumbs

1 cup finely torn kale (leaves only, stems discarded)

8 oz. tube sun-dried tomato purée

1/2 cup finely chopped onion

1/4 cup julienne-cut sun-dried tomatoes in olive oil, drained, blotted dry

1/4 cup Kowalski's Shredded Parmesan Cheese

1/4 cup chopped fresh basil

1 egg, slightly beaten

1 tbsp. minced garlic

1/4 tsp. Kowalski's Coarse Ground Black Pepper

In a large bowl, combine all ingredients. Shape ground beef mixture into 2 loaves; place on a parchment-lined jelly-roll pan. Bake in a preheated 350° oven until an instant-read meat thermometer inserted in the center of each loaf reaches 160° (about 60 min.). Let stand on counter, covered, 5 min.; cut into 1" thick slices.

Nutrition Information Per Serving

Total Calories	310
Total Fat	13 g
Saturated Fat	5 g
Sodium	415 mg
Fiber	3 g

Each serving also contains nearly 40% of the daily recommendation for these immune-boosting nutrients: vitamins A, C and B12, plus iron, selenium and zinc.

SERVES 6

EASY

BEEF TENDERLOIN
WITH DIJON AIOLI

2 lbs. beef tenderloin

- Kowalski's Extra Virgin Olive Oil

- kosher salt

- coarse ground black pepper

- *Dijon Aioli*

Rub tenderloin with olive oil and season generously with salt and pepper. Tie "tail" under for uniform thickness and even cooking. Roast in a preheated 425° oven or grill directly over high heat, lid down, 35-40 min. for rare (130° internal temperature) or 40-50 min. for medium (150° internal temperature). (If grilling, turn meat when grill marks form and meat releases easily from grates, until dark on all sides. Adjust heat down to medium-high if needed to prevent excess browning in last 20 min. or so.) Remove from heat; cover with foil and let stand 10-15 min. before slicing. Serve with *Dijon Aioli*.

DIJON AIOLI:
In small bowl, combine 1/2 cup mayonnaise, 1/2 cup Dijon mustard and 1 tsp. minced garlic; season with kosher salt and coarse ground black pepper to taste. Refrigerate, covered, until ready to use.
Makes 1 cup

SERVES 8

EASY

179

PORK TENDERLOIN DIANE

2 lbs. pork tenderloins

1 ½ tsp. soy sauce

1 ½ tsp. Kowalski's Extra Virgin
  Olive Oil

6 tbsp. butter, divided

1/4 cup finely minced shallots

1 cup veal demi-glace (3/4 cup
  hot water whisked with
  1 ½ oz. pkg. More than
  Gourmet Gold Classic
  French Demi-Glace)

2 tbsp. chopped fresh Italian
  parsley

1 ½ tbsp. Dijon mustard

2 tsp. Worcestershire sauce

1 tsp. fresh squeezed lemon
  juice

- kosher salt

- Kowalski's Coarse Ground
  Black Pepper

Rub tenderloins with soy sauce and olive oil; cut each into 8 medallions. In a large sauté pan over high heat, heat 3 tbsp. butter, swirling to coat pan. Sauté medallions in butter until browned on both sides (4-5 min. per side); transfer to a warm platter and cover with foil. In same sauté pan, add remaining 3 tbsp. butter and shallots; sauté until softened (about 1 min.). Deglaze pan with demi glace; stir in parsley, mustard, Worcestershire and lemon juice; season to taste with salt and pepper. Return medallions to pan to cover with sauce; serve immediately.

GOOD TO KNOW
• Find More than Gourmet Gold Classic French Demi-Glace in the Meat Department.

SERVES 8

FAST

ROAST PRIME RIB OF PORK
WITH APRICOT GLAZE

APRICOT GLAZE:

1 cup apricot preserves

1/4 cup Dijon mustard

2 tbsp. rice wine vinegar

1 tbsp. soy sauce

ROSEMARY-GARLIC RUBBED PORK:

1/4 cup chopped fresh rosemary

1/4 cup Kowalski's Extra Virgin
      Olive Oil

1 tbsp. kosher salt

2 tsp. minced garlic

3-4 lbs. prime rib of pork
      (8 ribs per rack)

In a small bowl, whisk together ingredients for glaze; set aside. In a small bowl, combine ingredients for rub (through garlic); place pork, skin side up, in a roasting pan. Spread rub evenly over pork. Roast in a preheated 325° oven until a meat thermometer inserted in the center of the roast registers 140° (20 min. per lb.). Brush with glaze during the last 15 min. of roasting time. Let rest, covered, about 10 min. Cut into individual chops.

SERVES 8

EASY

PORK LOIN ROAST
WITH SWEET ONIONS & MADEIRA WINE SAUCE

3 tbsp. butter

1 large sweet onion, thinly sliced

1 ¾ lbs. boneless pork loin
    rib-eye roast

2 tsp. Kowalski's North Woods
    Grill Seasoning Blend

1 cup Madeira wine

2 tbsp. chopped fresh Italian
    parsley

1/4 cup water

3 tbsp. flour

In a medium skillet, melt butter over medium heat; sauté onions until soft (8-10 min.); push onions to side of pan. Rub roast with seasoning; brown roast on both sides (about 3 min. per side). Place roast in a crockpot; top with onions, wine and parsley. Cover; cook on low heat 8 hrs. Remove pork and onions to a platter; let stand 15 min., covered. In small bowl, combine water and flour; add to juices in crockpot. Continue cooking on high heat until sauce is thickened (about 15 min.), stirring occasionally. Break pork into 6 chunks; serve topped with onions and sauce.

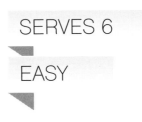

SERVES 6

EASY

GRILLED PORK RIBS

4 lbs. Kowalski's All Natural
   Pork Loin Back Ribs
   (2 racks), cut in half

3 cups barbeque sauce

Arrange ribs on a 10x15" jelly-roll pan. Pour sauce over ribs, turning to coat; cover with plastic wrap. Refrigerate 1-2 days. Wrap each rib section in foil; reserve sauce. Using indirect heat cooking method, heat grill to medium; turn half of grill off (or move coals to one side). Grill ribs over unheated side of grill, covered, until ribs are tender (2 ½-3 hrs.). Bring reserved barbeque sauce to a boil over medium heat; boil 5 min. Carefully remove ribs from foil to dinner plates; serve with warm sauce.

VARIATION

Oriental Ribs:

Whisk together 2 ¼ cups ketchup, 1/2 cup hoisin sauce, 1/4 cup superfine sugar, 1 tsp. minced garlic and 1 tsp. kosher salt to use in place of the barbeque sauce. Garnish finished ribs with toasted sesame seeds (available in the International Foods Aisle).

SERVES 4

EASY

PERFECT PORK CHOPS

4 pork chops, about 2 lbs.
    total weight (1" thick each)

- kosher salt and coarse
    ground black pepper,
    to taste

Season chops with salt and pepper. Arrange chops on a clean grill or grill pan preheated to high; cook, turning once when dark grill marks form and meat releases easily from grill grates, until slightly pink in center and meat reaches an internal temperature of 140° (10-14 min. total). Remove from heat and tent with foil for 10 min. before serving.

SERVES 4

EASY

FAST

PULLED PORK SANDWICHES **WITH LEMON COLESLAW**

2 tbsp. sour cream

2 tbsp. mayonnaise

1/2 tsp. lemon zest

1/4 cup lemon juice

1 tsp. superfine sugar

1/4 tsp. kosher salt

1/8 tsp. coarse ground
      black pepper

7 oz. bagged coleslaw

1/2 bunch green onions, sliced

1/4 cup chopped fresh cilantro

2 lbs. Kowalski's BBQ Pulled Pork

8 Kowalski's Hamburger Buns

In large bowl, combine first 7 ingredients; stir in coleslaw, green onions and cilantro, tossing to completely combine. Warm pulled pork in saucepan over medium heat until heated through, stirring occasionally (about 5 min.). Spoon pulled pork onto bottom of each hamburger bun; top with coleslaw. Top with other half of bun; serve immediately.

SERVES 8

EASY

FAST

185

SEVEN SECRETS FOR SUCCESSFUL GRILLING

Whether you're a seasoned old pro or afraid to even lift the lid, we're sharing a few simple tips that will change your grilling experience for the better! Read on to learn how to ensure your backyard barbeque best:

1. **Preheat your grill properly.** Gas grills need an average of 15 min. to heat to high. For best results, always heat fully to high, then adjust the heat down if needed. If you're using charcoal, wait until all the briquettes are white and ashy before moving them around.

2. **Clean your grill completely and at the right time** – when it's HOT. In most cases, a grill is hottest after it has been preheated. Doing it after your food is cooked might work, if the grill is very hot and if you aren't distracted by getting your food to the table. You will need to give stuck-on foods a few minutes to burn off (which is why doing it after preheating is preferred).

3. **Select the right foods for grilling.** Proteins with a lot of connective tissue that require a slow cooking over low heat and/or a longer cooking time (like roasts) aren't well suited to grilling. Neither are delicate, flakier fish with very little natural fat. Try firmer, naturally fatty fish such as salmon, tuna, sea bass or mahi mahi.

4. **Oil: The grates or the food? That IS the question.** If oil is required (not usually the case with burgers, steaks, sausages, chops, ribs, marinated chicken or tenderloins, etc.) it isn't terribly critical, but do oil the grates when cooking fish. Several swipes over hot grates with a paper towel dipped in (but NOT dripping with) oil until they are shiny should suffice.

5. **Turn your grilled foods properly.** For foods less than an inch thick, one turn is usually sufficient. In the case of fish, you may be able to cook it without turning (useful for delicate and/or skin-on fillets). Turn thicker, bone-in cuts evenly. Only turn foods when they release easily from the grill.

6. **Temp your foods!** This ensures not just doneness, but is critical to preventing OVER-doneness.

7. **Rest proteins to maintain moisture and allow for carryover cooking.** Even thinner chicken breasts and burgers will increase 5° after they are removed from the heat. Thicker foods and bone-in pieces will increase an average of 10°. Remove steaks, chops, ribs, chicken, fish, etc., and cover with foil for at least 5 min. Thicker, bone-in cuts and whole tenderloins can rest 15 min. or more and still maintain their heat.

WHAT ABOUT BRINING?

Brining is a great way to maintain moisture in certain cuts and proteins, but it is most popular with chicken and pork. Most any protein can be brined in a solution of 1 gallon water mixed with 1/3 cup sugar and 1/3 cup salt. As little as 20 min. is effective with pieces of chicken and fish. Pork benefits from as little as 30 min.

LOADED BACON-BBQ DOGS

6 grass-fed uncured beef hot
    dogs

2 tbsp. Kowalski's Original
    BBQ Sauce

6 Kowalski's Brat Buns
    (or White or Wheat Hot
    Dog Buns)

6 strips bacon, cooked crisp

- garnishes: sweet pickle relish,
    whole celery seeds, Dijon
    mustard, *Herbed Coleslaw*

Grill hot dogs over medium-high heat, covered, until dark grill marks form and dogs are thoroughly hot, turning 3-4 times (about 10 min.). Brush with BBQ sauce; grill 1-2 min. more until sauce is hot and starting to get sticky. Load dogs into buns with a strip of bacon; garnish as desired.

NOTE
• Find the recipe for *Herbed Coleslaw* in the Salads Section of this book. Kowalski's Herbed Coleslaw can also be purchased in the Deli Department.

SERVES 6

EASY

FAST

TERIYAKI BURGERS

1/2 cup teriyaki sauce

1/4 cup Kowalski's Pure Honey

1 lb. lean grass-fed beef

2 green onions, thinly sliced

3 tbsp. chopped fresh cilantro

1 clove garlic, finely minced

2 tsp. prepared Asian
chile-garlic paste

1/2 tsp. kosher salt

4 Kowalski's Wheat Burger
Buns, lightly toasted

- garnishes: finely shredded
green cabbage (such
as Dole Angel Hair
Coleslaw), *Quick Asian
Pickles* and *Ginger Aioli*

Whisk together teriyaki and honey in a small bowl; set aside. Combine next 6 ingredients through salt in a large bowl. Using your hands, mix thoroughly; form 4 patties. Grill burgers over medium-high heat, covered, until done (4-5 min. per side), turning twice and brushing each side with glaze in last 2 min. of cooking. Remove from heat; let stand 3-5 min., covered with foil, before serving. Serve on buns with desired garnishes.

SERVES 4

EASY

QUICK ASIAN PICKLES:

1/2 English cucumber, peeled and thinly sliced

1/2 tsp. kosher salt

1/2 carrot, peeled and thinly sliced

2 radishes, thinly sliced

3 tbsp. seasoned rice vinegar

3 tbsp. water

4 ½ tsp. sugar

- pinch crushed red pepper

In a small bowl, toss cucumbers with salt. Pour into a strainer set over a small bowl; let stand 45 min. Squeeze cucumbers dry with paper towels. In a medium bowl, toss dry cucumbers with carrots and radishes; set aside. In a small saucepan over medium-high heat, combine vinegar, water, sugar and pepper; bring to a boil. Reduce heat to low; simmer until reduced to 2-3 tbsp. (about 10 min.) Pour sauce over vegetables in a small bowl; refrigerate 30 min.

MAKES 1 cup

EASY

GINGER AIOLI:

1/2 cup mayonnaise

2 tsp. sweet pickle relish

2 tsp. finely minced fresh ginger

2 tsp. fresh lime juice

1 clove finely minced garlic

1/4 tsp. kosher salt

In a small bowl, stir together mayonnaise, relish, ginger and lime juice. Stir in garlic and salt. Store, covered, in the refrigerator until ready to use, up to 7 days.

MAKES 1/2 cup

EASY

FAST

189

JUICY BACON BLUE BURGERS

4 slices Kowalski's Bacon

1/2 sweet onion, sliced

1 lb. Kowalski's Premium
     All Natural 85% Lean
     Ground Beef

- Kowalski's North Woods
     Grill Seasoning Blend

1/3 cup Kowalski's Original
     BBQ Sauce

4 oz. Kowalski's Blue Cheese
     crumbles

4 Kowalski's Hamburger Buns

- Bibb lettuce

In a large skillet, fry bacon until slightly crisp (5-7 min.); drain on paper towels. Add onion to bacon drippings, sautéing until tender (3-5 min.); drain. Shape ground beef into 4 patties; sprinkle both sides with seasoning blend. Grill patties over medium heat, covered, to an internal temperature of 160° (10-15 min.), turning once, brushing both sides with BBQ sauce. Top with cheese during last 2 min. of grilling. Toast buns, cut side down, on grill rack until lightly browned (1-2 min.). Line bottom half of bun with lettuce; layer with burger, onions, bacon and top of bun.

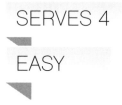

SERVES 4

EASY

FAJITA BURGERS

1/2 red bell pepper, cut into strips

1/2 yellow bell pepper, cut into strips

1/2 orange bell pepper, cut into strips

2 slices sweet yellow onion, separated

1 tbsp. Kowalski's Extra Virgin Olive Oil

1/2 tsp. kosher salt

1 ¼ lbs. Kowalski's Premium All Natural 85% Lean Ground Beef

1-2 tbsp. Kowalski's Chili Powder

4 slices Monterey Jack cheese

4 hamburger buns

4 tbsp. sour cream, divided

1/2 cup shredded lettuce, divided

4 tomato slices

In a medium bowl, combine first 6 ingredients; set aside. In a large bowl, combine ground beef and chili powder; shape into 4 patties. Place pepper mixture in a grill basket; grill over high heat until softened, stirring several times. Grill patties, covered, to a minimum internal temperature of 160° (4-5 min. per side). Top with cheese during last 3 min. of grilling. Spread cut side of top buns with sour cream; top with lettuce. Place burgers on bottom buns; top with tomato slice and grilled peppers.

SERVES 4

EASY

FAST

Pork Loin Roast with Sweet Onions & Madeira Wine Sauce (pg 182) and Dried Cherry & Almond Rice Pilaf (pg 261)

Chicken Saltimbocca (pg 197), Sautéed Kale with Pine Nuts & Dried Cranberries (pg 281) and Polenta & Parmesan Gratins (pg 293)

Lime & Honey Glazed Sea Bass
(pg 225)

Fajita Burgers (pg 191)

Teriyaki Burgers (pg 188)

Horseradish Steak Sandwiches
(pg 176)

Mexican Chicken Sandwiches
(pg 206)

Kowalski's Chicken Tacos
(pg 205)

Fish Tacos (pg 228)

Smoked Salmon & Egg Salad
on Rye (pg 215)

Mediterranean Sea Bass en Papillote (pg 226)

Roasted Chicken & Vegetables
(pg 194)

POULTRY

ROASTED CHICKEN & VEGETABLES

1 lb. pkg. baby carrots

8 baby red potatoes, quartered

1/2 sweet onion, sliced

3 medium celery stalks, trimmed, cut into 1" pieces

2 tbsp. plus 1 tsp. Kowalski's Extra Virgin Olive Oil, divided

2 ½ tsp. kosher salt, divided

1/4 tsp. Kowalski's Coarse Ground Black Pepper

2 tsp. chopped fresh thyme

2 tsp. minced garlic

4 lb. Kadejan All Natural Young Chicken

Line bottom of a broiler pan with foil; set aside. In a large bowl, toss carrots, potatoes, onion and celery with 2 tbsp. olive oil; season with 1 tsp. salt and the pepper. Spread evenly in bottom of foil-lined broiler pan. In a small bowl, combine thyme, garlic and 1/2 tsp. salt. Carefully loosen skin over breast of chicken; spread herb mixture under the skin. Arrange chicken, breast side up, on top rack of broiler pan. Rub skin with 1 tsp. salt; brush with 1 tsp. olive oil. Roast in a preheated 400° oven until an instant-read meat thermometer registers 165° (55-65 min.). Let stand, covered, 10 min. Move vegetables to a serving platter. Carve chicken; arrange on platter with vegetables.

SERVES 6

BUTTERMILK BRINED TURKEY BREAST

3 cups buttermilk, divided

1/4 cup hot sauce, optional

2 tbsp. kosher salt

4 ½ tsp. coarse ground
    black pepper

1 tbsp. garlic powder

1 tsp. cayenne pepper (optional)

2 ½-3 lb. turkey breast,
    bone in, skin on

In a medium microwave-safe mixing bowl, gently warm 1 cup buttermilk in the microwave, but do not boil. Whisk in next 5 ingredients, until salt is dissolved. Add remaining buttermilk and stir. If necessary, place in refrigerator until mixture is thoroughly cool. Place turkey in a large mixing bowl: cover with brine. Cover bowl and refrigerate 12-24 hrs. Remove the turkey breast from the brine; discard brine. Drain well and pat dry with paper towels. Bake in a preheated 325° oven for 75 min. Increase heat to 400°; cook until turkey registers 155° internal temperature and the skin is dark golden-brown (10-15 min. more). Remove from the oven; cover with foil and let rest 10-15 min. before carving (temperature will increase to 165° as the turkey stands).

SERVES 6

BRINED TURKEY

2 cups kosher salt

1 cup sugar

8 qts. water, divided

1 (10-12 lb.) turkey

1/2 cup melted butter

In a large stock pot, combine salt, sugar and 2 qts. water. Bring to a boil over high heat; remove from heat. Stir in remaining water; cool completely. Put brine and turkey into a container or brining bag large enough to completely cover turkey; refrigerate 8 hrs. or overnight. Remove turkey from brine; pat dry, but do not rinse. Discard brine. Place on rack in roasting pan, breast side up, tucking wings under body and tying legs together with butcher's twine; brush turkey with butter. Roast turkey in a preheated 325° oven, basting every 30 min., until deep golden-brown and a thermometer inserted in the thickest part of the thigh registers 165° (2 ½-3 hrs. or 15 min. per lb.). Let rest, covered with foil, 20 min. before carving.

SERVES 10

CHICKEN SALTIMBOCCA

4 boneless skinless chicken breasts, pounded to 1/4" thickness

1/2 tsp. kosher salt

1/4 tsp. Kowalski's Coarse Ground Black Pepper

1/3 cup flour

8 tbsp. butter, divided

4 tbsp. shaved Parmesan cheese, divided

4 thin slices prosciutto

1 ⅓ cups dry white wine

1 tbsp. chopped fresh sage

Season chicken breasts with salt and pepper; coat both sides of each breast with flour, shaking off excess. In a large skillet over medium-high heat, melt 4 tbsp. butter; add chicken breasts, sautéing until brown (about 8 min.), turning halfway through. Arrange breasts on a jelly-roll pan; set skillet aside. Divide cheese among breasts, topping each with slice of prosciutto; bake in a preheated 400° oven until chicken is cooked through (about 5 min.). While chicken is baking, add wine, sage and remaining 4 tbsp. butter to skillet; bring to a boil, reducing sauce to 2/3 cup, scraping up browned bits from bottom of pan (about 6 min.). Arrange each breast on a dinner plate; drizzle with sauce.

SERVES 4

PARMESAN CRUSTED CHICKEN **WITH HERBED BUTTER SAUCE**

1 cup breadcrumbs

1/2 cup panko breadcrumbs

1/3 cup Kowalski's Parmesan Cheese, freshly grated

1 ½ lbs. boneless skinless chicken breasts, pounded to an even 1/2" thickness

- kosher salt and coarse ground black pepper, to taste

1/2 cup flour

2 eggs, lightly beaten

5 tbsp. cold unsalted butter, divided

2 tbsp. minced shallot

1/4 cup dry white wine

1/4 cup heavy cream

1/4 cup low-sodium chicken broth

1 tsp. lemon juice

2-3 tsp. minced fresh sage

1 tsp. snipped fresh chives

1 tbsp. Kowalski's Extra Virgin Olive Oil

2 tbsp. chopped fresh Italian parsley

Combine breadcrumbs in a shallow dish; whisk in cheese and stir to combine. Season chicken liberally with salt and pepper. Place flour and eggs in separate shallow dishes. Working in batches, coat chicken in flour, shaking off excess. Dip floured chicken in egg, then coat with crumbs, pressing to adhere. Place chicken on a wire rack and let air-dry 15 min. In a small sauté pan over medium heat, melt 1 tbsp. butter. Sauté shallots until soft (2-3 min.). Whisk in wine, cream, broth and lemon juice; simmer over medium-low heat until reduced to about 1/3 cup (8-10 min.). Whisk in 3 tbsp. butter a bit at a time, whisking constantly. Stir in sage and chives; season with salt and pepper. Pour sauce into a glass measuring cup and place in a hot water bath to keep sauce warm until ready to serve. To cook chicken, melt remaining butter in oil in an extra-large skillet over medium-high heat. Sauté chicken until golden-brown and cooked through, turning once (about 4 min. per side). Move chicken to a warm platter; drizzle with sauce and garnish with parsley.

SERVES 4

BALSAMIC GLAZED CHICKEN,
ROASTED RED PEPPER & ONION CIABATTA SANDWICH

1 Kowalski's Signature Rotisserie Chicken

1 tbsp. olive oil

1 cup sweet onion slices

3 roasted sweet red peppers, cut into strips

1/2 cup balsamic vinegar

1 cup aioli

6 Kowalski's Take & Bake Ciabatta Rolls, sliced horizontally

6 slices provolone cheese, cut in half

Pick chicken meat from bones, discarding skin; shred into large pieces. Heat olive oil in a sauté pan over medium heat. Stir in onions; sauté 5 min. Add red pepper. Stir in vinegar; continue cooking until vinegar is syrupy (about 5 min.). Spread aioli on cut sides of each ciabatta roll; divide shredded chicken among bottom halves of each roll. Divide balsamic onion mixture among rolls. Arrange cheese slices over onion mixture; broil 6" from heat source until cheese is melted and slightly browned (1-2 min.). Top with top halves of ciabatta rolls; cut in half on the diagonal.

GOOD TO KNOW

• Roasted sweet red peppers are available in a jar in the olive section or on the Olive Bar. Whole peppers should be cut into strips for this recipe.

• Aioli is available in a jar in the mayonnaise section, or you can make your own by combining 1 cup mayonnaise and 5 cloves of finely minced garlic.

SERVES 6

EASY

FAST

LIGHT CHICKEN PICATTA
& ROASTED BROCCOLI

3/4 cup low-sodium chicken broth, divided

1/2 cup flour, divided

- kosher salt and coarse ground black pepper, to taste

1 ½ lbs. boneless skinless chicken breasts, pounded to an even 1/2" thickness

2 ½ tbsp. butter, divided

1 tbsp. Kowalski's Extra Virgin Olive Oil

1/4 cup finely chopped shallots

4 cloves garlic, thinly sliced

1/2 cup dry white wine

2 tbsp. fresh lemon juice

1 ½ tbsp. drained capers

3 tbsp. chopped fresh Italian parsley

- lemon slices, for garnish

- *Roasted Broccoli*

Stir 1/4 cup broth into 1 tsp. flour until smooth; set aside. Combine remaining flour, salt and pepper in a shallow dish. Dredge chicken in flour mixture; shake off excess. Melt 1 tbsp. butter and oil in a large skillet over medium-high heat. Sauté chicken in oil until dark golden-brown and cooked through, turning once (about 4 min. per side). Move chicken to a warm platter; keep warm. Add shallots to the pan; sauté 3 min., stirring frequently. Add garlic; sauté 1 min., stirring constantly. Add wine, scraping pan; bring to a boil. Cook, stirring often, until liquid almost evaporates. Add remaining broth to pan; bring to a boil. Cook until reduced by half (about 5 min.). Stir in flour-broth mixture; cook, stirring frequently, 1 min. until slightly thickened. Remove from heat; whisk in remaining butter, juice and capers. Drizzle sauce over chicken; sprinkle with parsley and garnish with lemon.

Nutrition Information Per Serving

Total Calories	280
Total Fat	12 g
Saturated Fat	4 g
Sodium	190 mg
Fiber	1 g

Rich in vitamins C and K, B vitamins and potassium.

ROASTED BROCCOLI:

2 cups of broccoli florets, cut into evenly sized 1 ½" pieces

- Kowalski's Extra Virgin Olive Oil

- Kosher salt and coarse ground black pepper, to taste

Completely but lightly coat broccol with oil. Season to taste with salt and pepper. Roast on a baking sheet lined with parchment paper in preheated 450° oven until browned and tender when pierced with a fork (10-15 min.).

SERVES 6

BAKED CHICKEN TENDERS
WITH SUNSHINE SAUCE

1 cup panko breadcrumbs

1/3 cup Kowalski's Parmesan Cheese, freshly grated

1 ½ tsp. Mrs. Dash Table Blend Salt-Free Seasoning Blend

1 tbsp. canola oil

1/2 cup flour

3 eggs whites, lightly beaten, whisked with 1 tbsp. water

1 lb. boneless skinless chicken breasts, cut into 1 ½" strips

- *Sunshine Sauce*

Spread breadcrumbs on a rimmed baking sheet; bake in a preheated 400° oven until golden-brown (about 6 min.). Transfer to a shallow dish; whisk in cheese and seasoning. Drizzle with oil; stir to combine. Place flour and eggs in separate shallow dishes. Working in batches, coat chicken in flour, shaking off excess. Dip floured chicken in egg, then coat with panko, pressing to adhere. Place chicken on a wire rack and let air-dry 15 min. Bake in preheated 400° oven on a baking sheet lined with parchment paper until chicken is golden-brown and cooked through (15-20 min.), flipping chicken and rotating pan halfway through. Serve with *Sunshine Sauce* for dipping.

SUNSHINE SAUCE:

In a small bowl, whisk together 1/4 cup each nonfat Greek yogurt and honey mustard with 2 tbsp. mayonnaise and 1/2 tsp. finely chopped fresh dill; add 1-2 tbsp. low-fat buttermilk to reach desired consistency. Season to taste with hot sauce, kosher salt and freshly ground Kowalski's Whole Black Peppercorns.

Nutrition Information Per Serving

Total Calories	401
Total Fat	15 g
Saturated Fat	4 g
Sodium	420 mg
Fiber	7 g

A good source of B vitamins, calcium, iron and vitamin A.

SERVES 4

EASY

TIPS & TRICKS FOR RAISING ADVENTUROUS EATERS

Her "In the Kitchen with the Kids" page has been a favorite feature of At Home with Kowalski's readers since Chef Perron joined us in 2011. Here she shares some key strategies for developing her own junior foodies:

• The more foods they're exposed to, the wider my kids' tastes range.

• My kids' palates are developing with the rest of their bodies. I didn't like lima beans or oatmeal as a kid, but I love them now. Similarly, they weren't born with an affinity for artichokes, salmon, bell peppers or mushrooms. That doesn't mean they won't like them someday.

• I can set a good example by eating a variety of foods myself and trying new foods whenever I can (even if I'm the only one at the table eating them).

• Kids who cook more try more. Sometimes it takes longer and it usually makes more of a mess, but when the kids ask to help with dinner, I let 'em. Admittedly, many of the things my kids like to help with are simple (or sweet) – cookies, cupcakes, pancakes, etc. – but even these are opportunities to teach basic skills and techniques that they'll be able to use someday to create more interesting (and hopefully healthier) dishes.

• My kids are happier when they get to pick dinner once a week. Yes, that means sometimes I eat macaroni and cheese, and we eat lots of tacos and spaghetti at my place. But when I once considered how I would feel if someone planned every meal for me, I had a little more empathy for my kids having to succumb to my tastes all the time.

• Kid-friendly foods don't have to be boring (for them or, importantly, me!). My kids' favorites become more interesting (and often healthier) when I choose whole grain pasta, make my own spaghetti sauce and offer lots of fresh taco accompaniments like cilantro, lime, chipotle salsa, avocado, beans and corn. I've even added spinach, carrots, tomatoes and peas in things like enchiladas, meat loaf, macaroni, pizza and chili. (Note: I try hard not to hide it. I don't want to encourage them to be suspicious of what I'm feeding them or think that there's something I need to cover up.)

• Kids will eat anything if it has Ranch dressing on it. When I can, I offer healthier options like hummus, salsa, guacamole – even ketchup. (Face it, dipping anything – even vegetables – is fun.)

• The grocery store is an amazing classroom; though it can sometimes be trying, slow and loud, I often involve my kids in shopping for food. I make sure they see me checking out new foods, ingredient lists and nutrition info in the aisles, and we practice their skills with cereal boxes, where they can each pick out their own (given certain nutritional parameters!).

• Kids who pick out their own food are more apt to eat it. When shopping, I have a rule that my kids can pick out anything in the produce section that catches their eye and I will buy it. This also provides a great opportunity to teach them how to pick ripe pears, cabbage, melon, avocados, etc. We apply similar skills to selecting great meat, seafood and bread, too.

KOWALSKI'S CHICKEN ENCHILADAS

32 oz. Kowalski's
    Enchilada Sauce, divided

- meat from 1/2 of a Kowalski's
    Signature Rotisserie
    Chicken, shredded

1 ½ cups shredded Monterey
    Jack cheese, divided

4 oz. can fire-roasted green
    chiles, drained

10 oz. pkg. corn tortillas
    (12 count)

- toppings, your choice:
    shredded lettuce, shredded
    Monterey Jack cheese,
    Kowalski's Salsa, diced
    avocado, roughly chopped
    fresh cilantro, lime wedges,
    sliced red onion and
    light sour cream

Pour 1 jar of enchilada sauce into bottom of 13x9" glass baking dish sprayed lightly with cooking spray. Pour remaining sauce into a bowl; warm slightly in the microwave then set aside. In a medium mixing bowl, mix chicken with 1 cup cheese and chiles; set aside. Dip 1 tortilla at a time into the bowl of warm sauce, top with filling and roll up. Place tortillas seam side down in prepared baking dish. Pour remaining sauce over top; sprinkle with reserved cheese. Bake in a preheated 400° oven until cheese is melted and bubbly and enchiladas are heated through (about 20 min.). Let stand 10 min. before serving topped with remaining ingredients to taste.

VARIATIONS

Beef Enchiladas:
Substitute 1 lb. ground beef and 1/2 cup onion for the chicken. Cook until beef is no longer pink and onions are tender; drain.

Cheese Enchiladas:
Substitute 12 oz. finely shredded Cheddar and Monterey Jack cheeses for the chicken.

SERVES 6

EASY

KOWALSKI'S CHICKEN TACOS

1/4 cup plus 2 tbsp. Kowalski's Hot Taco Sauce

1 tbsp. fresh squeezed lime juice

1 ½ tsp. cocoa powder

1/2 tsp. ground cinnamon

1/4 tsp. Kowalski's Coarse Ground Black Pepper

4 boneless skinless chicken breasts (about 1 ¼ lbs.), pounded to even 1/4" thickness

8 Kowalski's Flour Tortillas (6" each)

- toppings, your choice: shredded lettuce, shredded Monterey Jack cheese, Kowalski's Salsa, roughly chopped fresh cilantro, lime wedges, sliced red onion and light sour cream

In a medium bowl, whisk together first 5 ingredients through pepper. Cut each chicken breast in half to make 8 evenly shaped pieces; add to marinade, tossing to coat. Cover with plastic wrap; chill in the refrigerator 2 hrs. Discard marinade; grill chicken over medium heat, covered, until done (about 9 min.), turning once. Let stand, covered with foil, 5 min. Wrap tortillas in slightly damp paper towels; heat in the microwave until very warm (up to 45 sec.). Divide chicken among warm tortillas and top with remaining ingredients to taste; serve immediately.

Nutrition Information Per Serving (2 tacos)

Total Calories	385
Total Fat	10 g
Saturated Fat	3 g
Cholesterol	90 mg
Sodium	750 mg

A good source of B vitamins, iron, potassium, magnesium and calcium.

GOOD TO KNOW

• Find Kowalski's Flour Tortillas in the Dairy Department.

SERVES 4

GOOD FOODS FOR GOOD
Health

Signature

205

MEXICAN CHICKEN SANDWICHES

1/3 cup mayonnaise

1 tbsp. fresh squeezed lime juice

1 tsp. grated lime zest

- kosher salt and Kowalski's Coarse Ground Black Pepper, to taste

1 tbsp. Kowalski's Extra Virgin Olive Oil

1/2 cup canned black beans, rinsed and drained

2 tbsp. chopped red onion

2 tbsp. low-sodium chicken stock

1 tbsp. finely chopped fresh cilantro

1 tsp. ground cumin

1 ¼ lbs. boneless skinless chicken breasts, pounded to an even 1/2" thickness

2 tsp. chili powder

3/4 tsp. cayenne pepper

3 slices Pepper Jack cheese

1 Kowalski's Baguette, split horizontally, cut into 4 pieces

6-8 tomato slices

- Kowalski's Guacamole

In a small mixing bowl, whisk together mayonnaise, lime juice and lime zest; season with salt and pepper and set aside. Heat oil in a small skillet over medium heat; add beans and onion. Cook 5 min. Move bean mixture to a medium mixing bowl and add stock, cilantro and cumin; mash to a paste with salt and pepper to taste. Set aside. Season chicken with chili powder, cayenne, salt and pepper to taste; grill over high heat, covered, until cooked through (about 10 min.), turning once. Remove from grill; cover chicken with cheese and cover loosely with foil. Let stand 5 min. Spread half of each roll with bean paste and other half with a generous amount of lime mayonnaise. Top each roll with a piece of chicken, an equal amount of tomato and a generous dollop of guacamole. Serve immediately.

SERVES 4

KALBI CHICKEN LETTUCE WRAPS

MARINADE:

1 cup low-sodium soy sauce

1/4 cup superfine sugar

2 tbsp. chopped garlic

1 tbsp. minced ginger

1 tbsp. toasted sesame seeds

1 tbsp. vegetable oil

1 tbsp. toasted sesame oil

1/4-1/2 tsp. crushed red pepper

LETTUCE WRAPS:

1 lb. boneless skinless chicken breasts

8 oz. can sliced water chestnuts, drained

8 oz. pkg. fresh bean sprouts, rinsed

1/2 cup shredded carrot

1/4 cup red pepper strips

1 bunch green onions, chopped

1 oz. pkg. fresh cilantro, chopped

1 head Bibb or iceberg lettuce, rinsed, drained, leaves separated

In a medium glass bowl, combine marinade ingredients; add chicken, turning to coat. Refrigerate, covered, up to 12 hrs., turning several times. Reserve marinade. Grill chicken over medium heat, covered, until no longer pink in thickest part of breast (about 5 min. per side), turning 1-2 times. Cut chicken into thin strips; set aside. In a large skillet, bring reserved marinade to a boil over medium heat; add chicken and remaining ingredients except cilantro and lettuce. Cook until heated through (about 5 min.); stir in cilantro. Place chicken mixture in a bowl in the center of a serving platter; arrange lettuce leaves around edge of platter. Spoon chicken mixture onto each lettuce leaf; fold burrito-style.

SERVES 4

EASY

MOROCCAN CHICKEN SANDWICHES

1/2 cup chicken stock

1 tbsp. ground coriander

1 ½ tsp. ground cardamom

1 ½ tsp. ground cinnamon

1 cup dried chopped apricots

1 ½ cups shredded Kowalski's Signature Rotisserie Chicken

1 cup canned petite diced tomatoes, drained

1/3 cup chopped pitted green olives

1/4 cup raw, finely chopped almonds

2 tbsp. Kowalski's Extra Virgin Olive Oil

1 tbsp. red wine vinegar

- kosher salt and Kowalski's Coarse Ground Black Pepper, to taste

1 cup plain Greek yogurt

3 tbsp. fresh lemon juice

2 tbsp. chili powder

2 tbsp. finely chopped fresh Italian parsley

1/2 tsp. cumin

1/2 tsp. caraway seeds

- dash cayenne pepper

4 (1 oz. loaves) whole-grain pita bread, such as Joseph's Flax, Oat Bran and Whole Wheat Pita

2 cups pre-washed mixed baby greens

Warm stock in the microwave; whisk in coriander, cardamom and cinnamon and pour over apricots in a large mixing bowl. Set aside for 10 min. Add chicken, tomatoes, olives, almonds, oil and vinegar to apricot mixture; season with salt and pepper to taste and set aside. In another small mixing bowl, whisk yogurt with next 6 ingredients through cayenne; season with salt and pepper to taste. Cut a pocket in each pita; spread one side of each pocket with some yogurt mixture. Stuff each pita with an equal amount of greens and chicken mixture. Drizzle with extra yogurt mixture and serve immediately.

MOROCCAN CHICKEN SANDWICHES (CONTINUED)

NOTE

• For picnics, separately tote the prepared chicken mixture, yogurt dressing, greens and pita breads; quickly assemble sandwiches when it's time to eat.

Nutrition Information Per Serving

Total Calories	520
Total Fat	20 g
Sodium	650 mg
Fiber	10 mg

A good source of vitamins A, C, E, K, multiple B vitamins, calcium, magnesium, zinc and potassium.

SERVES 4

EASY

FAST

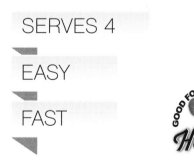

FISH & SEAFOOD

KOWALSKI'S BALSAMIC-GLAZED GRILLED SALMON

1/4 cup Kowalski's Balsamic Vinegar

1 tbsp. Kowalski's Honey

1 tbsp. sugar

2 tsp. soy sauce

- Kowalski's Extra Virgin Olive Oil

2 lbs. skin-on salmon fillet(s)

- kosher salt and coarse ground black pepper, to taste

- lemon wedges

Combine vinegar, honey, sugar and soy sauce in a small saucepan over medium-high heat; bring to a boil. Reduce heat to low and simmer, stirring occasionally, until reduced to about 1/4 cup (about 15 min.); skim off foam. Remove sauce from heat and cool to room temperature; set aside. Brush salmon lightly with oil and season with salt and pepper; grill fish, skin side down, over medium-high heat until flaky and fillet measures 125° (10-15 min, depending on thickness of fish). Transfer salmon to a platter, leaving skin behind; squeeze with lemon. Drizzle warm fish with balsamic sauce; serve immediately.

SERVES 8

EASY

Signature

BROILED SALMON

WITH MANGO SALSA

4 salmon fillets, 1" thick, about
    4 oz. each

2 tsp. olive oil

- kosher salt and coarse ground
    black pepper, to taste

1 cup Kowalski's Mango Salsa

Arrange salmon, skin side down, in a glass baking dish brushed with oil; sprinkle with salt and pepper. Broil salmon 6" from heat source in preheated oven until interior of fish turns opaque and fish reaches an internal temperature of 145° (about 10 min.). Serve topped with salsa.

SERVES 4

EASY

FAST

GOOD TO KNOW
• Kowalski's Mango Salsa is available
  in the Seafood Department.

SALMON **WITH CITRUS VINAIGRETTE**

1 lb. salmon fillet(s), skin removed

1 cup Kowalski's Citrus Vinaigrette

- chopped fresh cilantro, Italian parsley or basil

Place salmon in a large zipper-closure food storage bag with vinaigrette; seal and refrigerate 30 min., turning several times to coat. Remove salmon from bag; discard marinade. Grill salmon over medium-high heat, covered, until interior of fish turns opaque (about 10 min. per inch of thickness, measured at the thickest part). Sprinkle with fresh herbs; serve immediately.

SERVES 4

EASY

SMOKED SALMON & EGG SALAD ON RYE

6 hard-boiled eggs, roughly chopped

4 oz. Kowalski's Smoked Atlantic Salmon, flaked

1/4 cup chopped fresh chives

2 tsp. chopped fresh dill

1/4 tsp. kosher salt (or more to taste)

1/2 tsp. coarse ground black pepper

1/3 cup mayonnaise

6 slices pumpernickel or caraway rye bread

- optional garnishes: leaf lettuce, tomato slices, red onion and additional mayonnaise

In a large mixing bowl, mix together eggs, salmon, chives, dill, salt and pepper; fold in mayonnaise. Scoop salad onto 3 slices of bread; garnish as desired. Cover with the remaining bread slices. Serve immediately.

SERVES 3

EASY

FAST

Signature

CRUSTED SALMON

WITH ARTICHOKE AIOLI

1 cup mayonnaise

5 cloves garlic, finely minced

6 oz. jar marinated artichoke hearts, drained, finely chopped

1/4 cup panko breadcrumbs

1/4 tsp. kosher salt

1 lb. salmon fillet(s), skinned, cut into 4 pieces

1/4 cup Kowalski's Extra Virgin Olive Oil, divided

- grated lemon zest

In a small mixing bowl, combine first 3 ingredients; refrigerate, covered, until ready to use. In a shallow dish, combine breadcrumbs and salt. Brush both sides of salmon fillets with about half of the olive oil; dredge in crumbs. Heat remaining olive oil in a large skillet over medium heat; cook salmon in olive oil until fish is opaque in the center and crumb coating is crisp and brown (about 10 min. per inch of thickness), turning once. Top hot salmon fillets evenly with artichoke aioli; sprinkle with lemon zest. Serve immediately.

SERVES 4

EASY

FAST

TUNA STEAKS
WITH TROPICAL SALSA

4 tuna steaks, 1" thick

1/4 cup olive oil

2 tsp. Kowalski's Chile Lime
    Seasoning Blend

1 ½ cups diced fresh mango

1 ½ cups diced fresh pineapple

1/4 cup chopped sweet onion

2 tbsp. snipped fresh cilantro

1 tbsp. chopped jalapeño pepper

1/2 tsp. grated lime zest

1 tsp. fresh lime juice

1/2 tsp. kosher salt

Brush both sides of tuna with olive oil; sprinkle with seasoning blend. Refrigerate, covered, 30 min. In a medium mixing bowl, combine remaining ingredients; refrigerate, covered, until ready to use. Grill tuna over medium heat, covered, to desired doneness (4-8 min. total cooking time), turning once. Serve with salsa.

GOOD TO KNOW
• Kowalski's Chile Lime Seasoning Blend is available in the Meat Department.

SERVES 4

EASY

217

SALMON CAKES

8 oz. salmon fillet, poached, skinned and flaked

1 egg, beaten

1/3 cup chopped fresh Italian parsley

1/4 cup finely chopped shallots

2 tbsp. mayonnaise

1 tbsp. white wine Dijon mustard

1/8 tsp. cayenne pepper

2 ¼ cups panko breadcrumbs, divided

3 tbsp. vegetable oil

- Kowalski's Mango Salsa

In a large mixing bowl, combine salmon, egg, parsley, shallots, mayonnaise, mustard, cayenne and 1 ¼ cups breadcrumbs; refrigerate, covered, several hrs. to overnight. Shape mixture into 8 patties; roll each in remaining breadcrumbs. Heat oil in a large skillet over medium-high heat. Sauté patties until golden-brown, turning once. Serve with Mango Salsa.

GOOD TO KNOW
• Kowalski's Mango Salsa is available in the Seafood Department.

SERVES 8

EASY

WHITEFISH CROQUETTES
WITH LEMON-CAPER AIOLI

1 cup mayonnaise, divided

1/4 cup finely chopped fresh Italian parsley, divided

1 tbsp. fresh squeezed lemon juice

2 tsp. finely minced capers

3 cloves garlic, finely minced, divided

6 tbsp. Kowalski's Extra Virgin Olive Oil, divided

1 lb. halibut (or other firm white fish) fillet(s)

2 cups Italian seasoned breadcrumbs, divided

1 cup chopped green onion

2 tbsp. flour

1 ½ tsp. fresh grated lemon zest

3/4 tsp. kosher salt

1/4 tsp. Kowalski's Coarse Ground Black Pepper

2 eggs, lightly beaten

In a small mixing bowl, combine 1/2 cup mayonnaise, 1 tbsp. parsley, lemon juice, capers and 1/3 of the garlic; refrigerate aioli until ready to use. In a large skillet, heat 2 tbsp. olive oil over medium-high heat; add halibut and sauté just until opaque in center (about 4 min. per side for a 1" thick fillet). Remove fish from the pan, discarding skin; let stand until cool enough to handle (about 15 min.). Flake fish into a large mixing bowl; stir in remaining parsley and garlic, 1 cup breadcrumbs, green onion, flour, zest, remaining mayonnaise, salt and pepper. Mix in eggs; shape into 6 cakes (about 3" across), coating with remaining breadcrumbs, pressing in lightly. Heat remaining oil on a nonstick griddle over medium heat until oil shimmers but does not smoke; add cakes to pan, cooking until dark golden-brown and crispy on the edges (4-5 min. per side). Top each cake with a small dollop of reserved aioli.

NOTE
- To serve as an appetizer, shape the fish mixture into 32 cakes (about 1 ½" across).

SERVES 6

EASY

COOKING SCHOOL
HOW TO COOK ANY VARIETY OF FISH

For all types of reasons, many people are nervous when it comes to preparing fish at home. But cooking fish isn't all that complicated or difficult. It all boils down to one really key consideration: selecting the right type of cooking method for your desired fish, or vice versa. Though some people will argue otherwise, the truth is not all fish is well suited for grilling. If you have your heart set on walleye, you'll have an easier time with it if you sauté or bake it. If you really want to use your grill, you might be best off selecting salmon or tuna instead. It all depends on how naturally fatty and flaky your fish is. Sturdy, fattier fish works well on the grill because it holds together and doesn't need added moisture (liquid or oil). Conversely, delicate, lean fish is better in an actual pan where a little oil or cooking liquid is used to keep it moist.

With that in mind, you need only heed a few other tips:

• Just before cooking, season fish lightly with kosher salt and coarse ground black pepper to taste.

• Cook fish skin-side-down (unless skinless fillets are used).

• Cook just until the interior of the fish turns opaque and fish reaches an internal temperature of 145°. This takes about 10 min. per inch of thickness, regardless of cooking method.

• It usually isn't necessary to flip the fish unless it is very thick.

The following cooking methods and simple preparation directions are recommended for each of the noted fish types:

BROILING and GRILLING are great for: barramundi, grouper, mahi mahi, marlin, salmon, sea bass, swordfish, trout, tuna and whitefish.

> To BROIL fish: Brush oil on bottom of glass baking dish. Arrange fish, skin side down, in dish; sprinkle with salt and pepper. Broil 6" from heat source in preheated oven.

To GRILL fish: Best with skin-on fillets, but may be done with skinless pieces of very firm-fleshed fish, if desired. Brush it with olive oil to prevent sticking. Grill directly over heat on a grill preheated to medium-high heat.

BAKING is great for: nearly all varieties of fish.

To BAKE fish: To prevent fish from sticking to the pan, bake on a bed of vegetables or wrap in parchment paper along with an assortment of vegetables. Alternatively, you can lightly coat a baking sheet or pan with cooking spray or oil. Bake in a preheated 450° oven.

SAUTÉING is great for: barramundi, blue marlin, catfish, cod, flounder, grouper, haddock, halibut, snapper, sole, swordfish, tilapia, trout and walleye.

To SAUTÉ fish: Best for skinless fillets but may be done with skin-on fillets, if desired. Heat a small amount of butter, olive oil or a mixture of the two in a nonstick skillet over medium-high heat before adding fish.

HALIBUT
WITH BROWNED BUTTER CAPER SAUCE

1 cup flour

1 tsp. kosher salt

1/4 tsp. Kowalski's Coarse
    Ground Black Pepper

1 lb. halibut fillet(s), skin removed,
    cut into 4 pieces

8 tbsp. butter, divided

2 tbsp. fresh squeezed lemon
    juice

2 tbsp. capers, rinsed

In a shallow dish, combine flour, salt and pepper; dredge fillets in seasoned flour. In a large skillet, melt 4 tbsp. butter over medium-high heat. Sauté fillets until golden-brown and crispy (6-10 min.), turning once; transfer to a heated platter. Meanwhile, in a small skillet, heat remaining 4 tbsp. butter over medium heat until butter starts to bubble (about 2 min.). Increase heat to high; continue cooking, swirling pan constantly until butter is medium golden-brown (2-3 min.). Stir in lemon juice and capers. Serve fish immediately, drizzled with sauce.

SERVES 4

EASY

FAST

HALIBUT VERACRUZ
OVER RICE WITH ARUGULA

12 oz. halibut fillet(s), 1" thick, cut into 2 pieces

- kosher salt and coarse ground black pepper

3 tsp. olive oil, divided

1 cup chopped onion

1 jalapeño pepper, seeded and finely chopped

1 tsp. ground cumin

1 clove garlic, minced

2 tbsp. water

1 tbsp. chopped fresh cilantro

1 ½ tbsp. Kowalski's 100% Fresh Squeezed Orange Juice

1 tbsp. chopped pitted green olives

1 ½ tsp. fresh squeezed lime juice

2 tsp. drained capers

1 tbsp. tomato paste

1/2 cup drained canned petite diced tomatoes

3/4 cup basmati rice

1 tbsp. extra virgin olive oil

4 cups fresh arugula

1/4 cup freshly grated Parmesan cheese

Lightly season fish with salt and pepper; place in an 8" or 9" glass baking dish coated with 1 tsp. oil. In a large nonstick skillet over medium-high heat, heat 2 tsp. oil. Add onion and jalapeño; sauté 3 min. Add cumin and garlic; sauté 1 ½ min. Stir in next 8 ingredients through tomatoes; bring to a boil. Reduce heat; simmer until slightly thick (about 3 min.). Pour tomato mixture over fish; bake in preheated 400° oven until fish flakes easily with a fork (about 15 min.). While fish bakes, prepare rice in a rice cooker according to manufacturer's directions. Move to a large mixing bowl; toss with oil and arugula. Cover with plastic wrap; let stand 1 min. (arugula will wilt). Stir in cheese; season to taste with salt and pepper. Divide rice between 2 plates; top with fish and sauce.

SERVES 2

EASY

FAST

GRILLED HALIBUT

WITH ORANGE CILANTRO MARINADE OVER CITRUS QUINOA

2 ½ tbsp. Kowalski's 100% Fresh Squeezed Orange Juice

2 tbsp. walnut oil

1 ½ tbsp. fresh squeezed lemon juice

1 tsp. kosher salt

1 tbsp. chopped fresh cilantro, divided

1 lb. halibut fillet(s)

1 cup quinoa

2 cups Kowalski's 100% Fresh Squeezed Orange Juice

In a zipper-closure food storage bag, combine first 4 ingredients and about half of the cilantro; add halibut, turning to coat with marinade. Refrigerate 30 min. Cook quinoa in orange juice, following package directions. Grill halibut, skin side down, over high heat, covered, until interior of fish turns opaque (about 10 min. per inch of thickness, measured at the thickest part). Remove skin from halibut; divide into 4 pieces. Divide quinoa evenly between 4 dinner plates; arrange halibut over quinoa. Sprinkle with remaining cilantro; serve immediately.

Nutrition Information Per Serving

Total Calories	380
Fat	11 g
Saturated Fat	1 g
Omega-3 Fats	1 g
Sodium	500 mg

Each serving is a good source of these brain nutrients: vitamins B6, B12 and C, folate, iron, magnesium, zinc, selenium and potassium.

SERVES 4

EASY

LIME & HONEY GLAZED SEA BASS

1 ½ tsp. finely grated lime zest

1/4 cup fresh squeezed lime juice

2 tbsp. Kowalski's Pure Honey

2 tbsp. chopped fresh cilantro

1 tbsp. low-sodium soy sauce

1 tbsp. Kowalski's Extra Virgin Olive Oil

1 ½ lbs. fresh sea bass fillet(s), skin removed

1/2 tsp. kosher salt

In a small mixing bowl, combine first 6 ingredients. Pour half of the mixture into a zipper-closure food storage bag; set remainder aside. Place fillets in the bag with the marinade. Refrigerate 30 min., turning bag several times to coat fillets. Remove fillets from bag; discard marinade in bag. Arrange fish in a shallow baking dish. Bake in a preheated 450° oven until sea bass is just opaque in center (8-10 min.); sprinkle with salt. Drizzle warm fish with reserved marinade; serve immediately.

GOOD TO KNOW
• Two medium limes will yield about 1/4 cup of juice.

SERVES 4

EASY

MEDITERRANEAN SEA BASS EN PAPILLOTE

4 sheets parchment paper, about 15" square

1 lb. sea bass fillet(s), skin removed, cut into 4 pieces

4 tsp. Kowalski's Extra Virgin Olive Oil, divided

4 tsp. chopped fresh basil, divided

4 tsp. capers, rinsed and divided

2 tsp. snipped fresh rosemary, divided

2 tsp. chopped garlic, divided

12 grape tomatoes, halved, divided

1 tsp. kosher salt, divided

1/4 tsp. Kowalski's Coarse Ground Black Pepper, divided

- Cucina Viva Classic Balsamic Glaze

Divide ingredients in order listed, except balsamic glaze, among each sheet of parchment paper; fold parchment paper using small folds to create individual packets. Place packets on jelly-roll pan. Bake in a preheated 400° oven until fish flakes easily with a fork (about 15 min.). Open packets; drizzle fish with balsamic glaze. Serve immediately.

NOTE

• To make a parchment packet, bring opposite edges of the parchment sheet together above the contents; fold tightly together in one direction 2-3 times. Press folded edge against contents and flatten slightly outwards towards open ends. Fold open ends tightly in one direction 2-3 times each until entire packet is sealed.

SERVES 4

EASY

226

TILAPIA SANDWICH
WITH CRANBERRY COLESLAW & LEMON DILL AIOLI

1/3 cup flour

1 tsp. kosher salt

1/4 tsp. Kowalski's Coarse
 Ground Black Pepper

4 tilapia fillets

1-2 tbsp. Kowalski's Extra
 Virgin Olive Oil, as
 needed

4 demi ciabatta rolls, cut in
 half horizontally

- *Lemon Dill Aioli*

- *Cranberry Coleslaw*

In a shallow dish, combine flour, salt and pepper; coat both sides of each fillet in flour mixture. In a large nonstick skillet, heat 1 tbsp. oil over medium heat; sauté fillets until opaque (10 min. per inch of thickness of fish, measured at the thickest part), turning halfway through. Add additional tbsp. olive oil if needed before turning. Spread cut sides of rolls with *Lemon Dill Aioli*; top with fish and *Cranberry Coleslaw*. Cut in half on the diagonal; serve immediately.

Lemon Dill Aioli:

In small mixing bowl, combine 1 cup mayonnaise, 1 tbsp. minced garlic, 1 tbsp. chopped fresh dill and 1 tsp. fresh squeezed lemon juice; refrigerate, covered, until ready to use.

Cranberry Coleslaw:

In a small mixing bowl, combine 2 cups angel hair coleslaw, 1/4 cup chopped onion and 1/4 cup dried cranberries; refrigerate, covered, until ready to use.

SERVES 4

EASY

FAST

FISH TACOS

8 (6" diameter) whole wheat tortillas

8 tilapia fillets, cut in half lengthwise

3 tbsp. Kowalski's Extra Virgin Olive Oil, divided

1 tbsp. chili powder

1 tsp. kosher salt

1 tsp. chopped garlic

1/4 cup dry white wine

- shredded red cabbage

- shredded green cabbage

- *Pepper Avocado Salsa*

Heat tortillas, one at a time, in a large skillet over medium-high heat until softened (about 30 sec. per side). Wrap in a clean, slightly moist dish towel to keep them warm and soft. Brush tilapia fillets with 2 tbsp. olive oil; rub with chili powder and season with salt. Heat remaining oil and garlic in the skillet over medium-high heat. Cook fish 5 min.; flip over. Add wine; continue cooking until tilapia is no longer opaque (3-5 min., depending on thickness of fillets). Place one piece of tilapia on each warm tortilla; top with cabbage and *Pepper Avocado Salsa*. Fold in half; serve immediately.

Nutrition Information Per Serving

Total Calories	285
Total Fat	10 g
Sodium	580 mg

This dish contains nearly 75% of your daily vitamin D needs. It's rich in B vitamins, potassium, magnesium and vitamin K and contains antioxidants, beta-carotene, vitamin C and E.

 SERVES 4

PEPPER AVOCADO SALSA:

1/3 cup chopped sweet
    red pepper

1/3 cup chopped yellow pepper

1/3 cup chopped orange pepper

1 bunch green onions, sliced

1 jalapeño pepper, seeded, diced

1 avocado, peeled, cubed

1 oz. pkg. fresh cilantro,
    chopped (about 1/4 cup)

1 tbsp. minced garlic

1/4 cup fresh squeezed lime juice

2 tbsp. Kowalski's Extra Virgin
    Olive Oil

2 tbsp. superfine sugar

1 tsp. kosher salt

1 tsp. lime zest

In a medium mixing bowl, combine the first 8 ingredients. In a separate small mixing bowl, combine remaining ingredients; pour dressing over pepper mixture, gently stirring to combine. Refrigerate several hrs. before using.

MAKES 2 ½ cups

EASY

GOOD FOODS FOR GOOD
Health

229

BAY SCALLOP & PROSCIUTTO GRATINS

6 tbsp. butter, softened

1 tbsp. chopped garlic

2 tbsp. minced shallots

2 oz. thinly sliced prosciutto, chopped

4 tbsp. minced fresh Italian parsley, divided

2 tbsp. fresh squeezed lemon juice

1/2 cup dry white wine, divided

1 tsp. kosher salt

1/4 tsp. Kowalski's Coarse Ground Black Pepper

1/3 cup Kowalski's Extra Virgin Olive Oil

1 ½ lbs. fresh bay scallops

1/2 cup panko breadcrumbs

2 tbsp. butter, melted

6 lemon slices, for garnish

- French baguette

In a medium mixer bowl, combine softened butter, garlic, shallots, prosciutto, 3 tbsp. parsley, lemon juice, 2 tbsp. wine, salt and pepper with an electric mixer on low speed; slowly drizzle in olive oil until combined. Arrange 6 (6") oval ramekins on a rimmed baking sheet; place 1 tbsp. wine in each. Divide scallops among ramekins; spoon garlic butter evenly over scallops. Bake in a preheated 425° oven until the scallops are barely done (10-12 min.); remove from oven. Turn oven to broil. In a small mixing bowl, combine breadcrumbs and melted butter. Sprinkle crumb mixture over scallops; place ramekins under broiler until crumbs are browned and crisp (3-4 min.). Sprinkle with remaining parsley; garnish with lemon. Serve immediately with bread for dipping.

SERVES 6

FAST

SEARED SCALLOPS
ON ANGEL HAIR PASTA

3/4 cup low-sodium chicken broth, divided

1 tsp. flour

4 tbsp. unsalted butter, divided

1/4 cup finely chopped shallots

4 cloves garlic, thinly sliced

1/2 cup dry white wine

9 oz. pkg. Kowalski's Fresh Angel Hair Pasta (in the Dairy Department)

12 large sea scallops (about 1 ½ lbs. total)

- freshly ground Kowalski's Sea Salt and Kowalski's Black Peppercorns

2 tbsp. fresh lemon juice

3 tbsp. chopped fresh Italian parsley

- lemon wedges for garnish

Stir 1/4 cup broth into flour until smooth; set aside. In a large stockpot, bring lightly salted water to a boil. Melt 1 tbsp. butter in a large skillet over medium-high heat. Add shallots to pan; sauté 3 min., stirring frequently. Add garlic; sauté 1 min., stirring constantly. Add wine, scraping pan; bring to a boil. Cook, stirring often, until liquid almost evaporates. Add remaining broth to pan; bring to a boil. Cook until reduced by half (about 5 min.). While sauce cooks, add pasta to boiling water and cook according to package directions (when pasta is done, drain and keep warm). Meanwhile, melt 1 tbsp. butter in another large nonstick skillet over medium-high heat. Sprinkle scallops with salt and pepper. Add scallops to skillet; cook until golden and just opaque in center (1-2 min. per side). Transfer scallops to plate; tent with foil to keep warm. Stir flour-broth mixture into reduced sauce; cook, stirring frequently, 1 min. until slightly thickened. Remove from heat; whisk in remaining butter and juice. Add drained pasta to sauce and toss to coat. Transfer pasta to a large serving platter; arrange scallops on top. Sprinkle with parsley and garnish with lemon; serve immediately.

SERVES 4  EASY FAST

GRILLED SHRIMP
WITH TWO DIPPING SAUCES

2 tbsp. Kowalski's Extra Virgin Olive Oil

1 shallot, finely chopped

1 tbsp. fresh chopped Italian parsley

2 tsp. finely minced garlic

1 tsp. Dijon mustard

1/2 tsp. kosher salt

1/4 tsp. Kowalski's Coarse Ground Black Pepper

1 ½ lbs. fresh shrimp, (16-20 per lb.), peeled and deveined, tails on

- 12 (10") wooden skewers, soaked in water for 60 min.

- *Remoulade* and *Asian Dipping Sauce*

In a small mixing bowl, whisk together first 7 ingredients (through pepper); set aside. Divide shrimp among skewers, using two skewers for each serving to keep shrimp from rotating when grilled. Place skewers in gallon-sized zipper-closure food storage bag; pour marinade into bag and seal. Marinate shrimp for 1 hr. at room temperature or up to 24 hrs. in the refrigerator. Grill shrimp over medium-high heat, covered, just until shrimp are opaque in the center (2-2 ½ min. per side). Serve with choice of dipping sauce.

Asian Dipping Sauce:

Whisk together 2 tbsp. soy sauce, 1 tbsp. honey and 1 ½ tsp. each of rice Vinegar and fresh squeezed lime juice until honey dissolves. Whisk in 1/2 tsp. sesame oil. Stir in 1 tbsp. sliced green onions, 3/4 tsp. minced garlic and 1/4 tsp. crushed red pepper flakes.

Makes about 3/4 cup

Remoulade:

In a small bowl, whisk together 1/2 cup mayonnaise with 1 tbsp. each of sweet pickle relish, finely chopped Italian parsley, finely chopped shallot, tomato paste and fresh squeezed lemon juice. Whisk in 1/2 tsp. Dijon mustard; season to taste with kosher salt, Kowalski's Coarse Ground Black Pepper and paprika.

Makes about 3/4 cup

SERVES 6

EASY

232

GRILLED SHRIMP

WITH SUNNY MANGO SALAD

3 cups chopped fresh or jarred mangoes (about 3 mangoes, peeled and pitted)

1/2 cup chopped red onion

1 ½ cups diced mixture of red, yellow and orange peppers

1/4 cup chopped fresh cilantro

1/3 cup Kowalski's Citrus Vinaigrette Dressing

1/4 cup fresh squeezed lemon juice (1/2 lemon)

2 tbsp. Kowalski's Extra Virgin Olive Oil

1 shallot, finely chopped

1 tbsp. fresh chopped Italian parsley

1 tbsp. chopped fresh basil

2 tsp. minced garlic

1 tsp. Dijon mustard

1/2 tsp. dry mustard

1/2 tsp. kosher salt

1/8 Kowalski's Coarse Ground Black Pepper

1 ½ lbs. fresh shrimp, (16-20 per lb.), peeled and deveined, tails on

- 12 (10") wooden skewers, soaked in water for 60 min.

- jasmine rice for 6 people, cooked according to pkg. directions

In a large mixing bowl, combine first 4 ingredients; toss with dressing and refrigerate, covered, until ready to use. In a small mixing bowl, combine next 10 ingredients (through pepper); set aside. Divide shrimp among skewers, using two skewers for each serving to keep shrimp from rotating when grilled. Place skewers in a gallon-sized zipper-closure food storage bag; pour marinade into the bag and seal. Marinate shrimp for 1 hr. at room temperature or up to 24 hrs. in the refrigerator. Grill shrimp over medium-high heat, covered, just until shrimp are opaque in the center (2-2 ½ min. per side). Serve shrimp with rice and salad.

SERVES 6

KALBI SHRIMP & NOODLE STIRFRY

1 pkg. Ka-me Hokkien Stirfry Noodles (2 pouches), or similar prepared stirfry noodles (not dried noodles)

2 tbsp. peanut or sesame oil, divided

2 cloves peeled garlic, minced

1/4 tsp. crushed red pepper flakes

8 oz. (roughly 1 ½ cups, or 1/2 pkg.) Kowalski's Stoplight Peppers

5 oz. (roughly 1 ½ cups, or 1/2 pkg.) matchstick-cut carrots

3/4 lb. fresh tiger shrimp (26-30 per lb.), peeled and deveined

7 oz. (roughly 3 cups, or 1/2 pkg.) Dole Coleslaw Mix

4 green onions, very thinly sliced on the diagonal, divided

1/2 cup Kowalski's Signature Kalbi Marinade

1/3 cup coarsely chopped roasted peanuts

1/4 cup roughly torn fresh basil leaves

1/4 cup fresh cilantro leaves

Remove noodles from outer wrapper; pierce inner bag several times with a knife. Microwave 1 min.; set aside. Meanwhile, in a large skillet, heat half the oil over medium-high heat; add garlic, crushed red pepper, peppers and carrots. Stir-fry 2 min. Add remaining oil and shrimp; cook 1 min. Add coleslaw and half the onions, stir-frying until shrimp is pink and opaque (about 1 min.). Add noodles and marinade; toss to coat. Cook until everything is warm; garnish with remaining onions, peanuts and herbs. Serve immediately.

SERVES 4

EASY

FAST

SHRIMP SCAMPI

6 tbsp. butter

2 cloves garlic, crushed

- grated zest of 1 lemon

1/3 cup chicken broth

2 tbsp. fresh squeezed
      lemon juice

1 lb. fresh shrimp (21-25 per lb.),
      peeled and deveined

2 tbsp. chopped fresh
      Italian parsley

In a large skillet, heat butter over medium heat. Stir in garlic and lemon zest; sauté 2 min. Add broth, lemon juice and shrimp. Continue cooking just until shrimp turns pink and opaque (about 2 min.). Sprinkle with parsley. Serve immediately over rice or pasta.

SERVES 4

EASY

FAST

LOBSTER POTPIE

6 tbsp. unsalted butter

1/2 cup diced yellow onion

1/2 cup flour

1 ½ cups skim milk, room temp.

2 ½ cups seafood stock

3 ½ cups roughly chopped cooked fresh lobster tail meat (about 4 tails, 10-12 oz. each)

14 oz. pkg. each Alexia Sauté Reds and Alexia Harvest Vegetables, thawed, seasoning packets removed

2 tbsp. chopped fresh Italian parsley

2 tsp. chopped fresh thyme leaves

- kosher salt and Kowalski's Coarse Ground Black Pepper, to taste

1/2 of a 17 oz. pkg. of frozen puff pastry

1 egg

1 tbsp. water

In a large sauté pan, melt butter over medium-low heat; add onion, sautéing until soft and translucent (about 5 min.). Stir in flour (about 1 min.); very slowly whisk in milk and stock. Simmer on low, stirring often until sauce is thickened (about 10 min.). Stir in lobster, vegetables, parsley, thyme, salt and pepper; pour filling into a 3 qt. casserole. Place pastry over filling, draping over the edges of the dish. In small mixing bowl, beat egg and water with fork; brush pastry. Cut several 1/2" slits in top of the crust. Place baking dish on rimmed baking sheet: bake in a preheated 400° oven until pastry is golden-brown and filling is bubbly (23-27 min.). Serve warm.

GOOD TO KNOW
- Alexia potatoes and vegetables are available in the Frozen Foods Section.

SERVES 6

EASY

CIOPPINO-STYLE STEW

1 tbsp. Kowalski's Extra
    Virgin Olive Oil

1 small yellow onion, finely diced

2 cloves garlic, minced

2 cups clam juice

28 oz. can crushed tomatoes

1 ½ cups red wine, such
    as Shiraz

1 ½ tsp. Kowalski's Dried Oregano

2 tbsp. tomato paste

1/2 tsp. Kowalski's Crushed
    Red Pepper Flakes

1 bay leaf

1/2 cup chopped fresh Italian
    parsley

1 ½ tsp. kosher salt

1/2 tsp. Kowalski's Coarse
    Ground Black Pepper

3/4 lb. fresh mussels, scrubbed
    and debearded

3/4 lb. fresh halibut fillets, skin
    removed, cut into 1" cubes

1/2 lb. fresh shrimp (21-25 per lb.),
    peeled and deveined,
    tails off

10-12 oz. loaf sourdough bread

Heat oil in a 6 qt. pot over medium-low heat; sauté onion and garlic for 5-6 min. until tender, adjusting heat down as needed to prevent garlic from browning. Add next 10 ingredients through black pepper; bring to a boil. Add mussels and cook until they open wide (about 7 min.). Discard unopened mussels and bay leaf; add fish and shrimp. Reduce heat to a high simmer; cook until fish and shrimp are opaque (about 4 min.), stirring often. Serve with hunks of bread for dipping.

SERVES 6

EASY

FAST

237

PASTA & GRAINS

CHICKEN ALFREDO

WITH ROASTED TOMATOES, ARTICHOKES & PEAS

14 oz. chicken broth

1 pt. heavy cream

1 tbsp. Kowalski's Extra Virgin Olive Oil

1 lb. boneless skinless chicken breasts, cut into 1" pieces

1 tbsp. chopped garlic

1 tsp. kosher salt

1/4 tsp. Kowalski's Coarse Ground Black Pepper

7 oz. canned roasted tomatoes, drained

14 oz. canned quartered artichoke hearts, drained

1 cup frozen baby sweet peas, thawed

9 oz. pkg. Kowalski's Fresh Egg Fettuccini, cooked according to pkg. directions

- freshly shredded Kowalski's Parmesan Cheese

1/4 cup chopped fresh basil

In a large skillet, bring broth to a boil over medium heat; gradually stir in cream. Cook at a moderate simmer, without boiling, until thickened (25-30 min.), stirring occasionally. In a separate large skillet, heat olive oil over medium heat; stir in chicken and garlic. Sauté until chicken is thoroughly cooked (10-12 min.); season with salt and pepper. Stir in cream sauce mixture, tomatoes, artichokes and peas; continue cooking just until heated through. Toss sauce with cooked pasta; sprinkle with cheese and basil.

SERVES 4

EASY

Signature

240

LINGUINI
WITH KALE, ROASTED TOMATOES & CHICKEN

16 oz. dried linguine noodles

5 cups torn kale

7 oz. canned roasted tomatoes, coarsely chopped, including liquid

1/4-1/2 tsp. Kowalski's Crushed Red Pepper

3 large garlic cloves, chopped

2 cups coarsely chopped Kowalski's Signature Rotisserie Chicken Breast

1/2 tsp. Kowalski's Coarse Ground Black Pepper

- kosher salt, to taste

1 cup shaved Parmigiano-Reggiano cheese

2 tbsp. fresh squeezed lemon juice

1/4 cup pine nuts, toasted

In a large stockpot, cook pasta in boiling salted water according to package directions until nearly al dente. Add kale and cook an additional 2 min.; drain in a colander over a bowl, reserving 1/2 cup cooking liquid. In a large sauté pan, heat tomatoes, crushed red pepper and garlic over medium-low heat (1 min.), stirring frequently. Add pasta and kale, reserved cooking liquid, chicken, black pepper and salt; toss to combine. Stir in cheese and lemon juice; top with pine nuts. Serve immediately.

> ## GOOD TO KNOW
> • To quickly remove stem from center of a kale leaf, fold the leaf in half lengthwise and cut down along the rib to remove both leaves; tear into bite-sized pieces.

SERVES 4

EASY

FAST

FETTUCCINI
WITH SCALLOPS, ASPARAGUS & PANCETTA

9 oz. pkg. Kowalski's Fresh Egg Fettuccini Noodles

1 tsp. kosher salt, plus more for seasoning

3 oz. pancetta, coarsely chopped, divided

1 bunch fresh asparagus, ends trimmed, cut on the diagonal into 1" pieces

1 lb. fresh bay scallops, rinsed, patted dry

1/4 cup thinly sliced green onions, including some green tops

1 tsp. minced garlic

1/2 cup Kowalski's Grated Parmesan Cheese, plus more for serving

1/3 cup heavy cream

3 tbsp. Kowalski's Extra Virgin Olive Oil

1 ½ tsp. finely grated lemon peel

3 tbsp. fresh squeezed lemon juice

2 tbsp. chopped fresh Italian parsley

2 tbsp. chopped fresh basil

- Kowalski's Coarse Ground Black Pepper, to taste

Add pasta and 1 tsp. salt to a large pot of boiling water; return water to a boil and cook just until tender (2-3 min.). Drain, reserving 1/2 cup pasta cooking water. Return pasta to pot. In a large skillet, cook pancetta over medium heat until crisp (about 8 min.). Using a slotted spoon, transfer pancetta to paper towels to drain. Pour off all but 1 tsp. drippings from skillet. Add asparagus to skillet and sauté 3 min., stirring occasionally. Add scallops, green onions and garlic, sautéing until scallops turn opaque (2-3 min.); remove from heat. Add asparagus mixture, 1/4 cup pasta cooking liquid, 1/2 cup Parmesan cheese, cream, olive oil, lemon peel, lemon juice, parsley, basil and 1/2 of pancetta to pasta. Toss, adding remaining 1/4 cup cooking liquid if needed. Season with salt and pepper to taste. Top with remaining pancetta and serve with additional Parmesan cheese.

SERVES 4

FAST

FETTUCCINI CARBONARA

WITH PANCETTA & PEAS

3 oz. thinly sliced pancetta, cut into 1" wide strips

1 tsp. minced garlic

1 cup heavy cream

3 pasteurized egg yolks, beaten

1/3 cup Kowalski's Grated Parmesan Cheese, plus extra for serving

1 cup frozen peas, thawed

9 oz. pkg. Kowalski's Fresh Egg Fettuccini

- kosher salt, to taste

- Kowalski's Coarse Ground Black Pepper, to taste

Bring a large pot of salted water to a boil. In a large sauté pan over medium heat, cook pancetta and garlic until pancetta is browned and crisp (about 5 min.). Using a slotted spoon, transfer pancetta to a paper towel-lined plate; discard all but 2 tbsp. fat from skillet. Add cream to pan, scraping up browned bits from bottom of skillet; heat 2 min. Slowly whisk cream into a bowl of egg yolks; add 1/3 cup Parmesan cheese. Transfer mixture back to the sauté pan; continue heating over low heat 4 min., whisking constantly. Add peas to the boiling water, cooking just until tender (about 1 min.). Using a slotted spoon, transfer peas to small bowl. Cook fettuccini in boiling water according to pkg. directions; drain. Stir pasta, pancetta and peas into cream mixture, tossing to coat. Season with salt and pepper; serve immediately, sprinkling with additional Parmesan cheese.

SERVES 4

EASY

FAST

243

KOWALSKI'S SHRIMP PENNE

1/4 cup Kowalski's Extra Virgin Olive Oil

3/4 lb. fresh shrimp (26-30 per lb.), peeled and deveined

1 ½ tsp. crushed red pepper flakes

1 tsp. salt

3/4 cup heavy cream

1 ½ cups Kowalski's Tomato & Basil Pasta Sauce

24 oz. penne pasta, cooked according to pkg. directions, drained and kept hot

2 tbsp. chopped Italian parsley

In a large pot, heat olive oil over medium-high heat; add shrimp. Cook shrimp until they turn pink (about 2 min.), stirring often. Season with pepper flakes and salt. Stir in cream; continue cooking until cream is reduced a little (about 2 min.). Add sauce; bring to a simmer. Continue cooking until sauce is thick enough to coat the pasta (2-3 min.). Toss pasta with the sauce in the pot. Serve on a warm platter or portion into individual bowls, dividing the shrimp evenly; garnish with chopped parsley.

SERVES 4

EASY

FAST

RIGATONI WITH SAUSAGE

1 lb. Kowalski's All Natural Bulk Hot Italian Pork Sausage

1/2 cup chopped onion

1 tsp. chopped garlic

28 oz. can whole tomatoes

1/3 cup Kowalski's Extra Virgin Olive Oil

10 basil leaves

1 tbsp. butter

1/2 tsp. kosher salt

1/4 tsp. Kowalski's Coarse Ground Black Pepper

8 oz. dried rigatoni noodles

- shaved fresh Parmesan cheese

In a large sauté pan, cook and crumble sausage with onion and garlic until sausage is thoroughly cooked; drain and set aside. In a blender or food processor, purée tomatoes. In a 2 qt. saucepan, heat olive oil over medium heat; add basil leaves, cooking until wilted (10 sec.). Stir in tomatoes; bring to a boil. Cook, stirring occasionally, until slightly thickened (about 6 min.). Add butter, salt and pepper; stir in sausage, continuing to cook until heated through. Cook pasta according to pkg. directions; drain. Divide pasta among each of 4 dinner plates; spoon sauce over pasta. Garnish with Parmesan cheese.

SERVES 4

EASY

FAST

NOTE
- Our Wine Experts recommend a Valpolicella Classico wine with this entrée.

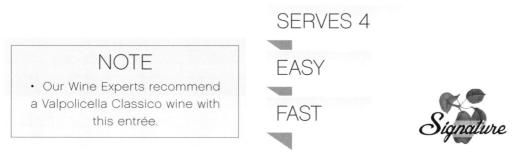

PESTO
CULINARY TIPS & IDEAS

- Toss with hot pasta. You can make a creamier sauce by whisking pesto with a few tablespoons of warm half-and-half, milk or pasta cooking water.

- Spread on a hot bagel.

- Serve on scrambled eggs, in omelets or on a frittata.

- Serve in place of butter or oil with crusty artisan-style bread.

- Use in place of or mixed with mayonnaise on sandwiches and wraps.

- Whisk into Caesar dressing.

- Spread on crostini for a quick appetizer.

- Use in place of traditional pizza sauce.

- Use as a garnish on soup.

- Serve on grilled or roasted meats.

- Pesto freezes very well; portion packaging makes it easy to remove and thaw smaller amounts when they're needed. Thaw frozen pesto in the refrigerator.

- Let pesto stand at room temperature for 30 minutes before using. Some separation or congealing of oil may occur in the refrigerator; blend room temperature sauce together to re-emulsify.

TRADITIONAL BASIL PESTO

3 oz. fresh basil leaves

1/2 cup pine nuts, toasted

1/2 cup grated Parmesan cheese

2 cloves garlic

1/2 cup extra virgin olive oil

- kosher salt and coarse ground black pepper, to taste

Combine first 4 ingredients in a food processor and blend until smooth. Slowly drizzle in oil through oil spout until mixture is glossy, very smooth and coats a metal spoon without running off quickly. Season to taste.

VARIATIONS

• Substitute another fresh herb (such as cilantro, oregano or Italian parsley) or spinach for all or part of the basil.

• Add drained sun-dried tomatoes, roasted red peppers, olives or artichokes.

• Use walnuts, almonds or pecans in place of the pine nuts.

• Try Asiago or Romano cheese in place of Parmesan.

MAKES 1 ¼ cups

EASY

FAST

GOOD TO KNOW

• Pesto may be covered with a thin layer of olive oil and stored in the refrigerator up to 3 days.

PENNE IN TOMATO-CREAM SAUCE **WITH ITALIAN SAUSAGE**

1 tbsp. unsalted butter

1 tbsp. olive oil

2/3 cup chopped onion

2 cloves garlic, finely minced

12 ½ oz. Kowalski's Signature Smoked Italian & Mozzarella Sausage, in 1/2" slices

2/3 cup dry white wine

14 ½ oz. canned petite diced tomatoes with their juice

1 cup heavy cream

1/2 tsp. kosher salt

1/4 tsp. coarse ground black pepper

1/4 cup chopped fresh Italian parsley, divided

1 lb. penne pasta

1 cup freshly grated Parmesan cheese

In an extra-large saucepan, heat butter and oil over medium-high heat; add onion, sautéing until tender (about 7 min.). Add garlic; cook until light golden-brown (1 ½-2 min.) Add sausage; sauté until golden-brown (about 7 min.). Add wine to the pan; bring to a boil, cooking until liquid nearly evaporates (about 2 min.). Add tomatoes; simmer 3 min. Add cream; simmer until sauce thickens slightly (about 5 min.). Stir in salt, pepper and 1/2 of the parsley. Meanwhile, cook pasta according to pkg. directions; drain. Add pasta to saucepan; stir into sauce with 3/4 of the cheese. Serve with remaining cheese and parsley.

SERVES 4

EASY

PUMPKIN TORTELLONI

WITH GORGONZOLA CREAM SAUCE

1/4 cup butter

2 tbsp. minced shallots

2 tsp. minced garlic

1 pt. heavy cream

1 cup Kowalski's Crumbled
    Gorgonzola Cheese

1/2 tsp. Kowalski's Coarse
    Ground Black Pepper

9 oz. pkg. Kowalski's Fresh
    Pumpkin Tortelloni

- chopped fresh basil

In a medium skillet over medium heat, melt butter; sauté shallots and garlic until translucent. Add cream to skillet; simmer, stirring constantly, until slightly thickened (3-4 min.). Add cheese; cook until cheese melts, stirring constantly. Season with pepper. Cook tortelloni according to pkg. directions; drain. Toss pasta with sauce; serve immediately, sprinkled with basil.

SERVES 4

EASY

FAST

249

MACARONI & CHEESE

FOR BIG KIDS

2 tbsp. unsalted butter, melted

1 cup corn flake crumbs

1/4 cup unsalted butter

1/4 cup finely minced onion

1/4 cup flour

2 ¾ cups half-and-half

1 tsp. kosher salt

1/8 tsp. coarse ground black pepper

2 cups (about 1/2 lb.) grated Cheddar cheese, divided

1 cup (about 1/3 lb.) grated fontina cheese, divided

1/4 cup grated Parmesan cheese, divided

16 oz. pkg. dried whole wheat penne rigate pasta

In a small bowl, mix 2 tbsp. melted butter with corn flake crumbs; set aside. In a large sauté pan over medium heat, melt 1/4 cup butter; sauté onions until tender (about 5 min.). Whisk in flour until smooth; gradually whisk in half-and-half. Bring to a boil; continue cooking until thickened (about 1 min.), stirring constantly. Stir in salt, pepper and most of each cheese, reserving some cheese for the top. Cook pasta in salted water according to pkg. directions; drain completely. Stir pasta into cheese sauce; pour into greased 13x9" baking dish. Sprinkle remaining cheese and corn flake mixture on top. Bake in a preheated 350° oven until browned on top (20-25 min.).

SERVES 6

EASY

TRADITIONAL LASAGNA

1 lb. lean ground beef

1 ½ tbsp. minced garlic

- kosher salt and coarse ground black pepper, to taste

2 ½ cups Kowalski's Tomato & Basil Pasta Sauce

15 oz. ricotta cheese, seasoned to taste with salt and pepper

2 eggs, beaten

30 oz. Alfredo sauce, divided

12 oz. pkg. Kowalski's Fresh Egg Lasagna Sheets, divided

8 oz. shredded mozzarella cheese

8 oz. fresh mozzarella cheese, thinly sliced

In a large skillet over medium heat, cook and crumble beef with garlic until dark brown and meat is thoroughly cooked (about 10 min.); season with salt and pepper. Stir pasta sauce into meat mixture; set aside. In a large mixing bowl, mix ricotta, egg and about 2/3 of the Alfredo sauce; set aside. Spread 1 cup of the meat sauce in the bottom of an extra-deep 13x9" baking dish or lasagna pan sprayed with cooking spray. Top with 2 pasta sheets. Layer half of the ricotta mixture with 1/3 of the remaining meat mixture and half of the shredded mozzarella. Cover with 2 more pasta sheets. Layer remaining ricotta, 1/2 the remaining meat and remaining shredded mozzarella. Cover with 2 more pasta sheets. Pour remaining meat sauce then remaining Alfredo sauce on top. Cover with sliced fresh mozzarella. Bake, covered, in a preheated 350° oven 45 min.; remove foil. Continue baking until cheese browns (10-15 min.). Let stand, loosely covered, at least 10 min. before serving.

SERVES 6

EASY

VEGGIE LASAGNA

6 Roma tomatoes, sliced into thirds

- kosher salt and coarse ground black pepper, to taste

1 lb. asparagus, trimmed

- olive oil

16 oz. sliced baby bella mushrooms

1 ½ tbsp. minced garlic

20 oz. frozen spinach, thawed, squeezed very dry

15 oz. ricotta cheese, seasoned to taste with salt and pepper

2 eggs, beaten

30 oz. Alfredo sauce, divided

12 oz. pkg. Kowalski's Fresh Egg Lasagna Sheets, divided

8 oz. shredded mozzarella cheese

8 oz. fresh mozzarella cheese, thinly sliced

Season tomatoes with salt and pepper. Bake on a parchment-lined baking sheet in a preheated 350° oven for a few min. until lightly browned; set aside. Toss asparagus with oil; season with salt and pepper. Grill over medium heat, covered, until browned and fork-tender (about 4 min.); set aside. In a large skillet over medium heat, sauté mushrooms and garlic in oil until dark brown (about 10 min.); season and set aside. In a large mixing bowl, mix spinach with ricotta, egg and about 2/3 of the Alfredo sauce; spread 1 cup of the spinach mixture in the bottom of an extra-deep 13x9" baking dish or lasagna pan sprayed with cooking spray. Top spinach mixture in pan with 2 pasta sheets. Layer 1/2 of the remaining spinach mixture with 1/2 of these ingredients: mushrooms, asparagus, tomatoes and shredded mozzarella. Cover with 2 more pasta sheets. Layer remaining spinach, mushrooms, asparagus, tomatoes and shredded mozzarella. Cover with 2 more pasta sheets. Pour remaining Alfredo sauce on top. Cover with sliced fresh mozzarella. Bake, covered, in a preheated 350° oven 45 min.; remove foil. Continue baking until cheese browns (10-15 min.). Let stand, loosely covered, at least 10 min. before serving.

SERVES 8

Signature

SEAFOOD LASAGNA

1/2 cup organic chicken broth

1/2 lb. bay scallops

2 tbsp. Kowalski's Extra Virgin Olive Oil, plus extra

1 ½ cups chopped onion

8 oz. pkg. sliced mushrooms

1 tbsp. minced garlic

1 tbsp. Kowalski's Italian Seasoning

1 lb. cooked shrimp, tails removed, chopped

6 ½ oz. canned white crab meat

12 oz. pkg. Kowalski's Fresh Egg Lasagna Sheets, divided

6 ½ oz. jar julienne-cut sun-dried tomatoes in olive oil and herbs, drained, and blotted dry, divided

30 oz. jarred Alfredo pasta sauce, divided

5 oz. organic baby spinach, divided

12 oz. shredded Italian blend cheese (such as with mozzarella, provolone, Asiago and Parmesan), divided

In a small skillet, bring chicken broth to a boil over medium heat. Add scallops, cooking just until they turn white (2-4 min.); set aside. In a large skillet, heat olive oil over medium heat; stir in onion, mushrooms, garlic and Italian seasoning, sautéing until onions are soft (about 3 min.). Add shrimp, crab meat and scallops, stirring to combine. Brush the bottom of a 13x9" glass baking dish with olive oil; line the bottom of the pan with 2 pasta sheets. Top with 1/2 of the seafood mixture, 1/2 of the sun-dried tomatoes, 1/2 of the Alfredo sauce, 1/2 of the spinach and 1 cup cheese. Layer with 2 additional lasagna sheets and remaining seafood mixture, sun-dried tomatoes, Alfredo sauce, spinach and 1 cup cheese; top with last 2 lasagna sheets. Bake, covered, in a preheated 350° oven 45 min.; remove foil. Top with remaining cheese and continue baking until cheese melts (10-15 min.). Let stand, covered, until set (about 10 min.).

SERVES 8

BASIC RISOTTO WITH VARIATIONS

6 cups *cooking liquid* (such as broth, stock, water or combo)

1 ½ tbsp. Kowalski's Extra Virgin Olive Oil

2 cups risotto rice, such as Arborio or Carnaroli

- *aromatics* (such as 1-1 ½ cups chopped onion and/or 2-4 cloves minced garlic)

1 cup dry white wine

- *stir-ins* (such as 1 cup cheese(s); Kowalski's fresh chopped herbs, kosher salt and Kowalski's Coarse Ground Black Pepper to taste; cooked vegetables or meats)

Bring cooking liquid to a simmer in a small saucepan; keep warm but do not boil. Heat oil in a large saucepan over medium heat. Add rice and aromatics; sauté 5 min. Add wine; cook until liquid evaporates. Add 2 cups cooking liquid to rice. Cook, stirring occasionally, until liquid is nearly absorbed (about 5 min.); if liquid takes much longer or much less than 5 min. to absorb, adjust heat up or down slightly. Add another 1 cup liquid; stirring occasionally and cooking until the liquid is almost gone again (another 5 min.). Continue adding liquid, 1 cup at a time, cooking until rice is tender (about 15 min. more). Stir in remaining ingredients until cheese is melted and ingredients are evenly heated through. Serve immediately while risotto is very hot.

See following pages for Risotto Variations.

NOTE
• More or less cooking liquid may be required.

SERVES 6

GORGONZOLA PISTACHIO RISOTTO

Cooking liquid:
- vegetable stock (or chicken broth)

Aromatics:
1 cup chopped red onion

2 cloves garlic, minced

Stir-ins:
1/2 cup grated Kowalski's Parmesan Cheese

1/2 cup crumbled Gorgonzola cheese

1/2 cup toasted roughly chopped shelled pistachios

- dash ground nutmeg

Use these ingredients as directed in the recipe for *Basic Risotto*.

LEMONY CHICKEN & PARMESAN RISOTTO

Cooking liquid:
- chicken broth

Aromatics:
1 cup chopped yellow onion

2 cloves garlic, minced

Stir-ins:
1 ½ cups shredded rotisserie chicken

1/3 cup frozen baby peas, thawed

1 cup grated Kowalski's Parmesan Cheese

1 tbsp. chopped fresh thyme

1 tbsp. lemon zest

Use these ingredients as directed in the recipe for *Basic Risotto*.

PORCINI & MASCARPONE RISOTTO

Cooking liquid:
3 cups boiling water

1 oz. dried porcini mushrooms

28 oz. low-sodium beef broth
    (or vegetable stock)

Aromatics:
1 ½ cups chopped shallots

4 cloves garlic, minced

Stir-ins:
1/2 cup grated Kowalski's
    Parmesan Cheese

1/2 cup mascarpone cheese

2 tbsp. chopped fresh thyme

Pour boiling water over mushrooms in a medium bowl and soak 10 min.; drain mushrooms, reserving 2 ½ cups liquid. Strain liquid in a fine mesh strainer to remove sediment. Combine strained mushroom soaking liquid with beef broth to create cooking liquid. Chop mushrooms; add to cooked risotto when other stir-ins are added.

Use these ingredients as directed in the recipe for *Basic Risotto*.

BUTTERNUT SQUASH RISOTTO **WITH PANCETTA & FRESH SAGE**

Cooking liquid:
- chicken broth

Aromatics:

1 cup chopped yellow onion

2 cloves garlic, minced

Stir-ins:
- roasted butternut squash
        (see *Roasted Vegetables*)

2 oz. thinly sliced pancetta,
        cooked crisp & crumbled

1 cup grated Kowalski's
        Parmesan Cheese

1 tbsp. thinly sliced fresh sage

Cook the pancetta first and reserve drippings. Add Kowalski's Extra Virgin Olive Oil, if needed, to make 1 ½ tbsp. of fat in which to cook the rice and aromatics.

Use these ingredients as directed in the recipe for *Basic Risotto*.

KRIS'S FAMILY FAVORITE PASTA DINNER

1 lb. Italian seasoned
    ground turkey

16 oz. long-cut pasta (such as
    spaghetti, linguine or
    fettuccine)

5 ¼ cups (about 1 ½ jars)
    Kowalski's Tomato &
    Basil Pasta Sauce

- Kowalski's Parmesan Cheese,
    shredded or grated,
    to taste

- freshly ground Kowalski's
    Sea Salt and Black
    Peppercorns

In a large skillet over medium heat, cook and crumble turkey until brown and completely cooked through. Meanwhile, prepare pasta in salted water according to pkg. directions. Drain pasta; keep warm. Add pasta sauce to turkey in the pan; cook and stir over medium-low heat until hot. Scoop noodles onto serving dish(es); ladle sauce on top. Serve immediately, passing cheese, salt and pepper at the table.

SERVES 6

EASY

FAST

GRAINS
CULINARY TIPS & IDEAS

- Cook grains in flavorful liquids instead of water. Stocks and broths work. So does water mixed with a little tomato paste, fruit or vegetable juice or even tea.

- To enhance a grain's nuttiness and texture, toast grains over low heat with a bit of olive oil for just a few minutes before adding your cooking liquid.

- To create another layer of fabulous flavor, add lightly sautéed aromatics like onion, garlic and peppers (even hot peppers) to grains before adding liquids.

- Stir in chopped dried fruits, toasted nuts or fresh herbs to cooked grains.

- Try cooked grains such as quinoa, brown rice or red rice in meatballs or meatloaf in place of some of the breadcrumbs.

FRUITED WILD RICE PILAF

WITH KOWALSKI'S SIGNATURE WILD RICE

2 tbsp. Kowalski's Extra Virgin Olive Oil, divided

1 ½ cups chopped celery

1 cup chopped yellow onion

2 cloves garlic, finely minced

1 cup Kowalski's Wild Rice

4 cups vegetable or chicken stock

1 ½ tbsp. julienned fresh sage

1 cup basmati rice

1/2 cup chopped dried apricots

1/4 cup chopped dried cherries

1/4 cup dried cranberries

1/2 cup chopped pecans, toasted

3/4 tsp. kosher salt

1/2 tsp. Kowalski's Coarse Ground Black Pepper

In a 6 qt. saucepan, heat 1 tbsp. oil over medium-high heat. Add celery, onion, garlic and wild rice to the pan; sauté until vegetables are nearly translucent and rice is softened slightly (about 4 min.). Add stock and sage; bring to a boil. Reduce heat; cover and simmer 35 min. Stir in basmati rice; increase heat to bring pot to a boil. Reduce heat; simmer, covered, until liquid is absorbed (about 20 min.). Remove from heat; let stand, covered, 10 min. Drizzle with remaining oil; stir in remaining ingredients.

SERVES 12

EASY

DRIED CHERRY & ALMOND RICE PILAF

3 tbsp. butter

1/4 cup chopped onion

1 tsp. kosher salt

1 ½ cups brown rice

2 ¼ cups low-sodium
    chicken broth

1 tsp. orange zest

3/4 cup dried tart cherries

1/2 cup sliced almonds

2 tbsp. chopped fresh
    Italian parsley

In a large skillet, melt butter over medium heat. Cook onions until soft (about 5 min.); season with salt. Stir in rice; cook until onions become translucent (about 3 min.). Add broth to the skillet with orange zest. Bring to a boil over medium-high heat; reduce heat to low. Continue cooking, covered, until rice is tender (15-20 min.). Add cherries to the pan; remove from heat. Let stand, covered, 10 min. Sprinkle with almonds and parsley; toss with a fork.

SERVES 6

EASY

FRIED RICE

3 tbsp. vegetable or canola oil, divided

2 eggs, beaten

1/2 tsp. kosher salt

2 cups cold, cooked Lotus Foods Bhutan Red Rice, or brown rice

2 cups cold, cooked jasmine rice

1 tsp. minced garlic

1/2 cup sliced green onions

1/4 cup chopped fresh cilantro

3 tbsp. soy sauce

Heat a wok or large nonstick skillet over medium heat until hot enough to instantly evaporate a drop of water. Add 1 tbsp. of oil to wok, tilting to coat surface; heat until very hot. Add eggs; when the edges begin to bubble, push the eggs to the center of the wok until completely cooked, breaking into small clumps. Season with salt; transfer to a covered bowl. Add remaining oil to wok; heat until hot. Add rice and garlic, stirring to coat with oil until heated through (about 3 min.). Stir in remaining ingredients and cooked eggs; serve immediately.

VARIATIONS

• Add 1/2 lb. leftover cooked shrimp, chicken or pork tenderloin along with the rice.

• Add 1/2 cup cooked carrots, broccoli, green beans or fresh pineapple chunks along with the rice.

• Substitute (or add) 1 tsp. fresh gingerroot for the garlic.

• Add toasted sesame seeds, peanuts or almonds to garnish.

SERVES 4

EASY

FAST

ARTISAN DRESSING

WITH WILD RICE & MUSHROOMS

6 cups chicken broth

3/4 cup water

4 ½ tbsp. chopped fresh
    thyme, divided

4 ½ tsp. chopped fresh
    sage, divided

1 ¼ cup Kowalski's Wild Rice,
    rinsed and drained

1 oz. pkg. dried mushrooms

3/4 cup butter

3/4 cup chopped celery

3/4 cup finely chopped onion

6 cups (about 10 oz.) Kowalski's
    Artisan Croutons (any flavor)

1 ½ tbsp. chopped fresh
    Italian parsley

- kosher salt and coarse
    ground black pepper,
    to taste

In a large saucepan, bring broth and water to a boil; stir in 2 tbsp. thyme, 2 tsp. sage, wild rice and mushrooms. Return to a boil; reduce heat and simmer, covered, until most of wild rice kernels open (45-55 min.). In a large skillet, melt butter; stir in celery and onions. Sauté until tender (about 10 min.). Stir celery mixture, croutons, parsley, seasonings, remaining thyme and sage into wild rice and mushrooms. Spoon into a greased 3 qt. casserole. Bake, covered, in a preheated 325° oven until heated through (40-45 min.).

SERVES 8

EASY

Signature

Tuna Steaks with Tropical Salsa
(pg 217)

Grilled Shrimp with Sunny Mango Salad (pg 233)

Kalbi Shrimp & Noodle Stir Fry (pg 234)

Halibut with Browned Butter Caper Sauce (pg 222)

Bay Scallop & Prosciutto Gratins
(pg 230)

Fettuccini with Scallops,
Asparagus & Pancetta (pg 242)

Butternut Squash Risotto with
Pancetta & Fresh Sage (pg 257)

Gorgonzola Pistachio Risotto
(pg 255)

Fettuccini Carbonara with
Pancetta & Peas (pg 243)

Chicken Alfredo with Roasted
Tomatoes, Artichokes & Peas (pg 240)

Veggie Lasagna (pg 252)

Spiced Roast Carrots (pg 268), Fruited Wild Rice Pilaf with Kowalski's Signature Wild Rice (pg 260) and Roasted Squash & Arugula Salad (pg 154)

Herb Roasted Mushrooms (pg 279)

Maple Blue Butternut Squash
(pg 266)

VEGETABLES & SIDES

MAPLE BLUE BUTTERNUT SQUASH

3 lbs. butternut squash

1 tbsp. unsalted butter

2 tbsp. brown sugar

1 tsp. kosher salt

1/4 tsp. Kowalski's Four Pepper Blend Peppercorns, finely crushed

1/2 cup blue cheese crumbles, divided

1/4 cup Kowalski's 100% Pure Maple Syrup, divided

Cut 1" slit in squash; microwave to soften skin (about 4 min.). Cut ends off squash; remove skin. Cut in half; scoop out seeds. Cut squash into 1/2" cubes (about 4 cups). In a large skillet, melt butter over medium heat; stir in brown sugar until dissolved (about 2 min.). Add squash cubes, salt and pepper; cook over medium-high heat, stirring occasionally, until lightly browned on edges (10-12 min.). Divide squash among 4 individual ramekins; top with cheese and maple syrup. Preheat broiler; broil squash 6" from heat source until cheese is melted (about 2 min.). Serve immediately.

SERVES 4

EASY

ORANGE-GLAZED CARROTS

32 oz. bag baby carrots

1/4 cup brown sugar

2 tbsp. butter

1 tbsp. light corn syrup

2 tsp. orange zest

2 tbsp. chopped fresh
    Italian parsley

Cut carrots lengthwise into quarters. In a large saucepan, cook carrots in simmering water (enough to just cover the carrots) until just crisp-tender (10-12 min.); drain. In a large skillet, combine brown sugar, butter, corn syrup and orange zest; cook and stir over medium heat until butter is melted and sugar is thoroughly dissolved. Stir in cooked carrots and parsley, tossing to coat.

GOOD TO KNOW

• Zest is the outermost skin layer of citrus fruit, which is removed with a tool called a "zester." Only the colored portion of the skin (not the white pith) is considered the zest.

• For do-ahead convenience, carrots can be glazed and refrigerated, covered, several hours before serving. To reheat, microwave, covered, until heated through (about 5 min.).

SERVES 10

EASY

FAST

SPICED ROAST CARROTS

2 tbsp. water

1 tbsp. Kowalski's Extra Virgin
      Olive Oil

1 tbsp. unsalted butter, diced

2 garlic cloves, thinly sliced

1 small jalapeño, seeded,
      coarsely chopped

1 tsp. honey

1/2 tsp. Kowalski's Chili Powder

1/2 tsp. Kowalski's Ground Cumin

1/4 tsp. kosher salt

1/4 tsp. coarse ground black
      pepper

2 lbs. small green-top carrots,
      scrubbed, cut on the
      diagonal into 2" pieces,
      including root ends and
      1 ½" of tops

2 tbsp. coarsely chopped
      fresh Italian parsley
      (optional)

Whisk first 10 ingredients in a large bowl; add carrots and toss to coat. Pour onto a large rimmed baking sheet; cover with foil. Roast in a preheated 400° oven until carrots are nearly tender (about 30 min.). Remove foil; roast, uncovered, stirring occasionally until carrots are dark on the edges (15-18 min.). Sprinkle with parsley, if desired.

SERVES 6

EASY

BRUSSELS SPROUTS
WITH PANCETTA & HONEY

5 cups trimmed and halved
Brussels sprouts

4 oz. chopped pancetta

1/4 cup chicken broth

1/2 tsp. coarse ground black
pepper

1/4 tsp. kosher salt

3 tbsp. Kowalski's Honey

Cook Brussels sprouts in a large pot of boiling water for 2 min. Remove Brussels from water with a slotted spoon; drain and plunge into an ice bath until cool to the touch. Drain; pat dry. In a large sauté pan, cook pancetta over medium heat until crisp and browned; remove from pan, leaving drippings. Add Brussels and broth to pan; cover and cook 8 min. Add pancetta back to the pan. Season with pepper and salt; drizzle with honey.

SERVES 10

EASY

FAST

CREAMED SPINACH GRATINS

2 tbsp. butter, divided

1/2 cup chopped sweet
    yellow onion

2 tbsp. flour

1 cup skim milk

1/2 cup heavy cream

5 ¼ oz. pkg. Boursin Herb
    & Garlic Cheese

10 oz. pkg. frozen chopped
    spinach, thawed and
    squeezed very dry

2 tbsp. shredded Parmesan
    cheese

1 tsp. lemon zest

1/2 tsp. kosher salt

1/4 tsp. seasoned pepper

2/3 cup panko breadcrumbs

In a large sauté pan, melt 1 tbsp. butter over medium heat; cook onions until soft (about 5 min.). Stir in flour to coat onions; cook about 1 min. Gradually whisk milk and cream into onion mixture, stirring constantly; simmer sauce 1 min. Stir in Boursin cheese a little at a time until melted; remove pan from heat. Stir in spinach, Parmesan, lemon zest, salt and pepper. Divide mixture among 4 (4 oz.) greased ramekins. Microwave remaining butter in a small bowl until melted; stir in crumbs. Top spinach mixture with crumbs. Bake ramekins in a preheated 425° oven on a jelly-roll pan until crumbs are golden-brown (20-25 min.); serve immediately.

SERVES 4

EASY

KALBI-GLAZED BRUSSELS SPROUTS

1 lb. Brussels sprouts, trimmed and halved

3 tbsp. Kowalski's Extra Virgin Olive Oil

1 tsp. kosher salt

1/2 tsp. Kowalski's Coarse Ground Black Pepper

1/4 tsp. crushed red pepper flakes

1/4 cup Kowalski's Kalbi Marinade

In a large bowl, toss Brussels with oil; season with salt and peppers. Roast on a parchment-lined baking sheet in a preheated 400° oven until crisp and darkened on the edges and tender at the base (about 20 min.), stirring once. Move hot sprouts to a large mixing bowl; toss with marinade to coat. Serve immediately.

SERVES 10

EASY

FAST

Signature

271

HARICOT VERT
IN CITRUS SAUCE

2 lbs. haricot vert

3 tbsp. butter

1/4 cup minced shallots

1 tsp. minced garlic

1/2 cup fresh squeezed
      orange juice

2 tsp. orange zest

1 tsp. salt

1/4 tsp. fresh ground black
       pepper

Trim ends from haricot vert; rinse in cold water. In a large Dutch oven, bring salted water to a boil; add haricot vert. Blanch 3-4 min.; remove from hot water and quickly chill in ice water to stop cooking. Drain; pat dry. Store in zipper-closure food storage bag in refrigerator up to 1 day. Melt butter in a large skillet over medium heat. Add shallot and garlic; cook until tender (about 5 min.). Stir in haricot vert and remaining ingredients; sauté until heated through (about 5 min.). Serve immediately.

GOOD TO KNOW

• *Haricot vert* is the French term for *green string bean*, *haricot* meaning *bean* and *vert* translating as *green*. They are very thin fresh green beans.

• Regular fresh green beans can be substituted in this recipe; just increase the blanching time to 6-8 min.

SERVES 8

EASY

FAST

CITRUS
CULINARY TIPS & IDEAS

Citrus is a great accent in recipes like *Haricot Vert in Citrus Sauce, Fresh Asparagus with Lemon* and countless others of our favorite dishes. If there is a bright spot in a cold Minnesota winter, it has to be citrus fruit. It can be no coincidence that most citrus fruit resembles the sun! Oranges, lemon, lime, grapefruit, tangerines, clementines and kumquats are in season through the winter months and can provide a bright, happy note in wintry dishes including grains, fish, salads and baked goods. Of course, these sunny beauties are also great as a snack or make a perfectly simple and satisfying dessert on their own. Here are some great tips and recipes for enjoying your favorite citrus fruits all winter long:

• Cut orange segments for eating by slicing "between the poles," not through them; then slice into easy-to-eat wedges.

• Add lemon and lime zest to rice and grain dishes, salad dressings and salads.

• For the most pronounced citrus flavor in baked goods, use zest in the batter. Citrus juice becomes very muted in baked products. For even more fruity oomph, brush muffins, quick breads and cakes with a citrusy simple syrup (made from equal parts citrus juice and dissolved sugar) and/or make a simple citrus glaze with 1 cup powdered sugar and 3-4 teaspoons citrus juice.

• To supreme citrus fruit, slice off the ends down to the flesh and place one of these flat ends on a stable cutting board. Use a sharp knife to cut down toward the board (between the cut ends), moving the knife with the contour of the fruit to remove all of the peel and white pith, down to the brightly colored flesh. Hold the peeled fruit in one hand over a large bowl (membranes running across your open palm). Using a sharp knife in your other/cutting hand, carefully cut down into the fruit alongside the membranes to release the segments into the bowl below. Squeeze the remnants of the fruit (the membranes) over the bowl to extract every last drop of juice.

• To get the most juice from your citrus, squeeze them at room temperature or microwave them for up to 10 seconds first.

• When you want to use the juice and zest of a citrus fruit, zest first before squeezing the fruit to extract the juice.

• You can save a zested citrus fruit, but wrap it well in plastic and use as soon as possible. The juice in a zested lemon will oxidize and turn bitter quickly.

FRESH ASPARAGUS

WITH LEMON

2 bunches asparagus

2 tbsp. Kowalski's Extra
　　　Virgin Olive Oil

1 tbsp. minced garlic

1/4 cup fresh squeezed
　　　lemon juice

1/4 cup Chardonnay wine

1 tsp. kosher salt

1 ½ tsp. lemon zest

Snap off the bottoms of the asparagus spears. In a large sauté pan, heat olive oil over medium heat; sauté garlic (about 2 min.). Add asparagus, tossing to coat; cook until starting to soften (4-5 min., depending on the size of the spears). Add lemon juice and wine; cover and continue cooking until cooked through (3-5 min.). Season with salt and sprinkle with lemon zest before serving.

SERVES 8

EASY

FAST

SPICY GREEN BEANS

1 lb. haricot vert

2 tbsp. low-sodium soy sauce

1 tbsp. rice vinegar

1 tbsp. superfine sugar

1 tbsp. toasted sesame oil

2 tbsp. minced garlic

3/4 tsp. kosher salt

1/4 - 1/2 tsp. crushed red
pepper (optional)

Microwave beans in package according to package directions (about 3 min.); set aside. In a small bowl, combine soy sauce, rice vinegar and sugar; set aside. In a large sauté pan, heat sesame oil, garlic and green beans over medium-high heat, stirring frequently (2 min.). Add soy sauce mixture; continue cooking until sauce thickens and glazes the beans (about 2 min.), stirring constantly. Season with salt and crushed red pepper, if desired.

GOOD TO KNOW

• *Haricot vert* is the French term for *green string bean*, *haricot* meaning *bean* and *vert* translating as *green*. They are very thin fresh green beans.

• Regular fresh green beans can be substituted in this recipe; just increase the blanching time to 6-8 min.

SERVES 6

EASY

FAST

ALABAMA BAKED BEANS

1/2 lb. bacon, chopped

1 yellow onion, chopped

3/4 cup ketchup

1/3 cup molasses

1/2 cup tomato sauce

1/2 cup brown sugar

1/4 cup apple cider vinegar

1 tbsp. Worcestershire sauce

1 tbsp. Dijon mustard

1 tsp. hot sauce (optional)

1 tsp. kosher salt

1 tsp. Kowalski's Coarse Ground
    Black Pepper

30 oz. canned navy beans,
    rinsed and drained

In a large oven-safe pan over medium-high heat, cook and stir bacon until crisp (about 7 min.). Add onion; cook until softened (about 5 min.). Stir in ketchup, molasses, tomato sauce, brown sugar, vinegar, Worcestershire, mustard, hot sauce, salt and pepper. Bring to a simmer; cook 5 min. Stir in beans until well coated; cover and bake in a preheated 325° oven 1 hr. Uncover; bake 15 min. more. Cool 10 min. before serving.

SERVES 10

EASY

Signature

GRILLED CORN ON THE COB **WITH FRESH HERB BUTTER**

1/2 cup softened butter

2 tbsp. chopped fresh herbs of your choice

1/4 tsp. lime zest

8 ears corn on the cob

- kosher salt, to taste

In a small mixing bowl, combine first 3 ingredients; refrigerate several hrs. Peel off all of the husks on each ear of corn except for the layer touching the kernels; remove silk and pull remaining husks back up over corn. Soak corn in cold water about 1 hr. before grilling. Grill corn over medium heat, covered, until kernels yield gently to pressure (8-10 min.), turning each ear a quarter turn every 2 min. Carefully remove husks; serve with herb butter and salt.

GOOD TO KNOW

• To cook corn on top of the stove, remove husks and silk. Plunge into boiling water; cook until kernels yield gently to pressure (3-5 min.). Serve immediately with herb butter and salt.

• To microwave corn, remove husks and silk from four ears of corn. In a shallow-sided microwavable dish, melt 3 tbsp. butter; add corn, turning to coat completely with butter. Cover dish with plastic wrap. Microwave until kernels yield gently to pressure (6-8 min.). Add 2 min. per ear for additional corn, or subtract if you wish to cook fewer ears.

SERVES 8

EASY

GRILLED FENNEL & RED POTATOES

1 fennel bulb, sliced, reserving feathery fronds

8 Kowalski's B-size Red Potatoes, scrubbed, cut into quarters

2 tbsp. Kowalski's Extra Virgin Olive Oil

1 tsp. kosher salt

1/4 tsp. Kowalski's Coarse Ground Black Pepper

In a large bowl, combine all ingredients except fennel fronds. Grill over high heat in a grill basket, covered, until potatoes are tender and fennel has golden-brown edges (25-30 min.), stirring occasionally. Garnish with fennel fronds.

SERVES 4

EASY

HERB ROASTED MUSHROOMS

1 ¾ lbs. shiitake, baby
    portabella, oyster or
    cremini mushrooms (or
    combination), stemmed,
    cut into 1 ½" inch pieces

2 fresh rosemary sprigs,
    cut into 1/2" pieces

5 garlic cloves, thinly sliced

1/2 cup Kowalski's Extra Virgin
    Olive Oil

- kosher salt and Kowalski's
    Coarse Ground Black
    Pepper, to taste

2 tbsp. chopped fresh
    Italian parsley

In a large mixing bowl, toss mushrooms, rosemary and garlic with oil; sprinkle with salt and pepper. Roast mushrooms on two parchment-lined baking sheets in a preheated 450° oven until dark brown (about 25 min.), stirring occasionally. Remove rosemary stems; adjust seasonings and garnish with parsley.

MUSHROOMS CULINARY TIPS & IDEAS

• Store loose mushrooms in a paper bag in the refrigerator to keep them as dry as possible. Loose or packaged, they should last 4-5 days.

• Wait to clean mushrooms until you're ready to use them. To clean, use a soft brush to remove any traces of peat moss or soil.

• If you want mushrooms to brown, give them plenty of room in your sauté pan; otherwise they'll steam. Salt draws moisture out of mushrooms. Save seasoning until the end.

• To make paper thin slices, place mushrooms on a baking sheet in the freezer for 5 minutes, then slice.

SERVES 6

EASY

CLASSIC EGGPLANT PARMESAN

3 cups panko breadcrumbs

1 tsp. Kowalski's Bold
      Italian Seasoning

2 eggs

2 tbsp. water

3 lbs. eggplant, cut into
      1/2" thick slices

- Kowalski's Extra Virgin
      Olive Oil

2 (26 oz.) jars Kowalski's
      Thick & Hearty Tomato
      & Basil Pasta Sauce

1 lb. Kowalski's Fresh Mozzarella,
      thinly sliced, torn into
      small pieces

6 oz. pkg. fancy shredded Italian
      blend cheese

1 tsp. lemon zest

- chopped fresh Italian parsley

In a shallow pan, combine breadcrumbs and Italian seasoning; set aside. In a medium mixing bowl, combine eggs and water; dip eggplant slices in egg mixture, then coat with breadcrumbs. In a large skillet, heat 2 tbsp. olive oil over medium heat; working in several batches, cook eggplant slices until golden on both sides (8-10 min.), turning once and adding oil as needed. Drain eggplant slices on paper towels. Spread 1 cup pasta sauce in bottom of a 13x9" glass baking dish. Arrange half of fried eggplant slices in baking dish; top with half of fresh mozzarella and shredded cheese. Repeat layers with remaining pasta sauce, eggplant, mozzarella and shredded cheese. Bake in a preheated 400° oven until sauce is bubbling (about 45 min.). Let stand, covered, 15 min.; sprinkle top with lemon zest and parsley before serving.

NOTE
• This dish can be assembled and refrigerated, covered, up to 24 hrs. before baking.

SERVES 8

Signature

SAUTÉED KALE

WITH PINE NUTS & DRIED CRANBERRIES

2 bunches fresh kale

2 tbsp. Kowalski's Extra Virgin
    Olive Oil

1/2 large red onion, chopped

1 clove garlic, minced

- kosher salt, to taste

- Kowalski's Coarse Ground
    Black Pepper, to taste

2 tbsp. pine nuts, toasted

1/2 cup dried cranberries

Fold each kale leaf in half lengthwise; tear stem away along crease and discard. Coarsely tear leaves; set aside. In a large sauté pan, heat olive oil over medium-high heat. Add onion and garlic; sauté until onion is soft (about 5 min.). Add half of kale; continue cooking until kale wilts (2-3 min.), tossing often. Add remaining kale; cook until kale is just tender and still bright green (about 3 min. longer). Season with salt and pepper; stir in pine nuts and dried cranberries. Serve immediately.

SERVES 4

EASY

FAST

SAUTÉED SWISS CHARD

1 large bunch of fresh Swiss
    chard, rinsed thoroughly,
    tough stems discarded

2 tbsp. olive oil

1 clove garlic, thinly sliced

1/8 tsp. crushed red pepper

2 tbsp. water

1 tsp. unsalted butter

- kosher salt and freshly ground
    Kowalski's Coarse Ground
    Black Pepper, to taste

Roughly chop chard leaves into strips 1"
wide. Heat olive oil in a medium saucepan
over medium heat; add garlic and red
pepper. Sauté 1 min. Add chard leaves;
cover. Cook 5 min.; add water. Flip the leaves;
return cover to pan. Cook until tender (about
5 min.). Add butter; season to taste with salt
and pepper. Serve immediately.

SERVES 2

EASY

FAST

**DARK LEAFY GREENS
CULINARY TIPS & IDEAS**

• Colored chard (red stems and veins) is usually a bit milder in flavor than
traditional green chard.

• Toss chopped kale, chard, spinach or collard greens into soups,
casseroles and egg dishes.

• Remove the stems, especially from kale and collard greens, and you drastically
reduce cooking time – up to 75%!

• Cook greens like kale in a small amount of vegetable or chicken stock over low
heat until just tender. Drizzle cooked greens with a little extra virgin olive oil to add
flavor and richness.

BASIC GRILLED VEGETABLES

Cut evenly; completely but lightly coat veggies with oil. Season to taste. Grill over medium heat, covered, turning several times until browned and tender when pierced with a fork.

WHAT TO GRILL	HOW TO PREPARE IT	COOK TIME
BELL PEPPERS	Remove seeds, membranes and stems; cut into 1" strips	6-8 min.
CARROTS	Do not peel; blanch in boiling water 3-4 min. (halve or quarter lengthwise if very thick)	10-12 min.
CORN ON THE COB	Remove silks and husks, except husk layer touching kernels; soak in water 1 hr.	8-10 min.
GREEN ONIONS	Trim ends, but leave whole	6-8 min.
ONIONS	Trim ends and peel; cut into slices 1/4" thick	4-6 min.
PORTABELLA MUSHROOMS	Clean out most of the gills with the tip of a spoon; grill gill-side-down first	6-8 min.
POTATOES	Pierce with a fork and microwave 5 min.; cut into 3/4" wedges.	10-12 min.
SWEET POTATOES	Pierce with a fork and microwave 5 min.; cut into 3/4" wedges	10-12 min.
ZUCCHINI & YELLOW SQUASH	Trim ends; cut lengthwise into planks 1/4" thick	3-4 min.

EASY

BASIC ROASTED VEGETABLES

Cut evenly; completely but lightly coat veggies with oil. Season to taste. Roast on baking sheet lined with parchment in preheated 450° oven until browned and tender when pierced with a fork.

WHAT TO ROAST	HOW TO PREPARE IT	COOK TIME
ACORN SQUASH	Cut in half; roast skin-side-down	50 min.
ASPARAGUS	Trim woody ends	10-15 min.
BEETS	Leave whole; scrub but don't peel (remove skins after cooked/cooled)	60-90 min.
BROCCOLI	Cut 1 ½" florets	10-15 min.
BRUSSELS SPROUTS	Trim and halve lengthwise	20-25 min.
BUTTERNUT SQUASH	Cut in half lengthwise; roast skin-side-down or cut into 1" cubes	25 min.
CARROTS	Peel; cut into 1" pieces	18-20 min.
CAULIFLOWER	Cut 1 ½" florets	25-35 min.
MUSHROOMS	Clean well; trim stems from shiitakes, if desired	15-25 min.
PARSNIPS	Peel, cut into 2" sections then halve or quarter depending on thickness	60-70 min.
POTATOES	Do not peel; cut into 1/2" pieces (fingerlings and baby reds work best for roasting)	30-35 min.
RUTABAGAS OR TURNIPS	Peel turnips only; cut both into 1" wedges	60-70 min.
SWEET POTATOES	Peel; cut into 1/2" pieces; cover with foil	20 min.
TOMATOES	Roast unpeeled, whole (time shown is for large tomatoes; grape tomatoes and cherry tomatoes may take 5-7 min. or less)	20-25 min.
ZUCCHINI & YELLOW SQUASH	Halve lengthwise; cut into 1 ½" pieces	20 min.

ARTISAN BREAD DRESSING

WITH CRANBERRIES, SQUASH & PEPITAS

1 tbsp. Kowalski's Extra Virgin Olive Oil

1 cup chopped yellow onion

2 ribs celery, diced

1 ½ lb. butternut squash, peeled, halved, seeded, in 1" dice (about 3 cups)

1 Granny Smith apple, peeled, cored, in 1" dice (1 ½ cups)

16 oz. Kowalski's Artisan Croutons, any flavor (about 9 cups)

1/2 cup Kowalski's Dried Cranberries

1/3 cup raw pepitas (pumpkin seeds), toasted

1 tbsp. chopped fresh sage

1 tsp. kosher salt

1/4 tsp. Kowalski's Coarse Ground Black Pepper

1 cup low-sodium chicken broth

In a large sauté pan, heat olive oil over medium heat. Stir in onion, celery, squash and apples; cook, stirring constantly, until onion softens (4-5 min.). Stir remaining ingredients into onion mixture. Scoop mixture into a 13x9" glass baking dish sprayed lightly with nonstick cooking spray; bake, covered, until heated through (40-45 min.).

GOOD TO KNOW

- Find Kowalski's Croutons in the Bakery or Produce Departments.

- Find Kowalski's Dried Cranberries in the Bulk Foods Section.

SERVES 12

EASY

SALSA DI PARMA TOPPED DUCHESS POTATOES

2 lbs. organic red potatoes, peeled, quartered

1 tbsp. plus 1 tsp. kosher salt, divided

2 tbsp. milk

2 tbsp. butter

1 egg, beaten

1 cup Kowalski's Salsa di Parma, divided

Place potatoes in a large saucepan; cover with cold water and sprinkle with 1 tbsp. salt. Bring to a boil over high heat; reduce heat and simmer until tender when pierced with a fork (about 20 min.). Drain potatoes; add milk, butter, egg and remaining salt to pan. Using a hand potato masher, mash potatoes until no lumps remain. Spoon potato mixture into a zipper-closure food storage bag; using scissors, snip off one corner of bag, making a small opening. On a parchment-lined rimmed baking sheet, pipe potato mixture into 8 circular mounds. Using the back of a teaspoon, make a well in the center of each mound; fill each with 2 tbsp. Salsa di Parma. Place pan in freezer, covered, until potatoes are firm; keep frozen until needed. Bake in a preheated 425° oven until lightly browned on top (12-15 min.). Serve immediately.

NOTES

• Potatoes hold their shape better during baking if they are baked from frozen.

• Salsa di Parma can be purchased in the Deli Department.

SERVES 8

ASIAGO AU GRATIN POTATOES

2 lbs. Kowalski's Yukon Gold
    Potatoes

1/4 cup butter

1 tbsp. flour

1 tsp. salt

2 cups heavy cream

2 cups shredded Asiago cheese

Arrange potatoes in a large saucepan; cover with cold water. Bring to a boil; cook potatoes until tender (30-35 min.). Drain; let potatoes stand until cool enough to handle. In a medium saucepan, melt butter over medium heat; stir in flour and salt. Cook, stirring constantly, until bubbly. Stir in cream; heat to boiling, stirring constantly. Boil and stir 1 min; remove from heat. Stir in cheese; continue stirring until melted. Peel and slice potatoes. Alternately layer potatoes and sauce in a buttered 13x9" glass baking dish, ending with sauce on top. Bake, uncovered, in a preheated 350° oven until bubbly and thoroughly hot (30-35 min.).

NOTES

• This dish can be assembled and refrigerated, covered, for several hrs. before baking.

• The Asiago sauce will separate if the potatoes are reheated after the initial baking.

STEAKHOUSE BAKED POTATO:
Rub an Idaho russet potato lightly with olive oil; sprinkle with sea salt. Prick several times with a fork. Bake on a baking sheet in a preheated 350° oven until a knife easily pierces all the way to the center (60-90 min. depending greatly on the size and shape of the potato).

SERVES 6

EASY

ROASTED FINGERLINGS & BABY CARROTS

3 lbs. organic fingerling potatoes, scrubbed, quartered

16 oz. bag organic baby-cut carrots, halved lengthwise

8 oz. bag cipolline onions, blanched, peeled, quartered

1/4 cup butter, melted

1/4 cup olive oil

1 tbsp. minced organic garlic

1 ½ tsp. salt

1 tsp. coarse ground Kowalski's Four Pepper Blend Peppercorns

1 tsp. chopped fresh organic rosemary

1 tsp. chopped fresh organic thyme

In a large roasting pan or bottom of a broiler pan, combine first 8 ingredients, tossing to coat. Roast in a preheated 425° oven, stirring every 10 min. until vegetables are fork-tender and slightly browned (about 30 min.). Sprinkle with rosemary and thyme, tossing to coat.

GOOD TO KNOW

- To blanch cipolline onions, place onions in boiling water; boil for 5 min. Plunge into ice-cold water. Cut off root ends; slip off skins.

- Fingerling potatoes should be cooked with their skins intact.

SERVES 8

EASY

CREAMY THYME POTATO GRATIN

3 lbs. Kowalski's Yukon Gold
    Potatoes (about 8
    medium potatoes),
    peeled, sliced 1/4" thick

6 tbsp. cold butter, cut into
    small pieces, divided

4 tbsp. flour, divided

3 tbsp. chopped fresh thyme,
    divided

2 tsp. salt, divided

1/2 tsp. Kowalski's Coarse
    Black Pepper, divided

3 cups half-and-half

1 cup panko breadcrumbs

2 tbsp. melted butter

Layer 1/3 of potato slices in bottom of a greased 13x9" glass baking dish; top with 2 tbsp. butter and sprinkle with 2 tbsp. flour, 1 tbsp. thyme, 1 tsp. salt and 1/4 tsp. pepper. Repeat layers twice, eliminating flour, salt and pepper from the top layer; pour half-and-half over top. Bake, loosely covered, in a preheated 350° oven until bubbly (about 45 min.). In a small bowl, combine breadcrumbs and melted butter; sprinkle evenly over potatoes. Continue baking, uncovered, until topping is browned (12-15 min.); sprinkle with remaining thyme. Serve immediately.

SERVES 8

MASHED POTATOES
CULINARY TIPS & IDEAS

What's the secret to the fluffy, creamy, smooth and tasty side dish everyone loves? Read on for some tips for tasty taters:

• Waxy potatoes, such as Yukon Gold, are recommended for those who like mashed potatoes with texture, such as smashed potatoes. They are generally more flavorful than mealy potatoes, but due to their high natural moisture content, they turn gluey with less mashing.

• Mealy potatoes, such as Idaho and russet potatoes, have a higher starch content and lower natural moisture, so they can withstand a little more handling (mashing). They are recommended for those who like smoother, creamier mashed potatoes.

• One pound of potatoes will make approximately 2 cups of mashed potatoes.

• Be sure to cut potatoes uniformly before cooking so the pieces cook evenly.

• Start cooking potatoes in cold water to ensure that the pieces cook evenly throughout.

• If you are leaving the skins on in your mashed potatoes, be sure to cut your spuds into smaller pieces so you don't end up with unappealingly large pieces of potato peel in your finished dish.

• Cook potatoes in stock or broth to add an extra layer of flavor to your finished potatoes. You can also use broth in place of all or part of your milk or cream.

• After draining, return potatoes to the pot and shake over heat to remove any remaining moisture before mashing or ricing.

• Food processors and electric mixers will turn cooked potatoes into glue! (This is why everyone says they want their mashed potatoes to be like their grandmother's – she didn't own either!) If you don't have a potato ricer, use a hand masher instead. Both disrupt the potato cells less, releasing less starch.

• Mash potatoes to desired consistency before adding any milk, cream, butter, sour cream, etc., because the liquid will act to set the texture of the potatoes.

• When adding milk or cream to mashed potatoes, heat just to a simmer, but do not boil.

• Buttermilk used in place of milk or cream gives a tangy, sour cream-like flavor with less calories and fat.

GARLIC CHIVE MASHED POTATOES

1 ½ lbs. Kowalski's Russet
    Potatoes, peeled,
    quartered

2 cloves garlic, peeled, quartered

1 tsp. salt

1/4-1/3 cup hot milk

2 tbsp. butter, room temperature

1 tbsp. chopped fresh chives

Place potatoes and garlic in a large saucepan; cover with cold water and sprinkle with salt. Bring to a boil over high heat; reduce heat to medium. Cover and continue cooking until potatoes are tender when pierced with a fork (15-20 min.); drain. Place pan over low heat just until excess moisture in pan evaporates (1-2 min.). Mash with hand potato masher until no lumps remain. Stir in milk, butter and chives until potatoes reach desired consistency.

SERVES 8

EASY

GRILLED DUTCH YELLOW BABY POTATOES

24 oz. bag Melissa's Dutch
    Yellow Baby Potatoes

2 tbsp. olive oil

1 tbsp. chopped fresh thyme

1 tsp. minced garlic

Place potatoes in a large saucepan and cover with cold water. Bring to a boil over high heat; reduce heat to medium. Cover and continue cooking until potatoes are tender when pierced with a fork (15-20 min.). Drain and air-dry thoroughly; cut cooled potatoes in half. Toss with remaining ingredients. Grill potatoes in a grill basket over high heat, covered, until slightly charred (about 20 min.), stirring occasionally.

SERVES 4

SHREDDED SWEET POTATO & PARSNIP PANCAKES

2 cups peeled, shredded sweet potatoes (about 1 large sweet potato)

2 cups peeled, shredded parsnips (about 2 medium parsnips)

1/4 cup whole wheat flour

1/4 cup finely chopped sweet onion

1 tbsp. chopped fresh thyme

1/4 tsp. kosher salt

1/8 tsp. Kowalski's Coarse Black Pepper

1 egg, beaten

4 tsp. Kowalski's Extra Virgin Olive Oil, divided

- applesauce

In a large mixing bowl, combine first 8 ingredients. In a large sauté pan, heat 2 tsp. oil over medium heat; place 6 (1/4 cup) portions of sweet potato mixture in oil, pressing with back of spatula to flatten into 2-3" pancakes. Cook until crispy and golden (3 min. per side). Repeat with remaining mixture. Spoon a dollop of applesauce over each pancake.

Nutrition Information Per Serving

Total Calories	90
Total Fat	3 g
Saturated Fat	0 g
Sodium	94 mg
Fiber	3 g

Each serving is also an incredible source of antioxidant beta-carotene and a good source of vitamin C.

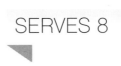 SERVES 8

POLENTA & PARMESAN GRATINS

2 cups milk

2 cups water

1/4 cup unsalted butter

1 ½ tsp. kosher salt

1 ½ tsp. chopped fresh rosemary

1 cup polenta (not instant)

1 egg

1 cup shaved Parmesan cheese, divided

3/4 cup heavy cream, divided

In a medium saucepan, bring milk, water and butter to a boil; add salt and rosemary. Gradually whisk in polenta until smooth; bring to a simmer, whisking until thickened. Continue cooking over low heat (15 min.), stirring constantly; remove from heat and cool (10 min.), stirring occasionally. Whisk egg and 1/2 cup Parmesan cheese into polenta; divide polenta among 8 (5") greased ramekins. When completely cool, refrigerate, covered, until firm (at least 2 hrs. or overnight). Pour 1 ½ tbsp. cream over polenta in each ramekin; top with remaining Parmesan. Bake in a preheated 400° oven until top is puffed and golden (15-20 min.); let stand, covered with foil (5 min.), before serving.

NOTE

• The ramekins can be refrigerated for up to 2 days or frozen for 2 months before baking. If frozen, defrost in the refrigerator before baking.

SERVES 8

COOKIES

KOWALSKI'S DATE CORN FLAKE COOKIES

1 cup shortening

1/2 cup sugar

3/4 cup brown sugar

1 ½ tsp. baking powder

1 tsp. baking soda

1/2 tsp. salt

1/2 tsp. vanilla

1 egg

2 ¾ cups cake flour

8 oz. chopped dried dates

1 cup (about 4 oz.) chopped walnuts

3 tbsp. water

2 ½ cups corn flakes

In an electric mixer fitted with the paddle attachment, cream first 7 ingredients through vanilla on medium-high speed until light and fluffy but not starting to separate (about 2 min.). Scrape bowl, then add egg; beat until incorporated, then 1 min. more. Scrape bowl; add flour, dates, walnuts and water. Mix just until flour is incorporated (1-2 min.). Add corn flakes; mix just until combined. Drop 12 evenly sized, rounded spoonfuls 2" apart on 2 parchment-lined baking sheets. Lightly flatten dough to form patties about 2 ½" across and 1/2" thick. Bake pans one at a time in a preheated 360° oven until the edges are set and cookies are puffed and golden at the bottom (9-11 min.); cookies may appear underbaked in the cracks. Remove from oven and cool on pans 2 min. until set. Cool completely on wire racks.

NOTE:
• If you don't have a digital control for setting your oven temperature, set your dial slightly less than halfway between 350° and 375°. Check cookies often and use given indicators for doneness.

MAKES 12

EASY

FAST

SALTED PEANUT BUTTER
CHOCOLATE CHUNK COOKIES

1 cup plus 2 tbsp. flour

1 tsp. baking soda

1/2 tsp. kosher salt

10 tbsp. unsalted butter, at room temperature

3/4 cup dark brown sugar

1/2 cup sugar

1 egg plus 1 yolk

3/4 cup Kowalski's Refrigerated Creamy Peanut Butter, at room temperature, stirred

1 tsp. vanilla extract

1/2 cup semisweet chocolate chunks

- sea salt (optional)

In a medium mixing bowl, whisk together flour, soda and salt; set aside. With an electric mixer, beat butter and sugars until light and fluffy. Add egg and yolk, then peanut butter, then vanilla; beat just until well combined. Add dry ingredients; beat on low speed just until you can no longer see flour. Mix in chocolate. Drop 24 evenly sized rounded spoonfuls (or use a #40 cookie scoop) 2" apart on 3 parchment-lined baking sheets; sprinkle with salt. Bake pans one at a time in a preheated 350° oven until just barely set and slightly puffy (7-9 min.), rotating pan halfway through. Cookies will appear slightly underbaked when done. Cool completely on pans set on wire racks.

GOOD TO KNOW

• For the most beautiful cookies, lightly press a few chocolate pieces into the dough balls just before baking.

• Find Kowalski's Refrigerated Peanut Butter in the Dairy Department.

MAKES 24

EASY

FAST

Signature

MOLASSES COOKIES

2 ¼ cups flour

1 tsp. baking soda

1 ½ tsp. Kowalski's Ground Ginger

1 ¼ tsp. Kowalski's Ground Cinnamon

1/2 tsp. Kowalski's Ground Cloves

1/4 tsp. Kowalski's Ground Allspice

1/4 tsp. Kowalski's Coarse Ground Black Pepper

1/4 tsp. kosher salt

12 tbsp. unsalted butter, room temperature

1/3 cup brown sugar

1/3 cup sugar, plus more for rolling

1 egg yolk, room temperature

1 tsp. pure vanilla extract

1/2 cup unsulfured molasses

In a medium mixing bowl, whisk together first 8 ingredients; set aside. In a large mixing bowl, cream butter and sugars with an electric mixer until smooth and light. Add egg and vanilla; beat until well combined. Add molasses; beat until well combined. Add dry ingredients; beat on low speed just until you can no longer see flour. Using your hands, roll 24 evenly sized balls (about 1 ½"); roll balls in sugar. Place 2" apart on 2 parchment-lined baking sheets. Bake in a preheated 375° oven until just barely set and puffy (10-11 min.), turning and switching pans halfway through; cool on pan 5 min. Cool completely on wire racks. Store in an airtight container at room temperature up to 1 week.

MAKES 24

EASY

FAST

PUMPKIN COOKIES
WITH BROWN BUTTER ICING

2 ¾ cups flour

4 tsp. Kowalski's Vietnamese Ground Cinnamon

2 tsp. baking powder

1 tsp. allspice

1 tsp. baking soda

1 tsp. salt

1 ½ cups sugar

1 ¼ cups unsalted butter, room temperature

3 tbsp. dark molasses

2 tsp. vanilla extract

4 eggs

1 ¼ cups pumpkin purée

1/2 cup buttermilk

1 cup chopped walnuts

- *Brown Butter Icing*

In a medium mixing bowl, combine first 6 ingredients; set aside. In a large mixing bowl, beat sugar, butter, molasses and vanilla with an electric mixer until creamy. Add eggs, one at a time, beating after each addition; beat in pumpkin. Add dry mixture alternately with buttermilk, beating until thoroughly combined; stir in walnuts. Drop dough by rounded tablespoonfuls 2" apart on parchment-lined baking sheets. Bake in a preheated 325° oven until a toothpick inserted in the center comes out clean (12-14 min.); cool completely on the baking sheet before frosting with icing.

BROWN BUTTER ICING: Sift 4 cups confectioner's sugar and 1/4 tsp. salt into a large mixing bowl; add 1 tsp. vanilla and set aside. In a large sauté pan, melt 1 cup butter over medium heat until the solids start to turn golden-brown (about 10 min.), swirling pan to prevent burning. Slowly pour browned butter into sugar while stirring. Stir in 4-5 tbsp. milk by hand until frosting is of spreading consistency.

MAKES 48

FAST

CINNAMON SUGAR COOKIES

1 ¾ cups sugar, divided

1 tbsp. Kowalski's Vietnamese
Cinnamon

1/2 cup shortening

1/2 cup unsalted butter,
room temperature

2 eggs

2 ¾ cups flour

2 tsp. cream of tartar

1 tsp. baking soda

1/4 tsp. salt

In a small bowl, combine 1/4 cup sugar and cinnamon; set aside. In a large mixer bowl, beat remaining sugar, shortening, butter and eggs with an electric mixer on medium speed. Stir in remaining ingredients. Shape dough into 1 ¼" balls; roll in cinnamon sugar. Place 2" apart on parchment-lined baking sheets. Bake in a preheated 400° oven until centers are almost set (about 10 min.). Cool completely on wire racks.

MAKES 48

FAST

EASY

CRANBERRY BLONDIES

3/4 cup butter, melted

2 eggs

4 tsp. vanilla

1 ½ cups flour

1 ½ cups brown sugar

1 tsp. baking powder

1/2 tsp. salt

1 cup white chocolate chips

1/2 cup chopped pecans

- *Cream Cheese Frosting*

1/2 cup dried cranberries, chopped

1 tbsp. chopped orange zest

Line a 13x9" baking pan with parchment paper, extending up over ends of pan. In a large mixing bowl, stir together butter, eggs and vanilla until thoroughly combined; set aside. In a small mixing bowl, combine flour, brown sugar, baking powder and salt; stir into butter mixture until thoroughly combined. Add chips and pecans; stir to combine. Spread evenly into the prepared pan; bake in a preheated 350° oven until top is shiny, cracked and light golden-brown (25-30 min.). Cool completely in pan; lift bars out of pan with ends of parchment paper. Frost with *Cream Cheese Frosting*; garnish with cranberries and orange zest. Cut into bars.

CREAM CHEESE FROSTING: In a medium mixing bowl, beat 3 oz. softened cream cheese, 2 tbsp. room temperature butter, 1 tsp. milk and 1/2 tsp. vanilla extract with an electric mixer on low speed until creamy. Gradually beat in 2 cups confectioner's sugar on low speed until frosting is smooth and spreadable.

MAKES 24

EASY

COOKIES READY FOR THEIR CLOSE-UP

Whether you're gifting cookies, participating in an exchange or just want an attractive selection for a holiday gathering, office party or coffee with the neighbors, we've got some simple tips for making your treats as pretty as can be. Simple can be very sophisticated, and some more straightforward recipes and designs can be super-chic.

• Try cookies that don't require decoration after they're baked, such as our *Molasses Cookies* or *Chewy Candied Ginger Cookies**. Both are formed into balls and rolled in sugar before baking so they always turn out perfectly round and sparkle like freshly frosted windowpanes.

• Consider shaped cookies like pinwheels and jam-filled or chocolate-filled thumbprints, such as our *Turtle Thumbprints*.

• Drizzle shortbread with melted chocolate. Try our recipe for *Orange Shortbread Cookies with Chocolate Chips** or *Chocolate-Dipped Shortbread Bites**.

• Any cookie can be dusted with a few layers of confectioner's sugar for a look reminiscent of a midwinter snowfall. Once they are set and quite cool, dust them heavily on the tops only or on all sides with a sifter, repeating as necessary to achieve desired effect. Ball-shaped cookies can be gently shaken with sugar in a zipper-closure food storage bag. Try our recipe for *Spiced Chocolate Snowballs**.

FOR CUT-OUT COOKIES:

• Stick to simple shapes like balls, stars, trees, snowmen or gingerbread men. Avoid complicated shapes like snowflakes, Santas, reindeer and sleighs, which can lose their definition when baked.

• Ice cut-out cookies in a single color and sprinkle with décors if desired. Or try 2-3 colors of icing marbled together with a toothpick for an abstract look. Try white with blue; red with white and green; or white with chocolate.

• Avoid piping or overly fussy techniques.

• Try sprinkling cut-out cookies with décors and colored sugar before baking.

• Dip cookies in melted chocolate and sprinkle with crushed pistachios, other nuts or even chopped dried fruits.

* Recipes at www.kowalskis.com

TURTLE THUMBPRINTS

2 cups confectioner's sugar,
   sifted

2 cups butter, room temperature

2 eggs, separated

1/4 cup milk

2 tsp. pure vanilla extract

2 ½ cups flour

1 cup unsweetened cocoa

1 tsp. salt

2 ½ cups chopped pecans

12 ¼ oz. jar caramel sauce

7 oz. carton Baker's Dipping
   Chocolate

In a large mixing bowl, beat powdered sugar and butter with an electric mixer on medium speed until creamy; beat in egg yolks, milk and vanilla until thoroughly combined; set aside. In a medium bowl, combine flour, cocoa and salt; add to butter mixture, beating until blended. Refrigerate dough until slightly firm (about 1 hr.). Beat egg whites in a small bowl with fork. Shape rounded tablespoons of dough into 1 ½" balls; dip balls into egg white, then roll in nuts. Place 1" apart on parchment-lined baking sheets; press thumb into center of each cookie to make an indentation. Bake in a preheated 350° oven until set (10-12 min.); quickly remake indentations with a rounded 1/2 tsp. measuring spoon if necessary. Carefully remove cookies to cooling rack to cool completely. Fill each cookie with 1/2 tsp. caramel topping. Place chocolate disks in zipper-closure food storage bag; microwave according to pkg. directions, squeezing bag every 15 sec. until completely melted. With scissors, snip small corner off of bag. Drizzle melted chocolate over cookies; let chocolate set. Store cookies in an airtight container in the refrigerator up to several days.

MAKES 60

NOTE
• The plastic cork from a wine bottle
will make perfect indentations in
each cookie.

ALMOND TOFFEE BARS

14 tbsp. unsalted butter, divided, at room temperature

3/4 cup brown sugar

1 egg yolk, at room temperature

1 ½ cups flour

1/4 tsp. kosher salt

14 oz. can sweetened condensed milk

12 oz. bag mini semisweet chocolate chips

8 oz. bag Heath English Toffee Bits (not chocolate-covered toffee bits)

In a medium mixing bowl, using an electric mixer, beat 12 tbsp. butter with sugar until light and fluffy. Add egg yolk; mix just until fully incorporated. In a separate small mixing bowl, mix together flour and salt; add to bowl with the butter mixture; stir until no traces of flour remain. Press mixture evenly and firmly into bottom of a 9x13" nonstick pan (sides only sprayed with cooking spray). Bake in a preheated 350° oven until light golden-brown (12-16 min.). Remove from oven; allow to cool slightly (leave the oven on). In a small saucepan over medium heat, combine sweetened condensed milk and remaining butter; cook, stirring frequently with a silicone spatula, until bubbly, then 5 min. more until thick. Pour evenly over crust; bake 10 min. Remove from oven; sprinkle evenly with chocolate chips. Return to oven; bake 3-5 min. until chocolate begins to melt. Remove from oven; spread chocolate with a knife evenly over the surface of the filling. Sprinkle toffee pieces evenly over melted chocolate, pressing in lightly. Cool at room temperature 30 min. Cool completely in the refrigerator; cut into 1 ½ x 4" bars. Store in the refrigerator, tightly covered, up to 5 days.

MAKES 24

EASY

PEPPERMINT BROWNIE CRISPS

18 ⅓ oz. pkg. fudge brownie mix

1/2 cup flour

1/4 cup vegetable oil

3 tbsp. water

2 eggs

15 mint-flavored hard candies,
        coarsely crushed, divided

In a large mixing bowl, combine first 5 ingredients, mixing by hand. Scoop 1 tbsp. of batter onto greased cookie sheet, swirling to create a circle; repeat with 5 additional tbsp. of batter. Bake in a preheated 350° oven until edges are set and centers are firm (9-10 min.); remove from oven and sprinkle tops with crushed mints. Cool on cookie sheet 5 min.; remove to wire rack to cool completely. Repeat with remaining batter.

GOOD TO KNOW

- To keep cookies crisp, store in an airtight container with parchment paper between the layers.

- For gift giving, stack 6 cookies in a clear plastic bag with squares of parchment between each cookie; tie with a colorful ribbon.

MAKES 24

EASY

FAST

ROOT BEER FLOAT COOKIE SANDWICHES

1 cup sugar

1 cup brown sugar

1/2 cup butter, room temperature

1/2 cup shortening

1/2 cup buttermilk

2 eggs

2 tsp. root beer extract

1 tsp. vanilla

4 cups flour

1 tsp. baking soda

1/4 tsp. salt

- vanilla ice cream

In a large mixing bowl, combine sugar, brown sugar, butter, shortening, buttermilk, eggs, root beer extract and vanilla; beat with an electric mixer on medium speed until well blended. Stir in flour, soda and salt; continue beating on low speed until a soft dough forms. Scoop rounded tablespoons of dough 2" apart onto parchment-lined baking sheets; bake in a preheated 375° oven until centers are set (10-12 min.), rotating cookie sheets halfway through baking time. Remove from cookie sheets onto cooling rack; cool completely. Place a scoop of ice cream on half of the cookies; top with remaining cookies. Place on a parchment-lined baking sheet; freeze, covered, until ready to serve.

NOTE

• Cookie may be frosted rather than made into sandwiches. To make frosting, beat 4 cups confectioner's sugar, 4 tbsp. half-and-half and 4 tsp. root beer extract until frosting is of spreading consistency, adding additional half-and-half if needed.

MAKES 18

EASY

306

CAMPFIRE CLOTHESPIN S'MORES

9 graham crackers, each cracker carefully broken in half

7 oz. carton Baker's Real Dark or Real Milk Chocolate Dipping Chocolate

7 oz. jar marshmallow crème

Clip a clothespin on one end of each graham cracker; set aside. Melt dipping chocolate according to package directions. Dip half of each cracker in melted chocolate; place on parchment paper to set chocolate. Spread marshmallow crème over chocolate; toast marshmallow with torch until golden-brown.

ALSO NEEDED

• 18 wooden snap-style clothespins

• parchment paper

• small kitchen torch

MAKES 18

EASY

FAST

OATMEAL RAISIN COOKIES

1/2 cup unsalted butter,
    room temperature

1/2 cup dark brown sugar

1/2 cup sugar

1 egg

1 ½ tsp. pure vanilla extract

1 cup flour

1/2 tsp. baking soda

1/2 tsp. kosher salt

1/2 tsp. baking powder

1 ½ cup oats

1 cup raisins

In a medium mixing bowl, using an electric mixer, beat softened butter with sugars until smooth and light (about 1 ½ min.). Add egg and vanilla; beat until well combined (about 30 sec.). In a separate small mixing bowl, whisk together flour, soda, salt, baking powder and oats; mix into butter and egg mixture just until you can no longer see white. Stir in raisins by hand. Drop 18 evenly sized rounded spoonfuls 2" apart on 2 parchment lined baking sheets. Bake in a preheated 350° oven until just set (12-13 min.), turning pans halfway through. Remove from oven; cool on pan 2 min., then cool completely on wire racks.

MAKES 18

EASY

FAST

CHOCOLATE CHIP COOKIES

1 cup plus 2 tbsp. flour

1/2 tsp. baking soda

1/2 tsp. kosher salt

8 tbsp. unsalted butter, at
room temperature

1/2 cup brown sugar

1/4 cup sugar

1 egg

1 tsp. vanilla extract

1 cup semisweet chocolate chips

In a medium mixing bowl, whisk together flour, soda and salt; set aside. With electric mixer, beat butter and sugars until light and fluffy. Scrape bowl. Add egg, then vanilla; beat just until well combined. Add dry ingredients; beat on low speed just until you can no longer see flour. Mix in chocolate. Drop 18 evenly sized rounded spoonfuls (or use a #40 cookie scoop) 2" apart on 2 parchment-lined baking sheets. Bake pans one at a time in a preheated 375° oven until just barely set and slightly puffy (about 9 min.), rotating pan halfway through. Cool 2 min. on pans, then cool completely on wire racks.

NOTE

• For the most beautiful cookies, lightly press a few chocolate pieces into the dough balls just before baking.

MAKES 18

EASY

FAST

DESSERTS

APPLE GALETTE WITH CRÈME FRAÎCHE

1 refrigerated pie crust

1 egg, beaten with 1 tbsp. water

3 unpeeled apples, cored, sliced 1/4" thick

1 ½ tbsp. flour

3 tbsp. sugar

1 tsp. Kowalski's Ground Cinnamon

1/4 tsp. Kowalski's Ground Nutmeg

1/4 tsp. Kowalski's Ground Ginger

1 tbsp. butter, cut into small pieces

10 oz. carton crème fraîche

- brown sugar, optional

Follow directions on the package for unwrapping and unrolling crust; roll into a 14" circle on a parchment-lined baking sheet. Brush crust with egg wash, reserving unused portion. In a large mixing bowl, combine apples, flour, sugar and spices; toss to thoroughly coat. Pour apple mixture into center of pastry. Dot evenly with butter. Pull the edge of the pastry up over apples, leaving the center uncovered; pleat edge of pastry. Brush crust with remaining egg mixture. Bake in a preheated 375° oven until crust is golden-brown (35-40 min.). Cool 20 min. Cut into slices; top with crème fraîche. Sprinkle with brown sugar, if desired.

VARIATION
Peach Galette:
Replace apple mixture with 3 peeled, pitted, sliced peaches tossed with 3 tbsp. brown sugar and 1/8 tsp. Kowalski's Vietnamese Ground Cinnamon.

SERVES 6

EASY

EASY APPLE PIE

3/4 cup brown sugar

3 tbsp. flour

1 tsp. Kowalski's Ground
    Cinnamon

3/4 tsp. kosher salt

1/2 tsp. Kowalski's Ground Nutmeg

1/4 tsp. Kowalski's Allspice

8 tart apples (such as Haralson),
    peeled, cored, sliced
    1/2" thick

14 oz. pkg. refrigerated
    pie crusts

1 egg white, lightly beaten

1 tbsp. turbinado sugar

In a large mixing bowl, combine first 6 ingredients; add apples, tossing to combine. Set apple mixture aside. Adjust oven rack to lowest position; place a rimmed baking sheet on the rack and preheat oven to 425°. Line a 9" deep-dish pie pan with one crust; fill with apples. Top with the second crust, tucking top crust under the edge of the bottom crust; pinch crusts together to seal. Flute edge of crust with fingers. Cut 6-8 slits in the crust; brush with egg and sprinkle with sugar. Place pie on the preheated baking sheet; bake until the crust is a dark golden-brown (40-45 min.), covering the edges of the crust with strips of foil to prevent overbrowning in last 10-15 min., if needed. Transfer pie to a wire rack; cool 2 hrs. before serving.

SERVES 8

EASY

PUMPKIN PIE

1/2 recipe *Perfect Pie Crust*

15 oz. canned unsweetened pumpkin purée (about 2 cups)

3/4 cup light brown sugar

3 eggs, lightly beaten

1 ¼ cups half-and-half

1 ½ tsp. ground cinnamon

1/2 tsp. ground ginger

1/2 tsp. allspice

1/4 tsp. ground nutmeg

1/2 tsp. salt

On a lightly floured surface, roll one piece of chilled dough with a rolling pin into a 12" circle about 1/8" thick. Transfer dough to a 9" pie plate, trimming edges to leave about 1" over the edge. Tuck overhanging dough underneath itself to form a thick edge that is even with the rim; flute the edge, if desired. Freeze crust 30 min. Put a piece of parchment paper or foil over the pie shell and fill with dried beans or pie weights. Bake on a baking sheet on the center rack in a preheated 400° oven until set (about 20 min.). Remove from the oven; remove parchment and beans. Continue baking until crust is light golden-brown (about 10 min. more). Cool on a rack. Lower the oven temperature to 350°. In a large mixing bowl, whisk together pumpkin, brown sugar, eggs, half-and-half, spices and salt until smooth. Return pie shell to the baking sheet; pour in the filling. Bake on the lower oven rack until the edges of the filling are set but the center is still slightly loose (about 50-60 min.). If the edge of the crust get very dark, cover edges only with aluminum foil. Cool on a rack. Serve at room temperature or slightly warm.

SERVES 8

EASY

PERFECT PIE CRUST

2 cups flour

3/4 tsp. kosher salt

- zest of 1/2 lemon

3 tbsp. shortening

1/2 cup unsalted butter,
    cold, cubed

1 egg yolk

1 tbsp. lemon juice

1/2 cup ice water, approx.

In a medium mixing bowl, whisk together first 3 ingredients; add to a food processor. Add shortening to bowl of processor and pulse just until combined; toss in pieces of butter and pulse crust mixture until it resembles coarse crumbs with chunks of butter remaining. Pour crumbs back into mixing bowl. Add yolk and juice to ice water in a separate small bowl and whisk together. Add liquid to crust mixture 1 tbsp. at a time as you toss crumbs with a fork. Stop adding liquid when you can take a small piece of the mixture between your hands and lightly squeeze it together; it should neither fall apart nor stick to your hands. Pour into two equal piles onto two pieces of plastic wrap (mixture will still be fairly loose). Pull opposite ends of one piece of plastic wrap together and squeeze crust mixture together to form a ball, continuing to squeeze until all of the crumbs are stuck together; repeat with second pile. Gently knead doughs to form two smooth, round balls; flatten slightly into disc shapes and wrap separately in plastic wrap. Refrigerate at least 30 min. up to 1 week until ready to use, or freeze tightly wrapped dough up to 3 months. To use frozen dough, thaw wrapped dough overnight in the refrigerator before rolling and baking according to recipe.

MAKES 2 (8-9") crusts

CARAMEL COFFEE ICE CREAM PIE

1 ½ cups finely chopped pecans, plus more for garnish

1/4 cup superfine sugar

1 egg white, lightly beaten

1 pt. coffee ice cream, softened

1/2 cup caramel sauce, such as Stonewall Kitchen Coffee Caramel Sauce

1 pt. French vanilla ice cream, softened

- hot fudge sauce

In a medium mixing bowl, combine 1 ½ cups pecans and sugar; fold in egg white. Press into a 9" pie plate sprayed lightly with cooking spray. Bake in a preheated 400° oven until browned (about 12 min.); cool completely. Spread coffee ice cream in bottom of cooled crust; top evenly with caramel sauce. Freeze pie 5 min. to set caramel. Spread vanilla ice cream over caramel; freeze several hrs. to overnight. Serve drizzled with hot fudge and sprinkled with pecans.

SERVES 8

EASY

PROFITEROLES

WITH SALTY CARAMEL ICE CREAM

1 cup water

1/4 cup butter

1/2 tsp. salt

1 cup flour

4 eggs

- *Salty Caramel Ice Cream*

- hot fudge sauce, warmed

- Kowalski's Praline Pecans,
    coarsely chopped

In a medium saucepan, heat water, butter and salt to a rolling boil; beat in flour over low heat until mixture forms a ball (about 1 min.). Remove from heat; cool 5 min. Beat in eggs, one at a time, until smooth. Drop dough by rounded tablespoonfuls 2" apart on a parchment-lined baking sheet. Bake in a preheated 400° oven until puffed and golden-brown (35-40 min.). Remove from cookie sheet; cool completely on a wire rack. Slice off top 1/3 of each puff; remove soft dough from inside of both pieces. Fill bottom of each puff with ice cream; cover with top. Drizzle filled puffs with hot fudge; sprinkle with pecans.

SALTY CARAMEL ICE CREAM: Very lightly brush the bottom of a jelly-roll pan with vegetable oil; set aside. Spread 1/2 cup sugar in an even layer in the bottom of a heavy-bottomed saucepan; heat over medium heat until edges begin to melt. Carefully stir the liquefied sugar from the bottom and edges of the pan toward the center, stirring until dissolved; continue cooking, stirring occasionally, until sugar caramelizes and turns deep golden-brown (it won't take long). Quickly sprinkle 3/4 tsp. sea salt over caramel without stirring; immediately pour caramel onto the prepared jelly-roll pan, tilting pan to form a layer as thin as possible. Set aside to harden and cool; break into 1/2" pieces. Stir into 1 pt. softened vanilla ice cream; return to freezer until firm.

SERVES 6

317

FRESH FRUIT TART

4 Kowalski's Biscotti

1/4 cup sugar

4 tbsp. butter, melted

16 oz. mascarpone cheese,
    room temperature

1/2 cup Kowalski's Pure Honey

2 eggs

1/3 cup heavy cream

1/4 cup flour

1 cup fresh blueberries

1 cup fresh raspberries

1 peach, peeled, thinly sliced

1/2 cup apple jelly, melted in
    the microwave

Place biscotti in a zipper-closure food storage bag; use a rolling pin to crush cookies into fine crumbs. In a medium mixing bowl, combine crumbs, sugar and butter; press crumb mixture onto bottom and up sides of a 10" removable-bottom tart pan. In an electric mixer bowl, combine mascarpone, honey, eggs, cream and flour, beating until light and fluffy (about 2 min.). Spread cheese mixture over crumb crust. Bake in a preheated 350° oven until filling is set (20-25 min.); cool. Cover and refrigerate at least 2 hrs. Arrange fruit on top of filling; evenly drizzle melted jelly over fruit.

GOOD TO KNOW
- Kowalski's Biscotti is available in the Bakery Department.
- Mascarpone cheese is available in the Imported Cheese Department.

SERVES 8

EASY

Signature

318

ITALIAN COFFEE & ALMOND TART

1/2 of a 5.25 oz. box hard almond cookies (such as Anna's brand), crushed

1 ¼ cups graham cracker crumbs

3 tbsp. sugar

8 tbsp. unsalted butter, melted

1/2 cup milk

10 oz. pkg. mini marshmallows

1 tbsp. instant coffee

1 ½ tsp. vanilla extract

1 ½ cups heavy cream, whipped to stiff peaks

- chocolate dessert sauce, for drizzling

1/4 cup sliced almonds, toasted

In a medium mixing bowl, combine crushed cookies, graham cracker crumbs, sugar and butter; press into the base and halfway up sides of an 11" removeable-bottom tart pan. Bake in a preheated 350° oven until golden (7-8 min.); cool. In a medium saucepan over low heat, combine milk and marshmallows; stir until smooth. Add instant coffee and vanilla, stirring until smooth; cool completely. Fold whipped cream into marshmallow mixture. Pour filling into crust; chill 2 hrs. until set. Drizzle tart liberally with warmed chocolate sauce; scatter with almonds.

NOTE
• Substitute another hard almond-flavored cookie, such as hard Amaretti cookies, if desired.

SERVES 12

EASY

SIMPLE CHEESE TART

WITH HOLIDAY SAUCE

1 ¼ cups graham cracker crumbs

1 cup sugar, divided

5 tbsp. unsalted butter, melted

12 oz. cream cheese,
    room temperature

1 cup sour cream

1 ½ tbsp. fresh squeezed
    lemon juice

1 tsp. pure vanilla extract

12 ½ oz. jar Stonewall Kitchen
    Holiday Jam

1/4 cup water

In a medium mixing bowl, combine crumbs, 1/4 cup sugar and butter; toss with a fork until well blended. Press crumb mixture firmly onto bottom and up the sides of an 11" removable-bottom tart pan. Bake in a preheated 350° oven until crust is golden-brown and firm to the touch (6-8 min.); cool completely. Using an electric mixer, beat cheese until smooth; thoroughly mix in remaining sugar, sour cream, juice and vanilla. Spread filling in cooled crust; chill 4 hrs. Pour jam and water into a medium saucepan over medium-low heat; stir continuously until jam melts into a smooth sauce. Remove pan from heat and cool to room temperature. Drizzle sauce over chilled tart; serve immediately.

NOTE
• Substitute another high-quality fruit spread or jam, if desired.

SERVES 12

EASY

320

LEMON MERINGUE TART

- *Graham Pie Crust*

- *Lemon Curd*

- *Marshmallow Meringue*

Prepare recipes for *Graham Pie Crust*, *Lemon Curd* and *Marshmallow Meringue* as directed. Fill cooled crust with warm lemon curd; cool completely in refrigerator. Top with *Marshmallow Meringue*. If desired, broil tart 1-2 min. or use a kitchen torch to brown meringue.

SERVES 8

GRAHAM PIE CRUST

1 ¼ cups graham cracker crumbs

1/4 cup sugar

5 tbsp. unsalted butter, melted

In a medium mixing bowl, combine crumbs, sugar and butter; toss with a fork until well blended. Press crumb mixture firmly onto bottom and up the sides of an 11" removable-bottom tart pan or 9" pie plate. Bake in a preheated 350° oven until crust is golden-brown and firm to the touch (6-8 min.); cool completely.

MAKES 1 (9-11") crust

LEMON CURD

1 ½ cups sugar

3/4 cup fresh squeezed lemon juice

- dash kosher salt

8 egg yolks, beaten

1/2 cup unsalted butter, cold, cut into approx. 32 cubes

In a medium saucepan over medium-high heat, combine sugar, juice and salt; cook just until sugar dissolves, adjusting the heat down if needed to ensure mixture does not boil. Put egg yolks in a heat-safe glass bowl; stream in a few tablespoons of hot syrup very, very slowly, whisking constantly to temper the eggs. Add remaining syrup to the egg mixture very slowly, a few tablespoons at a time, whisking constantly. Pour the curd back into the saucepan and cook, stirring constantly with a silicone spatula, over medium-low heat until the mixture reaches 170° and the spatula leaves a faint, disappearing trail when dragged across the bottom (11-15 min.). Remove cooked curd from the heat and stir in cold butter a bit at a time until melted. Strain; move to a storage container. Press a bit of plastic wrap onto the surface of the curd. Cool completely in the refrigerator. May be stored up to 10 days.

MAKES about 2 ½ cups

MARSHMALLOW MERINGUE

4 egg whites

1 ½ cups sugar

1/4 cup cold water

1/2 tsp. cream of tartar

1/2 tsp. kosher salt

2 tsp. vanilla extract

In a double boiler over simmering water, whisk together egg whites, sugar, water, cream of tartar and salt. Heat to 160°, whisking constantly (7-12 min.). Pour hot meringue mixture and vanilla into the bowl of an electric mixer; beat on medium-high until cooled to room temperature and icing is shiny and stiff.

MAKES enough for 1 (9-11") tart or for filling & frosting 1 (8-9") 2-layer cake

FAST

MOCHA BROWNIE TART
À LA MODE

6 tbsp. butter

3 ¼ cups semisweet chocolate chips, divided

3 eggs

1 cup sugar

1 tbsp. instant espresso powder

1/2 tsp. vanilla

1/2 cup flour

1/4 tsp. baking powder

1/4 tsp. salt

1 cup coarsely chopped hazelnuts

3 tbsp. heavy cream

- coffee ice cream

In a medium microwave-safe bowl, melt butter in microwave; stir in 2 cups chocolate chips. Continue microwaving until chips have melted, stirring every 15 sec.; cool completely. In a large mixer bowl, beat eggs, sugar, espresso powder and vanilla with an electric mixer on medium speed until light and fluffy (about 3 min.); stir in cooled chocolate. In a small bowl, combine flour, baking powder and salt; stir flour mixture into chocolate mixture to combine. Stir in 1 cup chocolate chips and filberts. Pour into 10" removable-bottom tart pan sprayed lightly with cooking spray. Bake in a preheated 350° oven until top is puffed (30-40 min.). Cool in pan on a wire rack until completely cool (about 60 min.); carefully remove side of pan. In a small microwave-safe bowl, microwave remaining chocolate chips with cream until chips are melted (20-30 sec.), stirring to combine. When completely cool, cut tart into wedges; top with coffee ice cream and a drizzle of melted chocolate-cream mixture.

SERVES 10

EASY

CHOCOLATE TRUFFLE TARTLETS

14 oz. pkg. refrigerated pie crusts

3/4 cup heavy cream

12 oz. pkg. semisweet chocolate chips

1/2 pt. fresh raspberries

- fresh mint leaves

Unfold pie crusts; cut 4 (4 ½") circles from each crust. Carefully press circles into bottom and up side of 8 (4") ramekins; prick the bottom of each crust several times with a fork. Arrange on a jelly-roll pan; bake in a preheated 450° oven until lightly browned (5-6 min.). Cool in ramekins on cooling rack. Meanwhile, bring cream barely to a boil over low heat. Place chocolate chips in a medium bowl; pour hot cream over chips, stirring until chips are melted and completely combined. Divide chocolate mixture among ramekins; refrigerate, covered at least 1 hr. up to 24 hrs. Bring to room temperature before serving; top tartlets with raspberries and fresh mint.

VARIATION
Chocolate Salted Caramel Tartlets:

Omit raspberries and mint leaves; drizzle finished tartlets with melted caramel and sprinkle lightly with sea salt.

SERVES 8

EASY

CHOCOLATE CARAMEL MOLTEN CAKES

1/2 cup unsalted butter

4 oz. semi sweet dark
    chocolate, such as
    Scharffen Berger

2 pasteurized eggs, plus 2
    pasteurized egg yolks

1/4 cup sugar

2 tbsp. flour

1/4 tsp. vanilla

4 soft caramel candies, quartered

- caramel sauce

- whipped topping

- Kowalski's Honey Toasted
    Pecans, coarsely broken

In a medium microwave-safe bowl, microwave butter and chocolate until melted (about 2 min.); stir to combine. In a large mixing bowl, beat eggs, egg yolks and sugar with an electric mixer on high speed until thick and pale yellow. Fold flour, vanilla and chocolate mixture into the egg mixture. Butter 8 rosette muffin cups or standard muffin cups; fill each half full of batter. Place 2 pieces of caramel in the center of each cup; top with additional batter to the top of the cups. Bake on a baking sheet on the bottom rack of a preheated 450° oven until edges are set but centers are still wet (5-7 min.). Cool in pan 2 min. Invert muffin pan onto the baking sheet, but do not remove. Let stand 1 min.; carefully remove muffin pan. Drizzle caramel sauce on dessert plates. Transfer hot cakes to each plate with a wide spatula without holes. Top cake with whipped topping; garnish with pecans. Serve immediately.

SERVES 8

FAST

MOLTEN CHOCOLATE CAKES

16 tbsp. butter

4 bars (4 ¼ oz. each) Hershey's Special Dark Chocolate, broken into squares

4 pasteurized eggs, plus 4 pasteurized egg yolks

1/2 cup sugar

1/4 cup flour

1/2 tsp. pure vanilla extract

- vanilla ice cream

- fresh strawberries

In a medium microwave-safe bowl, microwave butter and chocolate until melted (3-4 min.); stir to combine. In a large mixing bowl, beat eggs, egg yolks and sugar with an electric mixer on high speed until thick and pale yellow. Fold flour, vanilla and chocolate mixture into the egg mixture; set aside. Butter 8 ramekins; divide batter evenly between cups. Cover each ramekin with foil; freeze until solid. Bake frozen cakes in a preheated 450° oven until edges are set but centers are liquid (15 min.). Serve with ice cream; garnish with strawberries.

SERVES 12

CHOCOLATE TIRAMISU

3/4 cup boiling water

1 tbsp. instant espresso powder

2 tbsp. Kahlúa

1/2 cup plus 2 tbsp. superfine sugar

16 oz. mascarpone cheese

2 cups heavy cream

1/4 cup Scharffen Berger Natural Cocoa Powder

1/2 tsp. pure vanilla extract

6 oz. packaged soft ladyfingers

2 oz. semi sweet dark chocolate, such as Scharffen Berger, divided

1/2 cup sliced almonds, toasted, divided

In a 2-cup glass measure, combine the first 3 ingredients with 2 tbsp. sugar; set aside. In a large mixer bowl, beat remaining sugar and the next 4 ingredients with an electric mixer on low speed until thoroughly combined. Continue beating on medium speed just until soft peaks form. Arrange half of the ladyfingers in a 7x11" glass baking dish. Brush half of the espresso mixture over ladyfingers. Spread half of the mascarpone mixture over ladyfingers; sprinkle with half of the shaved chocolate and half of the nuts. Repeat layers with remaining ingredients. Refrigerate, covered, several hrs. to overnight.

SERVES 10

EASY

CHOCOLATE MOUSSE

1 ⅔ cups heavy cream

2 tsp. vanilla extract

1/2 tsp. kosher salt

4 egg whites

1/2 cup sugar

6 oz. dark chocolate, melted and cooled to room temperature

In a large mixing bowl, beat cream, vanilla and salt until soft peaks form; set aside in the refrigerator until ready to use. In another large mixing bowl, beat egg whites to soft peaks. Add sugar to soft whites; beat to stiff peaks. Drizzle melted chocolate into egg whites; fold until nearly incorporated. Fold whipped cream into chocolate mixture. Divide mousse evenly between 6 serving dishes. Chill completely in refrigerator before serving.

GOOD TO KNOW

• To melt chocolate, microwave it on 50% power in 1 min. increments until smooth (about 3 min. total).

• If you are concerned about consuming the raw egg whites in this recipe, try substituting pasteurized eggs.

SERVES 6

EASY

FAST

CARAMEL APPLE BREAD PUDDING

18 Kowalski's Mini Morning Buns (2-3 days old), quartered

1 cup Kowalski's Honey Toasted Pecans, coarsely chopped

1/4 cup butter

1 cup brown sugar, divided

6 eggs

1 pt. half-and-half

1 tsp. vanilla

3 baking apples, peeled, cored, sliced

1/2 tsp. ground cinnamon

- caramel sauce, warmed

- mascarpone cheese

Arrange morning buns evenly in a 13x9" glass baking dish sprayed lightly with cooking spray; sprinkle pecans on top. In a small saucepan, melt butter and 1/4 cup brown sugar until sugar is dissolved; drizzle over morning buns. In a medium bowl, whisk together eggs, half-and-half, remaining brown sugar and vanilla; pour mixture over entire dish. Refrigerate, covered, at least 2 hrs. to overnight. Toss apple slices with cinnamon; arrange over morning buns. Bake, covered, in a preheated 350° oven 30 min.; uncover and continue baking until browned (15-20 min. longer). Cut into squares; serve with warm caramel sauce and a dollop of mascarpone.

SERVES 12

EASY

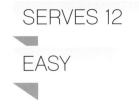

CHOCOLATE-CHERRY BREAD PUDDING

2/3 cup Kirsch, Grand Marnier or orange juice

1 ½ cups (about 10 oz.) dried cherries

1 loaf (roughly 12 oz.) challah, cut into 1 ½" pieces

1/4 cup unsalted butter, melted

10 oz. semi sweet dark chocolate, such as Scharffen Berger

6 eggs

2 cups half-and-half

1/2 cup mascarpone cheese

3/4 cup heavy cream

1 cup sugar

1 tsp. vanilla extract

In small saucepan, heat Kirsch over medium-low heat until just simmering; remove from heat. Stir in cherries; let stand, covered, 1 hr. In an extra-large mixing bowl, drizzle bread with butter; toss to coat. Pour half of the bread in a 3 qt. glass baking dish sprayed with cooking spray; scatter 2/3 of the chocolate over the bread. Spoon 2/3 of the cherries with the soaking liquid over the chocolate; top with remaining bread. In a large bowl, whisk together eggs, half-and-half, cheese, cream, sugar and vanilla; pour into baking dish. Cover with waxed paper and weigh paper down with sticks of butter or bags of shredded cheese, etc.; let stand 45 min. to overnight. Remove weights and wax paper; cover with foil. Bake in a preheated 350° oven 45 min.; uncover and bake until pudding is set and barely wiggles in the center (about 30 min. longer). Scatter remaining chocolate and soaked fruit on pudding; let stand 30 min. Serve warm.

GOOD TO KNOW
• Find challah on the Artisan Bread Table in the Bakery Department.

SERVES 16

CRÈME BRÛLÉE

4 cups heavy cream

8 egg yolks

1 ½ cups sugar, divided

1 tsp. vanilla extract

In a large saucepan, heat cream to a simmer over low heat. In a large mixing bowl, whisk egg yolks and 3/4 cup sugar until thick and pale yellow. Gradually whisk in the warm cream; add vanilla, stirring to combine. Pour mixture through a fine-mesh strainer. Pour into 8 (6 oz.) ramekins or custard cups. Place in a 13x9" baking dish; pour hot water around ramekins into baking dish until it reaches halfway up the ramekins. Bake, covered with foil, in a preheated 300° oven until custards are set around the edges but slightly loose in the center (40-50 min.). Cool on a wire rack; cover and refrigerate at least 4 hrs., up to 2 days. Sprinkle 1 ½ tbsp. sugar over the top of each ramekin. Caramelize sugar with kitchen torch until no dry sugar is visible. Let stand about 5 min. before serving to allow sugar to harden.

SERVES 8

CHOCOLATE CRÈME BRÛLÉE **WITH FRESH RASPBERRIES**

3 ½ cups heavy cream

1/2 of a 10 oz. pkg. of semisweet dark chocolate, such as Scharffen Berger

8 egg yolks

3/4 cup sugar

1 tsp. vanilla extract

32 fresh raspberries, divided

12 tbsp. superfine sugar, divided

In a large saucepan, heat cream over medium heat until mixture just begins to boil (about 8 min.); remove from heat and add chocolate. Let stand 5 min.; whisk until chocolate is melted and smooth. In a large bowl, whisk egg yolks and sugar until thick and pale yellow (about 4 min.); stir in vanilla. Gradually whisk hot cream mixture into yolk mixture. Place 4 raspberries in each of 8 (5 oz.) oval ramekins; divide chocolate mixture among ramekins. Place ramekins in 2 (13x9") baking dishes; pour hot water around ramekins into baking dishes until it reaches halfway up the ramekins. Bake, loosely covered with foil, in a preheated 350° oven until custards are set around the edges but slightly loose in the center (60-70 min.). Cool on a wire rack; cover and refrigerate up to 2 days, if desired. Sprinkle 1 ½ tbsp. sugar over the top of each ramekin. Caramelize sugar with kitchen torch until no dry sugar is visible. Let stand about 5 min. before serving to allow sugar to harden.

SERVES 8

SLICED CHOCOLATE
MOUSSE **OVER CRÈME ANGLAISE**

1 pt. heavy cream, divided

16 oz. dark baking chocolate,
    broken into small pieces

1/2 cup light corn syrup

1/2 cup unsalted butter

1/4 cup sifted powdered sugar

1 tsp. vanilla extract

- *Crème Anglaise*

6 oz. fresh raspberries

- fresh mint sprigs

Line a 9x5" loaf pan with plastic wrap, extending wrap over the sides of the pan; set aside. In a medium saucepan, cook 1/2 cup cream, chocolate, corn syrup and butter over low heat until chocolate melts (6-8 min.), stirring constantly; cool to room temperature. In a large mixing bowl, beat remaining cream, powdered sugar and vanilla with an electric mixer on high speed until stiff peaks form; fold in cooled chocolate mixture. Pour into prepared pan; refrigerate until firm (6-8 hrs.). Lift mousse out of pan with plastic wrap; let stand at room temperature 45 min. for easier slicing. Spoon a pool of *Crème Anglaise* onto serving plate(s); place sliced mousse over sauce; garnish with raspberries and mint.

CRÈME ANGLAISE:

In a medium mixing bowl, whisk 12 egg yolks and 1 cup superfine sugar until slightly thickened. In a medium saucepan, heat 1 qt. half-and-half over medium heat until small bubbles form around the edge of the pan. Slowly whisk hot half-and-half into egg mixture; return mixture to saucepan and continue cooking over medium heat, stirring constantly with heatproof rubber spatula until sauce is the consistency of heavy cream and reaches 170° on an instant-read thermometer (15-20 min.). Pour sauce through a fine-mesh strainer; stir in 2 tsp. vanilla. Refrigerate until completely cooled; cover until ready to use.

SERVES 16

CREAM PUFFS

1 cup water

1/4 cup butter

1/2 tsp. salt

1 cup flour

4 eggs

- *Vanilla Pastry Cream*

In a medium saucepan, heat water, butter and salt to a rolling boil; mix in flour by hand until mixture forms a ball. Remove from heat; cool 5 min. Beat in eggs by hand, one at a time, until smooth. Drop 6 evenly sized mounds 2" apart on a parchment-covered baking sheet. Bake in a preheated 400° oven until puffed and golden-brown (35-40 min.). Carefully remove from baking sheet; cool completely on a wire rack. Cut off tops; remove soft dough from inside of both halves. Fill bottom half of each puff with pastry cream; replace tops, dust with powdered sugar and drizzle with chocolate or caramel sauce, if desired. Serve immediately.

VANILLA PASTRY CREAM:

2/3 cup sugar
3 tbsp. cornstarch
5 egg yolks, beaten
2 cups whole milk
- dash salt
1 vanilla bean, split lengthwise
2 tbsp. unsalted butter

In a medium saucepan over medium heat, whisk together the first 6 ingredients, adding them to the pan in the order listed. Cook until bubbly (about 10 min.), stirring regularly at first, then constantly for the last 5 min. Continue to cook and whisk until boiling (about 2 min. more). Whisk the entire bottom of the pan (including the corners) constantly to avoid scorching and to prevent lumps. Boil 1 min.; remove from heat. Remove vanilla bean; whisk in butter. Transfer to a heatproof bowl; cover with plastic wrap touching the surface of the pastry cream. Chill completely in the refrigerator.
Makes enough for 1 (9") pie

SERVES 6

MINI PAVLOVAS

3 egg whites

1/4 tsp. cream of tartar

2/3 cup superfine sugar

1 tsp. vanilla extract

- fillings, your choice: *Lemon Curd, Sweetened Whipped Cream*, fresh berries, and/or *Balsamic Berry Sauce*

Beat egg whites and cream of tartar in a medium mixing bowl with an electric mixer on high speed until foamy. Beat in sugar, 1 tbsp. at a time; add vanilla. Beat until stiff and glossy. Drop by 1/4 cupfuls onto 2 parchment-lined baking sheets. Using the back of a spoon, shape into bird's nest-shaped bowls. Bake in a preheated 275° oven 1 hr.; turn off oven and leave meringues in oven with door closed (1 ½ hrs.). Cool completely at room temperature. Fill meringues with lemon curd and/or sweetened whipped cream; top with fresh berries or your favorite dessert sauce.

MAKES 10   EASY

SWEETENED WHIPPED CREAM

1 cup heavy cream

3 tbsp. sugar

In a medium mixing bowl, using an electric mixer, whip cream until soft peaks almost form; whisk in sugar.

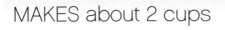

MAKES about 2 cups   EASY   FAST

Balsamic Berry Sauce (pg 337), Mini Palovas
(pg 336) and Sweetened Whipped Cream (pg 336)

Salted Peanut Butter Chocolate
Chunk Cookies (pg 297)

Molasses Cookies (pg 298)

Pumpkin Cookies with Brown Butter
Icing (pg 299)

Root Beer Float Cookie Sandwiches (pg 306)
and Campfire Clothespin S'mores (pg 307)

Cranberry Blondies (pg 301)

Profiteroles with Salty Caramel Ice Cream (pg 317)

Almond Toffee Bars (pg 304) and Strawberry Lemonade (pg 70)

Cream Puffs and Vanilla Pastry Cream (pg 335)

Chocolate Mousse (pg 329)

Chocolate Crème Brûlée with
Fresh Raspberries (pg 333)

Italian Coffee & Almond Tart
(pg 319)

Mocha Brownie Tart á la Mode
(pg 324)

Fresh Fruit Tart (pg 318)

Peach Galette (pg 312)

Caramel Apple Bread Pudding
(pg 330)

Chocolate Tiramisu (pg 328)

Lemon Meringue Tart (pg 321)

Mascarpone Berry Bruschetta
(pg 46)

BALSAMIC BERRY SAUCE

1 lb. strawberries, hulled and halved or quartered

1 pt. blueberries

6 oz. raspberries

6 oz. blackberries

1 oz. bunch fresh mint, tied together with kitchen string, some small leaves reserved for garnish, if desired

6 tbsp. brown sugar

6 tbsp. top-quality balsamic vinegar

3/4 tsp. Kowalski's Coarse Ground Black Pepper

In a large mixing bowl, mix fruit and mint. In a separate small mixing bowl, stir together sugar, vinegar and pepper; pour over fruit; let stand 1/2-1 hr., stirring occasionally. Remove mint bundle. Spoon sauce over yogurt, cake, ice cream or other desserts; garnish with mint leaves, if desired.

NOTES

• After washing, allow berries to air-dry thoroughly before adding sugar and vinegar to prevent diluting the syrup.

• Flavored balsamic vinegars (such as blueberry, blackberry or fig) are good alternatives.

• Try basil in place of the mint, if desired.

Nutrition Information Per Serving

| Total Calories | 60 |
| Total Fat | 0 g |

Contains half a day's recommended allowance of vitamin C.

SERVES 6

EASY

FAST

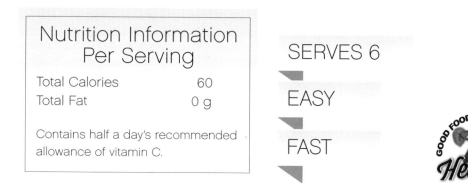

CHOCOLATE
CULINARY TIPS & IDEAS

• A two-tined meat fork is great for breaking chocolate into smaller pieces to speed up melting.

• The microwave is a quick way to melt chocolate. Heat 4-6 oz. of chocolate in a microwave-safe bowl on 50% power for 3 min., stirring once or twice.

• Keep utensils and bowls completely dry when melting chocolate. A single drop of water or steam can make chocolate seize or become grainy. Even a double boiler can splatter into chocolate and ruin it.

• Fix grainy melted chocolate by adding butter or warm water 1 tablespoon at a time until it can be whisked back to its smooth sheen.

• Never refrigerate or freeze chocolate. Wrap it tightly in plastic and store in a cool, dry place.

• Rapid changes in humidity or temperature will cause a harmless bloom (white powder) to form on the surface. Milk and white chocolate will keep for 6-12 months, while dark chocolate keeps for several years.

• To make easy chocolate curls, warm a large piece of chocolate in the microwave at 30% power 30 sec. to 1 min. Make long curls by dragging a vegetable peeler along the surface of the chocolate. Lift with a toothpick to place on top of desserts as a garnish.

TEMPERED CHOCOLATE

Tempering chocolate creates a smooth, hard, glossy finish on foods that are dipped into it. Chocolate is tempered by heating and cooling it to the proper temperatures:

Dark chocolate – Heat to 110°; lower temperature to 89°
Milk chocolate – Heat to 105°; lower temperature to 87°
White chocolate – Heat to 105°; lower temperature to 81°

To temper chocolate, first chop chocolate into small pieces of similar size. Gently heat 3/4 of the total amount of chocolate until melted, stirring every 30 sec. Start measuring temperature when chocolate starts to melt. When it reaches the appropriate temperature for the type of chocolate, remove it from the heat; vigorously stir in remaining 1/4 of chocolate, checking temperature until it lowers to tempering range based on the type of chocolate used. Properly tempered chocolate should begin to dry and set in 3-5 min.

BITTERSWEET CHOCOLATE ESPRESSO TRUFFLES

1 cup heavy cream

12 oz. bittersweet chocolate, such as Scharffen Berger, chopped

3 tbsp. cold unsalted butter, chopped

- pinch of salt

1/2 tsp. instant espresso powder, dissolved in 1/2 tsp. water

- choice of coatings: finely chopped chocolate-covered espresso beans, finely chopped candied ginger and/or confectioner's sugar sifted with cocoa powder and mixed with a pinch of kosher salt

In a heat-safe glass bowl set over a saucepan of simmering water, combine cream, chocolate, butter and salt (do not let bowl touch water). Let stand until the chocolate and butter are melted (about 5 min.); whisk until smooth and shiny. Remove from heat; whisk in espresso mixture. Cover with plastic; refrigerate until firm (about 3 hrs.). Line a large rimmed baking sheet with parchment paper. Drop 36 evenly sized scoops of truffle mixture onto the baking sheet. Chill until firm (about 1 hr.). Lightly moisten your hands with ice water; quickly roll truffles into balls. Roll truffles in desired coating(s). Truffles may be refrigerated for up to 3 days. Let refrigerated truffles stand at room temperature 15 min. before serving.

MAKES 36

EASY

SALTED CHOCOLATE CARAMELS

2 cups superfine sugar

2 cups heavy cream

3/4 cup light corn syrup

1/2 cup butter

2 oz. unsweetened baking chocolate, coarsely chopped

2 tsp. sea salt

Line bottom and sides of an 8x8" metal baking pan with 2 sheets of parchment paper extending up all sides. In a medium saucepan, bring sugar, cream, corn syrup and butter to a boil over medium-high heat; reduce heat to low. Stir in chocolate; let stand 1 min. Stir to completely melt chocolate. Continue cooking over medium heat, stirring frequently, to 245° on a candy thermometer or until a small amount of mixture dropped into a cup of very cold water forms a firm ball that holds its shape until pressed. Pour caramel into lined pan, being careful not to scrape bottom or side of saucepan. Let stand 10 min.; sprinkle evenly with sea salt. Cool completely in the pan on a wire rack (about 2 hrs.). Carefully invert caramel onto a clean, dry cutting board; peel off parchment paper. Turn caramel salt-side-up. Lightly oil blade of chef's knife; cut into 1" squares. Press additional sea salt onto caramels, if desired. Wrap caramels in 4" squares of wax paper, twisting ends.

MAKES 64 pieces

FUDGE

4 cups sugar

1 ⅓ cups milk

1/4 cup corn syrup

1/4 tsp. salt

4 oz. unsweetened baking
    chocolate

1/4 cup butter

2 tsp. vanilla extract

1 cup coarsely chopped
    walnuts, if desired

In a medium saucepan over medium heat, combine sugar, milk, corn syrup, salt and chocolate; cook, stirring constantly, until chocolate is melted and sugar is dissolved. Continue cooking, stirring occasionally, until mixture reaches 234° on a candy thermometer or until a small amount of mixture dropped into a cup of very cold water forms a soft ball that flattens when removed from water; remove from heat. Stir in butter. Cool mixture, without stirring, to 120° (about 1 hr.). Add vanilla; with a wooden spoon, beat vigorously and constantly until mixture is thick and dull (5-10 min.). Stir in nuts; spread in a buttered 8x8" baking pan. Let stand 1 hr. or until firm before cutting into 1" squares.

MAKES 64 pieces

ORGANIC YOGURT POPS

2 cups organic plain yogurt

3/4 cup frozen orange juice
concentrate, thawed

In a medium bowl, combine yogurt and juice concentrate; pour into 8 ice pop molds or small paper cups. Freeze until firm (at least 4 hrs.). Hold the mold for a minute to warm it, releasing the yogurt pop.

Nutrition Information
Per Serving

Total Calories	70
Total Fat	0 g
Sodium	40 mg

Offers more than 60% of the daily vitamin C requirement, plus calcium and folate.

NOTES

• Flavored yogurt or other flavors of juice concentrate may be substituted.

• If using paper cups, freeze for 1 hr. before inserting a popsicle stick into the center of each cup; continue freezing until frozen.

SERVES 8

EASY

LEMON-HONEY YOGURT PARFAITS

1/2 cup water

1/4 cup Kowalski's Pure Honey

1/4 cup fresh squeezed
     lemon juice

- grated zest of 1 lemon, plus
     extra for garnish

2 ½ cups nonfat plain
     Greek yogurt

1 ½ cups truwhip® whipped
     topping (or another
     whipped topping)

12 oz. fresh blueberries,
     raspberries or blackberries
     (or combination)

1/4 cup chopped toasted walnuts

1 ½ tsp. finely chopped fresh
     rosemary or thyme leaves
     or mint leaves for garnish
     (optional)

In a small saucepan, bring water, honey, juice and zest to a boil. Reduce heat; simmer until reduced to about 1/2 cup (8-10 min.). Remove from heat; cool 10 min. In a medium mixing bowl, whisk yogurt until smooth; gently fold in whipped topping. Divide half of yogurt mixture among 6 (6 oz.) glasses. Top yogurt evenly with berries and 1/2 of the nuts; drizzle with roughly half of the syrup. Top glasses with remaining nuts and herbs, if desired. Serve immediately.

Nutrition Information Per Serving

Total Calories	240
Total Fat	10 g
Saturated Fat	4 g
Sodium	30 mg

A good source of vitamins C and K, protein and calcium.

SERVES 6

EASY

FAST

GOOD TO KNOW

• Find truwhip® whipped topping in the Frozen Foods Department.

343

GRILLED STONE FRUIT

4 peaches, plums or nectarines,
halved and pitted

- melted butter

8 oz. mascarpone cheese

- brown sugar

Brush both sides of each stone fruit with
melted butter. Grill, cut side down, over
high heat, covered, until fruit softens (8-10
min.), turning halfway through. Fill warm
fruit halves with mascarpone; sprinkle with
brown sugar.

SERVES 4

EASY

FAST

PEARS
CULINARY TIPS & IDEAS

• Check the neck of the pear (around the stem) for ripeness. If it gives to gentle pressure, it is ready to enjoy.

• Bosc pears are firmer and generally better for cooking than Anjou. Anjou are best enjoyed fresh.

• To ripen, store pears in a brown paper bag at room temperature. Once ripe, store in the refrigerator for 3-5 days. You can speed ripening by adding an apple or banana to the bag.

• Slice and toss pears with green salads or slice and serve on sandwiches. (Eliminate or minimize browning by tossing cut pears with lemon or orange juice.)

• Pears complement many cheeses, including blue, Brie, fresh goat and fontina.

• Try grilling pears. Peel firm fruit. Brush cut or cored halves lightly with butter. Grill 5-10 minutes until tender. Drizzle with Kowalski's Pure Maple Syrup and serve with cinnamon or vanilla ice cream.

SPICED POACHED PEARS

4 cups water

- juice of 2 lemons, (about 1/2 cup)

1/2 cup fresh squeezed no-pulp orange juice

2 cups brown sugar

2 cinnamon sticks

5 whole cloves

5 whole peppercorns

3 whole allspice

- pinch of salt

6 pears, peeled, cored and halved lengthwise

In a large saucepan over medium-high heat, combine water, juices, sugar, spices and salt; bring to a boil, stirring to dissolve sugar. Reduce to a low simmer; add pears. Cook, turning fruit occasionally, until easily pierced with the tip of a paring knife, but not falling apart (15-20 min.). Transfer pears to a large bowl; set aside. Raise heat to high; boil until liquid is reduced to about 1 ½ cups (about 15 min.). Strain liquid to remove spices. Cool pears and syrup 15 min. at room temperature; pour syrup over pears. Refrigerate to chill completely.

NOTES

• Replace up to 3 cups of water with a fruity red wine (such as a Zinfandel) or a sweet dessert wine (such as Moscato).

• Try adding a bay leaf, split vanilla bean or whole nutmeg with or in place of other spices.

• Pears may also be poached whole (core removed). Increase cooking time slightly upward.

• Bartlett or Bosc pears are generally better for cooking than Anjou.

SERVES 6

PEARS FOSTER

2 tbsp. butter

4 ripe Bosc pears, peeled, halved and cored

1/4 cup brown sugar

1/4 tsp. Kowalski's Ground Cinnamon

1/2 cup dark rum

1 tbsp. brandy

- vanilla bean ice cream

Melt butter in a large skillet over low heat. Add pears; cook over low heat until tender when pierced with a fork (8-10 min.), turning to brown both sides; let stand, covered, 5 min. to soften. Stir in brown sugar and cinnamon. Place cooked pears in a serving dish; cover to keep warm. Off the heat, add rum and brandy to skillet; warm over medium heat. When hot, ignite with a long wooden match or long lighter tool; continue cooking until flame goes out. Arrange two pear halves in each of 4 individual serving bowls; top with ice cream. Drizzle evenly with warm sauce and serve immediately.

SERVES 4

EASY

FAST

Signature

347

A HANDY HERB PRIMER

Fresh herbs are a great way to add flavor to foods without adding unnecessary salt, sugar or fat. For some people, knowing which fresh herbs work well together and with what foods is a challenge. Here we examine popular herbs and discuss their key flavors and most effective uses:

Basil is one of the most popular herbs. It is sweet and tastes faintly of clove. Basil is great in Mediterranean dishes, especially Italian dishes (such as pasta), and with vegetables, particularly tomatoes and peas. Basil is the key herbal component in classic pesto.

Bay leaves are used in cooking for their distinctive flavor and fragrance, notably in Mediterranean and European cuisine, especially French. Bay is similar to oregano and thyme. The most common uses for bay leaves are in soups and stews, but they are also used in roasted or braised meat, seafood and vegetable dishes. Fresh bay leaves are very mild and aren't often used in cooking.

Chervil is a dark, licorice-y relative of parsley. Its intensity nicely accents chicken, beef and veal dishes, as well as eggs and some soups.

Chives are known for their mild, grassy, oniony flavor. They are tasty in a wide variety of dishes and pair well with many foods, including fish, chicken, sauces, soups, salads and potatoes.

Cilantro is a love-it-or-leave-it herb for many people, with its peppery, sharp flavor. It is often used in Latin and Eastern Asian cooking and is found in many salsa recipes. Some people complain raw cilantro has a "soapy" aftertaste, while others don't seem to notice. Dried cilantro is sometimes sold as coriander, and some who don't like fresh cilantro tolerate either dried coriander or ground coriander very well. Cooking cilantro in the base of a soup, sauté or stirfry will also give it a more mellow, less "soapy" taste.

Dill is strong, sharp and sweet. It is used often in Northern European cuisine in seafood dishes, cold soups, pasta and potato salads, pork sausage, dips and dressings, and in egg dishes. The fernlike leaves of dill are extremely aromatic and used much like caraway to flavor foods, most notably gravlax, borscht and pickles. Fresh dill is preferred to dill weed (dried dill). Dill seed tastes similar to dill leaves – faintly citrusy and somewhat floral – and is used like a spice in similar foods and regions.

Herbes de Provence refers to a blend of herbs common in the Provence region of France. It almost always includes savory, basil and fennel. Depending on the blend, it may also include thyme, marjoram, sage, lavender and rosemary.

Italian parsley is thought by many people to have a stronger flavor than regular "curly" parsley. It is grassy and sharp. It pairs well with a wide variety of foods and is often used in finishing dishes and as a garnish because of its universally appealing taste. Flat-leaf and curly parsley are close enough in flavor to be fairly interchangeable in recipes, but in modern recipes, curly parsley is often relegated to a garnish. Parsley is widely used in Middle Eastern, European and American cooking. It is commonly used on potatoes and in grain dishes for its color and suitability to a wide variety of foods. It is also popular on stews and casseroles and in breading for poultry, pork and fish. Parsley is one of the herbs used in traditional *bouquet garni*, a bundle of fresh herbs (commonly parsley with thyme and bay). It is used as an ingredient in stocks, soups and sauces and is a key ingredient in several Middle Eastern salads, particularly tabbouleh. It is also traditional in Italian *gremolata* (a mixture of parsley, garlic, and lemon zest) and Moroccan *chermoula*, where it is typically blended with cilantro, garlic, lemon and cumin.

Lemongrass is a mild, slightly gingery herb that is often used in Thai and other Oriental foods, such as stirfry and curry. Sometimes large pieces are used during cooking and removed before serving because lemongrass has a tougher texture and must be cooked for a long time to soften.

Marjoram is sometimes described as a milder oregano, but it is a bit sweeter and mintier. Those characteristics make it an ideal partner for peas, carrots and all varieties of meat and poultry. It is found less frequently in recipes than many other herbs but is very popular in classic French cooking. It isn't well known, but it is a key flavor component in classic ranch dressing recipes.

Oregano is found in many Latin and Mediterranean dishes, such as pizza and pasta, and in dishes containing chicken, lamb, beans and legumes. Dried oregano is often preferred over fresh oregano, as it is slightly more pungent. It is used frequently in Italian and Greek cuisines and is commonly paired with lemon and garlic in those foods. Oregano is sometimes referred to as "the pizza herb," a term that became popular after WWII when American soldiers who had served in Italy returned home with a penchant for the flavor. Unlike many herbs used in traditional Italian cooking, oregano pairs well with spicy foods, including many Mexican favorites. In general, oregano works well with meat, especially lamb, fish, tomato-based dishes and with vegetables. Many people prefer the flavor of dried oregano to fresh, though the fresh herb is especially beautiful as a garnish.

Rosemary has a bold, pine-y taste. It pairs wonderfully with lemon, nuts, poultry, beef, game, potatoes, vegetables and pasta and is a delicious accent in baked goods from breads to savory cookies and crackers. In the Mediterranean, faintly bitter and extremely aromatic rosemary is widely used in traditional regional cuisine.

Sage is a woodsy, dark, strongly scented herb that brings out the best in dark, hearty dishes. Try it in casseroles and pastas or with turkey, wild game and strong cheeses. Sage has a slight peppery flavor. It is used widely in British, Italian and Middle Eastern cooking for flavoring cheese, poultry, pork, stuffing, sausage and sauces. Sage can be used fresh, but it is common for the leaves to be dried, ground and rubbed to achieve a pleasantly soft texture. A majority of recipes containing sage involve the sage being cooked with the dish rather than enjoyed as an edible garnish or fresh-tasting finish. In such cases, rubbed sage is more appropriate.

Tarragon is slightly anise-flavored but with a mild sweetness, making it good for use with eggs, seafood, and in salad dressings and marinades for chicken. Along with parsley, chives and chervil, tarragon is one of the French *fines herbes*. Tarragon is popular in Mediterranean and classic French cuisine, and it is one of the notable herbs used to flavor traditional Béarnaise sauce.

Thyme is a classic herb used with potatoes, chicken, turkey, duck and in dishes like succotash. It is good in salad dressings, soups and stews. Thyme is also particularly good with mushrooms and eggs and in grain and bean dishes. It is often used in Middle Eastern and Mediterranean cooking and in Caribbean cuisine, including traditional Caribbean jerk seasoning. It is sometimes described as dark or woodsy with faintly floral, citrusy notes. Thyme also pairs very well with other herbs, making it a common ingredient in herb blends, including poultry seasoning and the popular French blend, *herbes de Provence*. Recipes frequently specify a number of thyme sprigs to be used, possibly whole (to be removed from the dish later). The equivalent amount of fresh leaves is about 1 tablespoon per six sprigs. Thyme leaves are easily removed from their woody stems by holding the tip of a stem and pulling backwards towards the base, using your fingertips to pluck the leaves off the tiny branch en masse. Thyme retains its flavor better than most fresh herbs do when they're dried, making dried thyme a useful substitute. A tablespoon of fresh thyme leaves equates to roughly 1 teaspoon of dried leaves or 3/4 teaspoon of ground thyme.

SECRET SPICES

While many people use a fair amount of cinnamon, they often wonder what to do with some of the less-frequently used bottles in their spice racks and cabinets. Here we discuss some less well-known spices, their key flavors and most effective uses:

Allspice berries resemble brown peppercorns. It is popular in Caribbean cuisine, where the sweet heat of allspice is a key flavor in traditional jerk seasoning. It is also used in sausage, cakes, curries and even chili. In a pinch you can approximate the flavor of ground allspice by combining 1 part finely ground black pepper with 2 parts each cinnamon, ground cloves and ground nutmeg. You can omit the pepper if you like and adjust the cloves and nutmeg down to as much as 1 part, to your own personal taste.

Ancho chili powder is so called because of the type of pepper used to make it – in this case, the ancho pepper (the dried form of a poblano). It has a medium heat and is used in many different cuisines, including Tex-Mex, Indian, Chinese and Thai.

Cardamom is the seedpod of a ginger-like plant. Within the football-shaped pods are several dozen sticky, black seeds. The pods can be used whole, but in Western cooking the seeds contained within the brown, black, green or bleached white pods are usually ground into a powder. The pod itself is generally not used, as it can impart unpleasant bitterness. Pungent, warm and aromatic with flavors of eucalyptus, camphor and lemon, cardamom is recognizable in recipes such as Dutch "windmill" cookies, various Scandinavian cakes and pastries, and in traditional Chai tea blends. It is also traditionally used in many Indian dishes, pickled herring and in punches and mulled wines.

Cloves are dried flower buds sold both whole and ground. Cloves are often used in Asian, African and Middle Eastern cooking to add flavor to meats and curries. They are also used in sweet and baked dishes, such as those with fruits like apples, pears, squash or pumpkin. They are extremely pungent, so recipes calling for cloves often require a very small amount. Whole cloves can be added to the poaching liquid for fruits, the brining liquid for meats or pickles, or used in homemade potpourri.

Crushed red pepper is sometimes labeled or referred to as crushed red pepper flakes. They are small, thin pieces of hot dried red peppers made from various combinations, including ancho, bell and cayenne peppers. Often there is a high ratio of seeds, which intensifies heat. Crushed red pepper is commonly sprinkled on pizza and pasta but is also used in pickles, soups, sauces and sausage.

Cumin is a plant closely related to parsley, caraway and dill. In ancient Greece and modern Morocco, ground cumin is found at the serving table, *a la* salt or pepper. It is especially popular in North African and Latin American cuisines and is often used as an ingredient in chili or curry powders. Cumin seeds are used whole and ground. In recipes, they add warmth and smokiness with a faintly musty aroma.

Curry refers to a blend of spices commonly used in Southeast Asian cuisine. Most recipes and producers of curry powder usually include coriander, turmeric, cumin and red pepper in their blends, but they may also have ginger, garlic, fennel seed, caraway, cinnamon, clove, mustard seed, nutmeg and other more exotic spices and varieties of pepper. Sometimes the hotter recipe for curry powder is labeled *Madras*. The sweeter, milder curry blend used in Indian cooking is known as *Garam Masala*. Curry powder as we know it is a Western invention, not an Indian one. In India – where a variety of spices found in modern curry powder are custom blended, roasted and ground for every dish prepared – curry powder doesn't really exist. Curry powder is intended to capture the flavor of Indian cooking without the painstaking effort of it – great for the modern cook who wants intense flavor, fast. Curry powder is used widely in Caribbean, Japanese, English and Australian cooking. It is found in recipes for soups, stews, sauces, marinades, meatloaf, burgers, chicken, tuna, pasta and even potato salads.

Garam Masala is a traditional Indian spice blend that differs widely throughout India. *Garam* is the Hindi word for "warm" or "hot," and this spice blend is used to bring warmth in recipes for curry, stirfry, vegetables, soups and stews, among others. No particular blend of Garam Masala is considered more authentic than another. While there are nearly endless combinations of Garam Masala, a typical Indian version will include these toasted, ground spices:

- black and white peppercorns
- cloves
- cinnamon
- black and white cumin seeds
- black, brown and green cardamom pods

Garam Masala may be blended into cream sauces (including curries) or sprinkled into rice and grain dishes or onto roasted potatoes or vegetables. When mixed to taste with a little Greek yogurt, it makes a uniquely spicy dip for grilled or roasted meats (especially lamb and pork) or chicken.

Ginger comes from the root of a tropical flowering plant. It is particularly hot and fragrant and is an important ingredient in Chinese, Korean, Japanese and many South Asian recipes. It provides an interesting counterpoint to flavors of lemon, chocolate or pumpkin, among other fruits. The flavors of fresh and dried ginger are somewhat different, with dried, ground ginger being six times as potent as its fresh counterpart. Powdered dry gingerroot is typically used as a flavoring for recipes such as gingerbread, gingersnaps and other cakes and cookies, as well as beverages like ginger ale, ginger beer and ginger tea.

Ground mustard is the powdered form of mustard seed, made from the seeds of the mustard plant. While it can be combined with water, salt, lemon juice and/or vinegar to make the condiment we know commonly as mustard, the availability of quality prepared mustard means most of us reserve our ground mustard for recipes, especially ones where you want mustard flavor without added liquid, moisture or acidity. It is commonly used in sauces, seasoning rubs and salad dressings. Ground mustard made from yellow mustard seeds is milder than the equivalent made with brown mustard seeds.

Paprika is a spice made from ground, dried bell peppers or chile peppers. While sweet paprika is most common these days, until the 1920s, hot paprika was the only kind available. Sweet paprika differs from hot in that most of the seeds of the peppers are removed before grinding. Though the seasoning is used in many food cultures to both color and flavor foods, it is most commonly associated with Hungarian and Spanish cuisines. It is used in rice dishes, stews, soups and the traditional Hungarian dish, *goulash*. In the United States, paprika is frequently sprinkled on foods as a garnish. For this reason, when many people think of paprika, they may automatically envision a deviled egg dusted with a bit of this bright red powder. Both Spanish and Hungarian paprika are available in mild, medium and spicy varieties. The Spanish are known for making a popular variety of smoked paprika called *pimentón de La Vera*. Hungary is a major producer, so Hungarian paprika is both commonly available and generally considered superior. Most Hungarian paprika sold in the U.S. is on the sweeter side. In recipes calling for paprika with no variety specified, Hungarian (sweet) paprika is generally suitable. Like many red-hued spices, paprika retains freshness better in your refrigerator than in your pantry.

Saffron is the dried, rust-colored stigma of a crocus flower. Each flower has three stigmas and must be hand harvested, which is largely why it is among the world's most expensive spices. It takes about 225,000 stigmas to make a pound of saffron. It is very popular in Mediterranean cuisine and is notably used for both its bright color and unique sweet, grassy flavor in both *risotto Milanese* and *paella*. It is preferred to buy saffron threads instead of powder for best quality. To evenly distribute saffron in a dish, it may be crushed into a fine powder or steeped in cooking liquid.

Sesame is a tall, flowering annual plant bearing tiny fruit capsules that naturally split open to release even tinier, flat, eye-shaped seeds about 3-4 mm long. There are thousands of varieties of sesame seeds, varying in size, form and color. Off-white is the most common color, but other common colors include tan, gold, gray, red and black. Light-colored seeds are common in Europe, the Americas, West Asia and the Indian subcontinent. Black and darker-colored sesame seeds are mostly produced in China and Southeast Asia. Sesame seeds are used commonly in bread, crackers, salads and snacks, especially in Asia and the Middle East. Sesame is actually the oldest oilseed crop known to humanity, with one of the highest oil contents of any seed. Sesame oil is one of the most stable vegetable oils, and it is used widely in cooking.

GREAT CULINARY TIPS & TRICKS

KITCHEN MANAGEMENT

• Keep a clean fridge and well-organized pantry. It helps if you can actually see everything in your fridge and freezer without having to pull things out or push things aside. Chances are if you can't see it, it's going to spoil before you remember to use it. Also, knowing what you have on hand can prevent running out at an inopportune time or picking up an unneeded quart of milk.

• Keep your kitchen safer by remembering to disinfect your cleaning tools, sponges and washcloths. Throw sponges, nylon dish scrubbers and vegetable scrubbers into the dishwasher every time you run it. Keep a plentiful supply of washcloths in a drawer near the sink so you won't be tempted to reuse a potentially dangerous wipe, and always wash kitchen linens in hot water.

• Take a cooking class. Improving even basic cooking techniques can help you understand how and why certain recipes work and is key to learning to create custom recipes and knowing if, when and how to substitute properly. The money spent on a good class can pay for itself in improved kitchen economy, efficiency and accuracy.

• Prepare to prepare. If using a recipe, read it several times before starting in. Make sure all of your ingredients are prepared (measured, chopped, etc.) according to the list of ingredients before starting. If a recipe calls for chopped onion, don't plan to chop it after you've begun. Have the required tools and equipment ready as well.

• A notebook dedicated to documenting your successes (and less-thans) with your recipes can prove to be an important kitchen "tool" if you're like me and your memory isn't quite what you think it should be a month after taking liberties with an old recipe or improvising a new one. If you like to take notes in your cookbooks (for recipes that come from cookbooks...) but don't like to write IN them, super-sticky Post-It® Notes are useful, too.

TIME SAVERS

• If you need to soften butter in a hurry, place the wrapped stick in a plastic storage bag and submerge it in a bowl of hot tap water for 3-5 minutes.

• Instead of chilling wine in the freezer, put it in a sink full of ice water (or use a bucket). It will cool a bit more quickly, and you won't have to worry that you'll forget about it in the freezer.

• Try this test kitchen trick for chopping herbs quickly without a board or knife: place stemmed, clean, fresh herbs in a small glass or ceramic ramekin or bowl. Using sharp kitchen shears, cut down into the bowl quickly and repeatedly until the herbs are chopped to the desired fineness.

• Remove the stems, especially from kale and collard greens, to drastically reduce cooking time by up to 75%.

QUALITY CONTROL

• Paprika, chili powder and cayenne pepper retain freshness better in a refrigerator than in your pantry.

• Store fresh herbs like flowers in a glass of water in the refrigerator. Depending on the variety, you can expect them to keep up to two weeks. Don't wash them until you are ready to use them, and give them plenty of time to dry. The excess moisture on the leaves of your fresh herbs isn't called for in your recipes! Spin them mostly dry in a salad spinner, then finish air-drying on a paper towel.

• Keep nuts and seeds (and nut flours, such as almond) in the freezer to prevent them from going rancid.

• Keep berries fresh a few days longer by gently washing them in 10 parts water and 1 part apple cider vinegar. Drain well and lay flat on a sheet pan covered with paper towels for up to 3 days.

• To ripen, store pears in a brown paper bag at room temperature. Once ripe, store in the refrigerator for 3-5 days. You can speed ripening by adding an apple or banana to the bag.

• If you're wondering if you should refrigerate a type of produce, take a tip from the experts who stock the department: if we cool it, so should you. Leave the avocados, mangos, bananas, tomatoes, potatoes and onions out of the fridge, but keep your greens, grapes and berries cold for best results. When in doubt, just ask!

• Hard-cooked eggs should be refrigerated no more than a week.

- One of the benefits of making homemade salad dressing is making just the amount you need, but if you have extra, most recipes will store safely in the refrigerator for at least 3 days. Do not store them for more than 2 weeks.

- Most home kitchen ovens are not accurately calibrated, which can cause frustration when recipes don't turn out properly. If your oven is too hot or too cold, it doesn't just mean your foods need to cook for less or more time; the correct temperature can ensure that baked goods brown and set properly and maintain your recipes' appropriate textures. A simple and inexpensive in-oven hanging oven thermometer will allow you to adjust your oven temperatures accordingly.

- Many recipes for seared scallops call for you to cut into them to test for doneness. You can also use an instant-read thermometer. Cook until the scallops reach an interior temperature of 115°. Accounting for the effect of carryover cooking, they should reach a perfect 125-130° after being removed from the pan.

- Keep a ruler in the kitchen. Yes, a ruler! Whether you are making Danish pastry, pie crust, veal cutlets, cookies or meatballs, ensuring foods are an even thickness and size is vital to recipe success. A stainless steel kitchen ruler is dishwasher-safe – an important consideration for something that may come into contact with potentially hazardous foods.

- A cooling rack is an essential tool in good baking, but it can also be useful when holding just-fried foods before serving. In both cases, the rack allows air to circulate around all sides of your food, helping them maintain their appropriate textures. Want to speed cleanup of your rack? Place a piece of parchment between it and your food.

- When making biscuits or shortcakes, don't twist your cutter! Twisting sideways while cutting the dough "seals" the edges, making it difficult for the biscuits to rise high. For the tallest biscuits, cut straight down and up.

- To avoid lumpy gravy, warm your liquid gently (don't boil) before adding it to your hot roux (fat/flour mixture), whisking it in very slowly. It's almost impossible to add it too slowly. Even if it looks like you are creating glue at first, the gravy will loosen up and be lump free as your proportion of liquid to roux grows and the temperature differential between the two evens out.

NOVEL IDEAS
- Make corn for a crowd in a cooler! Put shucked, cleaned corn in a cooler and cover with boiling water. Place the cover on the cooler and let stand for 30 minutes.

- When rehydrating dried tomatoes or mushrooms, save the soaking liquid. If you can, substitute it for water in the recipe in which you are using them, save and use in soups and stews, or use to boil dried pasta or make rice.

- Spreading butter on pancakes, waffles and French toast can be a pain, especially if you frequently forget to soften the butter. Melt 2 tbsp. of butter into 1 ½ cups of syrup in the microwave and you can skip this messy step without missing the buttery flavor. You'll probably use less butter, too!

- Dental floss can be a useful tool for slicing soft goat cheese into rounds or cutting blocks of cream cheese or butter into cubes. Place the floss under your cheese or butter and cross the ends together as if you were tying a knot, without tying an actual knot.

- Can't decide on brownies or chocolate chip cookies? Make both! Drop chocolate chip cookie dough by teaspoonfuls atop your brownie batter for a doubly delicious treat.

- Individually wrap and freeze extra buttermilk biscuits. Unwrap and microwave about 20 seconds (depending on size). Let stand 1 minute, then enjoy a quick breakfast or snack when you slather them with butter and honey or load with eggs and ham.

- Don't throw out the rind of your Parmesan cheese. It's great for adding a salty, nutty and slightly sweet flavor to soups and stews. You can store them in your freezer for months.

- Breaking a cork into a bottle of wine doesn't have to be a disaster. Pour wine through a very small fine-mesh sifter or a funnel lined with a coffee filter to strain out any offensive particles.

- To make the clearest possible ice at home, use distilled water and boil it. Not only is clear ice prettier, some studies suggest it melts slower.

- Use leftover fresh herbs to make a simple infused oil. Blanch 1 cup of fresh herbs in boiling water for 1 minute; allow them to air-dry on paper towels. Blend the herbs in a food processor with 1/2 cup of extra virgin olive oil and a pinch of kosher salt. Strain the oil through a strainer lined with a paper coffee filter. Refrigerate, tightly covered, for up to a week. Bring to room temperature before using as a dipping or drizzling oil or salad dressing.

- If you are trying to make whipped cream ahead of time and hold it before serving, don't overcompensate by whipping it extra-stiff. It won't help. If you are using it as a topping for a dessert, it's best to whip it right before use. Save time by pouring your cream into your mixing bowl and placing it and your beaters in the fridge until you're ready to go. If you need to incorporate it into a dish or are taking a finished dessert to an event, you can add 1/2 teaspoon plain, unflavored gelatin dissolved in 1 tablespoon water to your cream as it whips to give it a little extra staying power.

SUBSTITUTIONS

• Have a little leftover red wine? Use it in place of some of the stock or water in gravy, pan sauces, pot roasts, soups or stews.

• When substituting another liquid in a recipe that calls for wine, don't just use water – it lacks flavor and acidity needed to bring balance, brightness and sharpness to a dish. Use a combination of broth with red or white grape juice (for red or white wine) or broth with a splash of top-quality vinegar or lemon juice.

• The flavor of toasted sesame oil, which is made by expressing oil from toasted sesame seeds, is much darker and more intense than untoasted, or regular, sesame oil. Toasted sesame oil is most often used as a finishing oil, something to drizzle over a salad, soup or stirfry, for example. Using regular sesame oil won't pack the same "punch." Regular sesame oil is commonly used for frying, sautéing and salad dressings. If you want a more intense dressing, you could substitute toasted oil, but toasted sesame oil isn't recommended for frying or sautéing. Your finished dish might taste unpleasant at best, and at worst somewhat burnt.

• Red onions tend to be sharper and more tart than white or yellow onions, which are often used interchangeably. Both white and yellow onions are fairly mild, with yellow being a bit sweeter yet more pungent, depending on the variety. A particular variety of yellow onion, the Vidalia, is exceedingly mellow and sweet. Yellow onions aren't often eaten raw, and they can be hard on the nose and eyes due to their high sulfur content. If you are unsure of what type of onion a recipe calls for, you can almost always use yellow, especially if the recipe calls for the onions to be cooked (as in soups and stews). Red onions do not have a lot of heat and are most commonly eaten raw in salads and on sandwiches. In a pinch, you can surely substitute one for another.

• In recipes calling for pumpkin pie spice, you can substitute 1/2 as much cinnamon plus 1/4 as much each nutmeg and ground ginger and a dash of cloves (if desired).

• For lighter, fluffier and more tender pancakes, try using cold sparkling water in place of all or part of the water called for in your recipe.

• People often wonder if you can substitute Dutch process cocoa for natural cocoa powder. If your recipe doesn't call for baking powder or baking soda (or another acidic ingredient like buttermilk, sour cream, cream cheese, etc.), then yes. Recipes calling for natural cocoa powder usually require baking soda to neutralize the acidity, and recipes using Dutch process cocoa are most often made with more neutral baking powder because the cocoa itself has already been treated to tamp down the acidic and bitter natural taste of the cocoa.

• English cucumbers are easier to clean in that they don't have the same waxy coating that regular cukes do, and they have a thinner skin and less seeds, so they may be more desirable when eaten unpeeled or unseeded. If you do peel or seed English cucumbers, their thinner skin and lower seed count make that easier than conventional cukes, too. In any case, their flavors are pretty much the same, so use whichever you prefer. However, if your English cucumber recipe doesn't call for peeling or seeding, you might want to consider if your regular cucumber should be peeled and seeded anyway, and if so, if that will negatively impact your final result.

• Roquefort is to blue cheese what Champagne is to sparkling wine – it's made in a specific region in France, and laws protect the improper use of the word "Roquefort" to describe just any blue cheese. While purists will argue, it's probably not an issue to exchange one for the other in most recipes.

• Stir prepared tabbouleh (or tabouli) into cooked rice or other grains for a fast and flavorful side dish to pair with grilled beef, lamb or fish.

• Cut the fat in your favorite summer dips, pasta and potato salads by replacing half of the mayo or sour cream called for the recipe with low-fat or nonfat yogurt.

• Plain yogurt is a great substitute for buttermilk, milk or sour cream in most baked goods – especially in quick breads and muffins. Substitute in equal amounts.

• Lighten up the whipped cream on fruit desserts by folding it with an equal amount of whisked Greek yogurt. Take it one step further by using all natural whipped topping (such as truwhip®) or light whipped topping instead of the "real" stuff.

• You can incorporate more whole grains in your diet by substituting them for some of the breadcrumbs in meatloaf and meatball recipe or even burgers. Try raw oats or cooked grains such as barley, bulgur, wild rice and red quinoa.

• Swap frozen edamame for frozen peas or lima beans in just about any recipe. They have twice the protein of peas and are full of vitamins A, C and iron. Edamame are slightly less sweet than peas and slightly less starchy than lima beans.

• You can substitute whole wheat flour for all-purpose flour in baking recipes, but it works better in some recipes than others. Where you are looking for chew (in things like slicing breads, pizza crusts and some cookies), the extra protein in whole wheat can be a good thing. In lighter, airier recipes where a very soft and tender, open crumb is desired (as in cake, quick breads and muffins), whole wheat protein can make them tougher and less fluffy. In general, use whole wheat to replace *some* all-purpose flour, not all of it. In recipes where tenderness is critical (such as in cakes), use cake flour in place of part of the all-purpose flour and whole wheat in place of the other part – cake flour has even less protein than all-purpose, which will help to even things out. Recipes written specifically for whole wheat are a better bet, and you can find loads of them on the Internet.

INGREDIENTS
• Walnut and avocado oils make great alternatives to olive or canola oil in homemade salad dressings. They work especially well with lighter-colored vinegars such as apple cider, rice, Champagne, pear or even white balsamic.

• Nut oils make for great salad dressings, but they can spoil rapidly. Keep them in the refrigerator. Vegetable and canola oils are fine in a cool, dark pantry.

• Recipes calling for dry red wine will usually work with Cabernet Sauvignon, Merlot, Pinot Noir, Shiraz/Syrah or Zinfandel. Shiraz/Syrah and Zinfandel may also be considered fruity. Sauvignon Blanc, Chardonnay and Chenin Blanc are commonly cooked-with dry whites. As a rule of thumb, use a wine you would drink for cooking. (Most recipes don't call for a whole bottle, and you'll want something to do with the leftovers!) For help selecting a specific wine for cooking, ask our wine experts at our Oak Park Heights, Hennepin, Eagan and Woodbury Markets.

• If a recipe doesn't specify whether an herb is fresh or dried, you can guess which is preferred by noting when the herb is added. This will hold true for most herbs: if the herb is called for early in the cooking process (before heat is added), it's probably dried. The fresh, bright, grassy properties of fresh herbs are lost when cooked. Recipes calling for herbs at the end of preparation or just before serving probably require fresh. Another indicator would be the modifiers *chopped* or *minced*. Such prep is usually done to fresh herbs only. If you still can't tell, try fresh first. You may need to double the amount later if you feel the flavor is too muted. Don't start with dried unless you start with half as much. Because the flavor is concentrated in dried herbs, you could accidentally add too much.

• Spearmint and peppermint have different flavor sensations. Spearmint (from a plant with pointer leaves, *a la* spears) is more subtle and sweet, while peppermint has a stronger, more distinctive cooling sensation. Fresh mint, found in the Produce Department, is most often spearmint.

• Garlic powder is preferred over fresh garlic when oven-roasting potatoes, since it won't burn or turn bitter. Use about 1/2 teaspoon per 2 pounds of cut potatoes (even 1/2-3/4" pieces) tossed with 1 ½ tablespoons of oil and seasoned with salt and pepper to taste. Roast until crispy on the outside and tender on the inside, about 30 minutes in a preheated 500° oven.

• Brussels sprouts make a great addition to stirfry with their cabbagy essence. Use smaller sprouts and cut them in half before adding them to the pan.

• Parmesan cheese, fish sauce, soy sauce, tomato paste, anchovies, Cheddar cheese and Worcestershire sauce all have high concentrations of glutamates, which increase the "umami" effect in your recipes. Pairing one of these with mushrooms (particularly dried shiitake or porcini), beef or pork multiplies their effect.

• Cookies made with more brown sugar than white sugar are generally chewier than those made with more white sugar (which are usually crisper and more crumbly). Accordingly, you can increase the chew factor in your drop cookie recipes by switching out brown sugar for part or all of the white.

• To enhance a grain's nuttiness and texture, toast grains over low heat with a bit of olive oil for just a few minutes before adding your cooking liquid.

• USDA requirements for labeling chocolate are more lax than those in other countries, particularly European countries. As such, it's possible European chocolate labeled "milk" chocolate may be darker than an American-made product labeled "dark." Where available, use the percentage of cocoa liquor noted on the package to make your choice rather than the terms "dark" or "milk." The higher the percentage, the darker (and less sweet) the chocolate will be.

TOOLS AND TECHNIQUES

• When creaming butter and sugar for cookies or cakes, it's important to reach that light, fluffy texture called for in those recipes. But be careful not to go too far, where separation starts. Go past the point at which the mixture feels like wet cement, to the point where it looks puffy and feels light on your spatula when you scrape the bowl. For best results, be sure your butter is room temperature but doesn't look or feel mushy or greasy.

• Before using a thermometer you haven't used for a while, be sure to calibrate it. Fill a glass with half crushed ice and half water, then let stand for 2 minutes. Insert your thermometer without touching the glass and calibrate to 32°. (On digital models there is usually a button to press. With dial thermometers you usually turn the face and/or may have to use a pin to push a recessed button on the reverse.)

• To make fast work of egg salad, use your pastry cutter. It will also help keep your salad appropriately chunky.

• Use your Microplane™ "upside down" on top of your fruit to accumulate zest in the rimmed area opposite the cutting surface, making it easy to scoop out and measure.

• In a pinch you can use your wide-plane rasp grater (such as Microplane™) to sift confectioner's sugar over brownies, French toast and the like.

• When breading chicken cutlets or tenders, fish fillets, etc., place the breaded pieces on a wire rack to dry for 15-20 minutes before frying. This helps the coating stick to the chicken so that it doesn't fall away from it when you eat it.

• Prevent soggy-bottom pie crusts by cooling pies on a baking rack to help air circulate around the whole pie.

• If you want mushrooms to brown, give them plenty of room in your sauté pan, otherwise they'll steam. Salt draws moisture out of mushrooms. Save seasoning until the end.

• Pitting peaches, plums and apricots is easier with a melon baller. Cut the fruit through the poles around the pit as you would an avocado, twist to separate the halves and use the melon baller to scoop out the stone inside. Clingstone peaches are more difficult (as the name suggests, the pits "cling" to the flesh), so if ease is a priority, buy freestone varieties.

• Don't add filling to a pie crust until just before baking, to keep the crust from absorbing moisture and becoming soggy.

• Using a frozen pie crust? Bring it to room temperature for 1 hour before prebaking (for use with a no-bake cream filling or a baked custard filling) to prevent cracking.

• If you tend to overwork your homemade pie dough, try replacing a few teaspoons of your ice water with plain white vinegar to help keep it tender.

• Be sure to preheat your oven before baking and check your oven temperature for accuracy with an in-oven thermometer. A too-cool oven contributes to shrinking crusts.

• Bake pies until the crust is a dark golden-brown for the most flavorful results.

• Contrary to some logic, sharp knives are SAFER than dull knives – they stay where you put them and slice with less effort. Yes, a sharp knife will cut YOU worse, but there's less chance of that happening if you have the better control a sharp knife provides. That said, practice safe knife skills, especially using a stable cutting surface and finding flat planes to work with rather than rounded ones.

HEALTHY SWAPS

Suggestions for healthy ingredient swaps aren't terribly hard to come by, but they don't work for every type of recipe. Knowing when and where to make a substitute can mean the difference between a successful trade-out and a recipe disaster. Try the healthier ingredient substitutions below in the indicated situations for your best shot at success. Using substitutions in the right applications will result in less obvious changes. Still, if you find the flavor or textural changes too noticeable, try swapping less than the full amount – you still get credit for making a better choice!

In recipes calling for BUTTER, MARGARINE OR OIL in brownies, muffins, quick breads and cakes from a boxed mix,
Try instead: Prune purée, a 1:1 blend of applesauce and buttermilk, or butter spreads and shortenings specially formulated for baking that don't have trans fats.
Get these benefits: Less fat, cholesterol and calories.

In recipes calling for BUTTER OR MARGARINE in frosting,
Try instead: Marshmallow crème.
Get these benefits: Less fat, calories and cholesterol.

In recipes calling for BUTTER OR MARGARINE for baking and sautéing,
Try instead: Cooking spray and/or nonstick cookware.
Get these benefits: Less fat, calories and cholesterol.

In recipes calling for SHORTENING in cookies and pie crusts,
Try instead: Trans and saturated fat-free shortening or margarine.
Get these benefits: Less fat, especially trans fats.

In recipes calling for HEAVY CREAM in custards and desserts,
Try instead: Evaporated skim milk or fat-free half-and-half.
Get these benefits: Less fat.

In recipes calling for WHOLE MILK as a beverage, in sauces or in baked goods,
Try instead: Skim or low-fat milk.
Get these benefits: More protein and less fat.

In recipes calling for SOUR CREAM in dips and salad dressings,
Try instead: Equal parts low-fat yogurt and low-fat no-salt-added cottage cheese.
Get these benefits: Less fat, possibly less sodium and more protein (depending on choice).

In recipes calling for SOUR CREAM in sauces and some baked goods,
Try instead: Plain yogurt.
Get these benefits: Less fat and cholesterol and possibly more protein (depending on choice).

In recipes calling for CHEESE for sandwiches, salads, casseroles and pizza,
Try instead: 2% milk, low-fat or fat-free cheese.
Get these benefits: Less fat and cholesterol and possibly less sodium (depending on choice).

In recipes calling for CREAM CHEESE for spreading,
Try instead: Fat-free ricotta cheese, fat-free or low-fat cream cheese, Neufchâtel or puréed low-fat cottage cheese.
Get these benefits: Less fat and calories and possibly less sodium (depending on choice).

In recipes calling for a WHOLE EGG in baked goods, omelets and other egg dishes,
Try instead: 1/4 cup egg substitute or 2 egg whites.
Get these benefits: Less fat and cholesterol.
Note: For baked goods, check to see that the substitute contains lecithin, which acts as an emulsifier or thickener.

In recipes calling for ICEBERG LETTUCE in fresh salads,
Try instead: Arugula, dandelion greens, spinach or watercress.
Get these benefits: More vitamins, minerals and fiber (depending on choice).

In recipes calling for CABBAGE in soups, stews and casseroles,
Try instead: Collard greens, kale, chard, mustard greens or spinach.
Get these benefits: More vitamins, minerals and fiber (depending on choice).

In recipes calling for CANNED FRUIT IN HEAVY SYRUP in desserts and salads,
Try instead: Fruit canned in its own juices or in water, or fresh fruit.
Get these benefits: Less sugar (fewer carbs and calories).

In recipes calling for WHITE RICE in side dishes, casseroles, soups and salads,
Try instead: Brown rice, wild rice, bulgur or pearl barley.
Get these benefits: More fiber.

In recipes calling for BREADCRUMBS in meatballs, meatloaf and casseroles,
Try instead: Dry rolled oats or crushed bran cereal.
Get these benefits: More fiber.
Note: Also replace some of the meat in these dishes (see GROUND BEEF below) with cooked mushrooms, beans, whole grains and greens for even more benefits.

In recipes calling for MILK CHOCOLATE CHUNKS OR CHOCOLATE CHIPS in baking,
Try instead: 1/2 the amount of miniature semi-sweet chocolate chips or finely chopped dark chocolate.
Get these benefits: Fewer calories plus the health benefits of dark chocolate.

In recipes calling for SEASONING SALT, GARLIC SALT, CELERY SALT OR ONION SALT in entrées, side dishes, dips and sauces,
Try instead: Salt-free dried herb blends, fresh herbs, garlic, fresh peppers, herb-only seasonings (such as garlic or onion powder, celery seeds or onion flakes), or finely chopped fresh celery or onions.
Get these benefits: Lower sodium.

In recipes calling for PREPARED SOUPS OR SAUCES, SOY SAUCE, BOTTLED DRESSINGS, PACKAGED CRACKERS OR CANNED MEAT, FISH OR VEGETABLES,
Try instead: Low-sodium or reduced-sodium versions.
Get these benefits: Lower sodium.
Note: Some canned vegetables (especially beans, whole tomatoes and baby corn), even low-sodium choices, can be rinsed to further remove sodium before use.

In recipes calling for BACON in sandwiches, casseroles, egg dishes, soups and stews,
Try instead: Canadian bacon, turkey bacon, smoked turkey or prosciutto.
Get these benefits: Less fat, calories and sodium.
Note: Check labels carefully. Some Canadian bacon may contain more sodium than regular bacon.

In recipes calling for GROUND BEEF in meat sauces, burgers, meatloaf and tacos,
Try instead: Lean ground turkey breast or ground chicken, or extra-lean or lean ground beef.
Get these benefits: Less fat.
Note: Look for ground chicken and turkey made from white meat instead of dark meat.

In recipes calling for WHITE BREAD in sandwiches, meatballs, meatloaf and casseroles,
Try instead: Whole-grain bread.
Get these benefits: More fiber and protein.
Note: When comparing nutritional information on packaged bread, be sure to compare similar-sized loaves/slices, as they vary widely.

COOKING FOR COMPANY
TOP 10 TIPS

If you've hesitated to host a get-together for fear of the effort involved, we've got some helpful tips to make entertaining easy, and most importantly, fun. A small cocktail hour is the perfect type of party to test your abilities – it's short, doesn't require place settings and even non-cooks can pull it off. Whether you're hosting overnight guests or having a swank cocktail or dinner party, preparation is key to pulling it off with a smile. Here are some of our all-time best hostessing hints:

1. Don't make something for the first time unless you can try it in advance or you have a back-up plan.

2. Don't be afraid to get help. It's okay to ask a caterer to do just a few items for you – especially time-consuming, unique or specialty items. Ask friends to pitch in with specific, simple dishes that travel well. Ask friends to pitch in with specific dishes (great for hosts and hostesses who like to control the party – you'll avoid ending up with duplicates or dishes that don't compliment your menu). Ask for your guests to bring a specific wine, crackers or bread, or even give them a recipe for something simple that can be made ahead and travels well.

3. Don't serve too many dishes, and balance your workload with both make-ahead and no-cook recipes. Avoid any recipes that end with "Serve immediately."

4. If you are serving dinner, keep appetizers simple and light so as not to spoil everyone's appetite for the main meal. A few cheeses and a bowl of mixed nuts or a plate of sliced melon and a cracker/spread combo is plenty when paired with a glass of wine. If a cocktail party takes the place of a meal, plan on 8-12 pieces per person, depending on how long the party is.

5. Serve at least one sweet item. If you're serving dinner, serve a dessert. If it's a cocktail-style party, serve a smaller sweet of some sort. Mini desserts and assortments are popular, as are portable treats your guests can take home.

6. Buy prepped vegetables. They cost more, but they are worth it in the time they save you. Often the most time-consuming tasks in the kitchen involve peeling, dicing and shredding fruits and vegetables.

7. Plan for equipment needs. You can't bake three dishes at three temperatures at the same time if you only have a single oven!

8. Make store-bought items special with simple homemade sauces, condiments, etc. Serve rolls or bread from the bakery with herbed, whipped butter. Make a simple dessert sauce, dipping oil or vegetable dip. Not everything has to be homemade. Garnishes are key. A mere drizzle of oil, a sprig of fresh herbs or cluster of fresh fruit can personalize even the simplest plate, making it look interesting, appealing and unique. Garnishes are key. They can make even the simplest dish look more interesting, more refined and more unique. Try drizzling a plate of hummus with extra virgin olive oil and sprinkling with fresh oregano, crushed red pepper flakes, lemon zest, kosher salt and coarse ground black pepper.

9. Splurge on cheese. If you are serving a cheese board or cheese course, buy the best quality you can afford. Quality over quantity. Ask a Cheese Specialist for guidance in selecting accompaniments and crackers, too.

10. Know what foods are gluten free so you're ready when someone asks. Our Nutritionist shares tips on our website at **www.kowalskis.com**.

TIPS FOR SAFER FOOD

FOCUS ON THE FRIDGE

The FDA Food Safety Modernization Act aims to sharpen federal focus on preventing food contamination, but the responsibility for keeping food safe is ours as consumers as well. Educating ourselves about ways we can reduce the risks of contamination at home is a great first step. Here are some basics:

- Keep hot foods hot and cold foods cold.

- Know your safe meat temperatures and use an instant-read thermometer. Beef, lamb, pork and veal should not be served at less than 145° and chicken no less than 165°.

- In general, avoid guidance (especially in dated recipes) that calls for you to rinse meat before cooking. Rinsing meat just increases the risk that germs spread to your sink, faucet and countertops. If you must rinse raw seafood (to remove scales or tails, etc.) or raw poultry that has been brined, use extreme caution and be sure to sanitize your sink and surfaces as soon as you are done.

- Wash your fruits and veggies. Food poisoning is often linked to leafy greens, tomatoes, sprouts, berries and melons. Between 1990 and 2006, raw fruits and veggies caused more illness than beef and poultry combined. Remember that organic produce is just as likely as nonorganic produce to contain bacteria.

- Avoid cross-contamination by washing hands, cutting boards and utensils that touch raw animal products, such as meat, before they touch other foods. Switch utensils and cutting boards after each use if possible.

Perhaps the hardest-working appliance in the kitchen, the refrigerator, is a mighty machine which is critical in the fight to keep food safe. Keep your refrigerator at 40° or below and your freezer no warmer than 0°. Refrigerate leftovers within 2 hours of serving (1 hour if the air temperature is above 90°). Since it is best to cool foods slightly before adding them to a cold fridge, help speed along the cooling process by dividing food into smaller containers. Below we've included a guide to the life spans of various foods kept in the refrigerator. These storage times are based on optimal storage conditions. Heat, light and other factors may lessen timeframes. Don't forget to check package dating, too. Some foods may have package dates that are not consistent with these guidelines.

Finally, remember the most basic rule of all – "When in doubt, throw it out!"

REFRIGERATION GUIDELINES

BUTTER	1-2 months
MARGARINE	4-6 months
CHEESE	3-4 weeks (hard cheeses, such as Cheddar, etc.) 1 week (soft cheeses, such as Brie, etc.)
YOGURT	2 weeks
DELI SALADS	3-5 days
DELI MEATS	3-5 days
HARD/SUMMER SAUSAGE	7-10 days
LUNCH MEATS/HOT DOGS	2 weeks (unopened) 3-5 days (opened)
EGGS	4-5 weeks (fresh, in carton) 1 week (hard-cooked)
WHOLE CUTS OF MEAT	3-5 days
GROUND BEEF/MEAT	1-2 days
BACON	2 weeks (unopened) 1 week (opened)
FRESH FISH	1-2 days
FRESH POULTRY	1-2 days
ROTISSERIE CHICKEN	3-4 days
FRESH PRODUCE	Talk with our produce staff for specific guidelines. Generally 3-7 days depending on the type of fruit or vegetable.
LEFTOVERS	3-4 days
SALAD DRESSING	2-3 months (commercial) 2 weeks (homemade)
MAYONNAISE	2 months (opened)

TIPS FOR FREEZING FOODS SUCCESSFULLY

While you can freeze just about any food, not all foods are well suited to life in your refrigerator's colder cousin. Freezing expands and contracts the moisture contained inside the cell walls of frozen foods, the same way water expands then contracts when you freeze it as an ice cube. For this reason, many foods with weak cell structures will become limp, soggy or mushy after being frozen and thawed. Here are a few tips for ensuring the best results with various foods and dishes:

Cabbage, lettuce and most greens – Do not freeze. These will become limp and watery. For greens such as spinach, however, where the final application may be in a soup, stew, casserole, egg dish, etc., and the greens will be cooked until limp anyway, freeze away. Similarly, though herbs retain their flavor when frozen, they should only be considered when texture isn't a concern in their final use.

Berries – Freeze depending on your intended use. Berries will get soft when thawed, but if you intend to use them in jams, sauces, smoothies or another squishy recipe, they will be fine. When using thawed berries as a substitute for fresh ones, in general you should include the liquid that results from the thaw, unless your recipe says otherwise.

Bananas – Freeze bananas in their skins for use later in baked goods like muffins and quick breads, because they will be completely mushy when thawed.

Melons, stonefruits and pineapple – Slices or chunks will get mushy but will be fine for use in smoothies, pies, etc.

Milk-based sauces, custards and sour cream – These tend to separate or even curdle. If you are freezing a dish that is finished with milk, cream or sour cream, freeze it before adding those foods and finish the dish with them after it is thawed, if possible. An example is Swedish meatballs, into which you usually stir a bit of sour cream just before serving.

Onions, celery and peppers – These are watery and tend to lose their crispness when thawed. If they are going to be cooked after freezing, they may work satisfactorily. Pre-chopping and freezing them in portioned bags can be a big timesaver.

Cheeses – Blocks of cheese to be used for shredding or grating (such as Cheddar, mozzarella or Parmesan) freeze well.

Fresh meat and poultry – These freeze well and may in fact become more tender after being frozen.

Rice – Rice freezes very well if just barely undercooked to allow for a slight softening of the grain upon thawing. Cool well before freezing for best results.

Baked goods – Many baked goods freeze very well and, unlike most foods, can safely be thawed at room temperature. Unfrosted cakes and cookies usually freeze better than frosted ones.

Pasta dishes – Pasta dishes and other casserole-style dishes freeze well but will soften and absorb sauce as a result. To counter the effect, slightly undercook pastas and add extra sauce.

Eggs – While you can freeze both (raw eggs must be removed from their shells), these are fussy and it is generally not recommended to freeze eggs.

Butter – Freezes very well.

PANTRY STORAGE GUIDELINES

You've no doubt passed over a random can of tomatoes or tuna while rooting through your cupboards and wondered, "How long has *that* been in there?" followed closely by, "I wonder if this is still good?" Accordingly, we're suggesting the following guide for storing common foods. Keep in mind package dating, and remember that these guidelines assume optimal storage conditions. Exposure to light, heat, humidity, etc., can negatively impact storage. If you remove packaging or store the contents of packaged foods (like flour, sugar, etc.) in another container, it is recommended that you write the date on your storage container with a permanent marker on a piece of tape.

STAPLES, INCLUDING BAKING BASICS

BAKING POWDER AND BAKING SODA	18 months
BROWN SUGAR	4 months
DRIED HERBS	6 months
FLOUR	6-8 months
GROUND SPICES	1 year
HONEY	1 year (only 6-8 months when opened)
NUTS	3-4 months (shelled)
OATMEAL	6 months
OIL	6 months (only 1-3 months when opened)
SUGAR	2 years
VANILLA	1 year (only 6-8 months when opened)
VINEGAR	2 years (only 1 year when opened)
WHOLE SPICES	2 years

CANNED GOODS

CANNED FRUITS	1 year
CANNED SOUP	2 years
CANNED TOMATOES	1 year
CANNED TUNA	2 years
CANNED VEGETABLES	2 years

PASTA AND GRAINS

BREAD AND BUNS	3-5 days (not artisan breads)
BREAKFAST CEREAL	6-12 months (only 2-3 months when opened)
EGG NOODLES	6 months
GRAINS	6 months (other than white rice)

PASTA AND GRAINS

PASTA	1-2 years
WHITE RICE	1 year

MISCELLANEOUS

COFFEE	2 weeks
CONDIMENTS	1 year (only 6 months when opened, refrigerated)
JAMS AND JELLIES	1 year (only 6 months when opened, refrigerated)
PEANUT BUTTER	6-9 months (only 2-3 months when opened)
SALAD DRESSINGS	10-12 months (only 2-3 months when opened, refrigerated)
TEA BAGS	18 months